GOODWILL IN ACCOUNTING:
A History of the Issues and Problems

Hugh P. Hughes
School of Accountancy
Georgia State University

D1128019

Research Monograph No. 80
1982

Business Publishing Division
COLLEGE OF BUSINESS ADMINISTRATION
GEORGIA STATE UNIVERSITY
Atlanta, Georgia 30303

Library of Congress Cataloging in Publication Data

Hughes, Hugh P.
  Goodwill in Accounting.

  (Research monograph ; no. 80)
  Bibliography: p.
  Includes index.
  1. Good-will (in business, etc.)—Accounting.
I. Title. II. Series: Research monograph (Georgia State University.
College of Business Administration) ;
no. 80.

HF5681.G6H83   657'.7   81-23202
ISBN 0-88406-119-1   AACR2

Published by:
Business Publishing Division
College of Business Adminstration
Georgia State University
University Plaza
Atlanta, Georgia 30303
Telephone 404/658-4253

For Marilynn Collins

Contents

Preface

Ambrose Bierce once defined a historian as "a broad-gauge gossip," and while not pretending to be more than an accounting educator with interests in accounting history, I fully appreciate his remarks. This study was from start to finish a library research paper, and so, quite literally descending into dusty library stacks, I found that I had to begin "gossiping" with prehistoric times—a starting point I variously found intriguing, dismaying, puzzling, and enlightening. I have enjoyed and endured a love/hate relationship with the subject of goodwill even since.

For those interested in how this study came about, and as a possible aid for some PhD candidates who are attempting to formulate a dissertation, this monograph arose from my dissertation. As my professors instructed, I dutifully listed ten areas and topics of possible interest to me—which served as a basis of negotiation and exploration with them. Listed in the topics were "accounting history" and "goodwill." Among the ideas tossed about was the suggestion that I combine the two and see what resulted. To coin a phrase (and pardon the pun), the rest was history. The dissertation was completed in 1972 at a rather climactic time for accounting for goodwill—the Accounting Principles Board recently issued two pronouncements dealing with business combinations and intangibles. With the benefit of nine years of hindsight, I have updated and revised some of the material and conclusions. The added time has certainly given more historical perspective to the APB's work and even—if only temporarily—given some cloture to the history of goodwill accounting.

Several individuals were important to me in the preparation of this study—either offering direct assistance or influencing the manner in which I approached the subject. The late Dr. Rosser B. Melton, North Texas State University, was a very convincing scholar of Institutional Economics, and conversations with Dr. Herschel M. Anderson, North Texas State University, helped indicate to me the importance of Institutional Economics for accounting and accountancy. The late Dr. W. B. Flowers, University of Alabama, offered encouragement in the study of accounting history when the topic was not nearly so popular as it came to be. Dr. Robert J. Freeman, then of the University of Alabama, provided much guidance as dissertation chairman, and Dr. Marion Posey, then of the University of Alabama, was very helpful in the detailed organization of the study.

During the revision of this study, Dr. Al Roberts and Dr. Roger Hermanson, both of Georgia State University, read portions of the revised manuscript and offered valuable constructive comments. I appreciate very much the encouragement and assistance I received from Mr. Cary Bynum and Ms. Peggy Stanley of the Business Publishing Division.

When I first began this project in 1969, I believed that I would come up with the intrinsic nature of goodwill—maybe even define the asset for all time. Perhaps all of those writers were arguing and struggling toward some unforeseen Truth, and it was for me to chart the direction, extract the essence of their works, and obtain the ultimate answer that maybe all were moving unconsciously toward. My own personal exuberant and intellectual Charge of the Light Brigade was rewarded with frustration, disappointment, and—finally—relief. I at last came to accept fully that all of those unfortunate souls who struggled with goodwill's nature and treatment did so, not in some possibly great movement toward Truth, but because there was no one Truth and never will be. The origin of goodwill can be revealed through history, but its nature is a matter of personal interpretation.

Approaching my revision with this later view, and now having written it and reflected back on it, a paraphrase of an old Leiber and Stoller song title comes to mind—"Is That All There is to Goodwill?"

Chapter I

Introduction

Nature of the Problem

> No one can afford to be dogmatic about the treatment of goodwill. So many excellent authorities disagree absolutely as to the treatment of goodwill that it would seem as if almost any of the methods discussed would be justifiable.[1]

If everyone had shared Gilman's views expressed back in 1916, then perhaps this study would not have been necessary. Gilman's seemingly tolerant attitude toward goodwill's treatment was not shared, however, by many of his contemporaries and by, quite literally, a multitude of those to follow. By 1916, accounting for goodwill was already an "old" topic as accounting subjects go—it had been discussed continuously in accounting texts and periodic literature for over thirty years. By the early 1980s,—almost a century after initial accounting articles on goodwill appeared—approximately one thousand books and articles had been written that focused or touched on accounting for goodwill and closely related subjects, such as pooling of interests accounting.

Goodwill's accounting treatment was both a major problem and a significant reflection of many of the important issues to face accountants and the profession in the hundred years following the 1880s. The rise of the corporation, reliance on the cost principle, the emphasis on conservatism, problems with inflation, and the relationship of the Securities and Exchange Commission to the accounting profession and its rule-making bodies are just examples of the issues and events associated with goodwill.

By the sheer volume of discussion and the many topics to which it relates, accounting for goodwill may be viewed as a subject in need of thorough historical documentation. While previous writers have focused on specific problems at given points in time, these authors were not attempting an evolutionary treatment of either the theoretical concepts or accounting practices related to goodwill.

Objectives

The objectives of this study were (1) to develop a cohesive and comprehensive history of the issues and problems related to the accounting concept and treatment of goodwill; (2) to place these issues and problems within a historical and institutional perspective, analyzing the asset's treatment in terms of the then contemporary understanding of major accounting concepts; and (3) in light of the above, to inquire into the nature of goodwill in contemporary industrial society.

Scope and Limitations

Emphasis for the history was placed primarily on events in the United States and on the period beginning with the 1880s, when the first pertinent literature appeared. The literature was assumed to adequately and accurately describe and reflect the concepts underlying accounting practice.

Throughout the study, goodwill was acknowledged as a product of its environment—a reflection of the dominant form of business existing at any point in time. In order to analyze the nature of goodwill in the modern economy, the institutional framework and ideas of Thorstein Veblen and John Kenneth Galbraith were utilized as authoritative sources depicting the current business environment. Their ideas constituted a point of departure for an inquiry into the nature of goodwill.

Research Procedure and Major Sources of Data

The study necessitated an extensive gathering of articles and texts directly or indirectly touching upon the accounting aspects of goodwill. Other fields of inquiry were drawn on for background material insofar as they related to goodwill in accounting.

Goodwill may be viewed on three levels: (1) the nature of goodwill, (2) the accountant's perception of goodwill, and (3) the accountant's treatment of the asset in the accounts. The accountant's perception and treatment constituted the subject of discussion in five historical chapters. These topics were analyzed simultaneously since they were found to have always been closely related both in the literature and in practice. The nature of goodwill was considered in a separate chapter, though the subject occasionally was touched on in the historical section.

An inductive approach was used in the historical chapters. After an initial review of approximately one thousand books and articles, the framework described in the following section was developed. Issues discussed in the literature were placed within definite time periods and organized by topics that constituted the framework utilized consistently in each of these chapters.

The nature chapter was developed deductively from the theories of Veblen and Galbraith. But other sources were used for information concerning specific characteristics traditionally associated with goodwill.

The major sources of data included the libraries of the University of Alabama, the University of Texas at Austin, and the University of Illinois. Substantial reliance also was placed on many other libraries throughout the United States since a large number of the sources prior to 1920 were found only in a few libraries.

Organization of the Study

The study was developed in four major sections: background, history, nature, and conclusions.

Background

Legal, economic, and historical materials are described, compared, and contrasted in Chapter II to furnish the appropriate setting.

History

Time segments: The period under study was divided into five segments and each was discussed in a separate chapter. The literature published in each period was analyzed within the following framework.

1884-1909. The first segment represented the first quarter-century of thought on goodwill in Great Britain and the United States and was marked by the rise of the modern business corporation.

1910-1929. Writers in the second segment produced the first large outpouring of articles and discussion on the subject of goodwill. This discussion continued throughout the period, but the depression in 1929 definitely curtailed extensive debate.

1930-1944. This period began with the first extended discussions on matters of accounting theory and ended in a lull brought about by the concern with World War II. Out of this lull, however, came the first authoritative pronouncement on the subject of intangibles in 1944.

1945-1957. An important merger period began in the United States after the war, and several authoritative pronouncements concerned with business combinations and goodwill were issued during this period. Articles in increasing numbers were written on the subject of goodwill during these years.

1958-1980. A significant increase in the number of mergers in the United States took place in this period, and abusive practices associated with the employment of the pooling of interests accounting technique led to a climactic and bitter struggle within the accounting profession and the financial community at large, culminating in simultaneous issuance of two major opinions directly affecting accounting for business combinations and goodwill.

Internal Organization of Each History Chapter: Each of these chapters was organized as follows—

> *The Business Environment*
> *The Accounting Environment*
> *Developments Concerning Goodwill*
> > *Characteristics of the Literature*
> > *Issues and Problems*
> > > *Initial Valuation*
> > > *Subsequent Treatment*
> > > *Financial Presentation and Disclosure*
> > > *Auditing Considerations*
> > > *Tax Considerations*

The business environment and the accounting environment were discussed briefly within each chapter to provide a suitable setting for consideration of specific developments concerning goodwill. The literature revealed overall trends relating to goodwill, and these trends provided the basis for determining the characteristics of the literature. The bulk of each chapter was devoted to a discussion of each of the specific areas that serve as focal points for an analysis of the issues and problems surrounding goodwill in accounting. The five areas listed under "Issues and Problems" are present in every chapter, but in some chapters an extra topic was added to fit the special problems of the period. For example, the topic "The Rise of the Corporation" appears in the first segment, and a section on "Goodwill and Pooling of Interests Accounting" was added in the chapters concerning each of the last two time periods. The issues to which writers addressed themselves, the problems they encountered, and the solutions they proposed became the main concern for each time period.

Nature

The nature of goodwill has proven a very elusive topic for accountants and nonaccountants alike. Indeed, one can quite reasonably argue that much of the variation in accounting treatment is due directly to problems associated with defining the nature of goodwill. The subjectivity seemingly plaguing goodwill may be viewed as preventing precise definition until subjectivity is recognized as an important aspect of the asset's nature. A major goal of this chapter was to explain the subjectivity where possible or at least to provide an understanding of why it exists.

Following a deductive approach, Veblen's institutional theory was utilized as a basic framework for analyzing the nature of goodwill. Since Veblen's articles appeared in 1908, important changes have occurred, and the contemporary interpretation of Galbraith was presented to furnish a basis for some modern implications concerning the development and maintenance of goodwill. Finally, a number of characteristics traditionally associated with goodwill were examined in detail and reconsidered with regard to new developments in the economy.

1. Stephen Gilman, Principles of Accounting (Chicago: La Salle Extension University, 1916), p. 195.

Chapter **II**

Background

Although the first accounting literature on goodwill appears to have been written in the mid-1880s, goodwill had been a topic of commercial and legal interest for centuries. English courts were dealing with one aspect of the subject as early as 1417,[1] and the term "goodwill" has been in business use since at least 1571.[2] Thus, when writers began to concern themselves with accounting aspects of goodwill, they found numerous court decisions available for their use. Because they drew heavily from the precedents and guidelines established therein and the existing commercial environment as well, an evolutionary sketch of that environment and the important court cases constitute the subject of this chapter.

A Working Definition of Goodwill

Before beginning a history of goodwill, recognition must be given to the fact that the term has always proven troublesome to define. A primary reason for the problem is that the meaning of the term has changed over time, but even at the same point in time definitions have been formulated that may be termed at least different and in some cases conflicting. Therefore a "working definition" of goodwill is offered (and utilized throughout this monograph), which allows for inclusion of certain characteristics that are currently and commonly associated with the concept: goodwill may be thought of as the differential ability of one business, in comparison with another or an assumed average firm, to make a profit.

First of all, goodwill is associated with business enterprise. In early feudal times, lords possessed economic advantages in comparison with serfs, but these advantages were not enjoyed in an institution (the manor) with a profit-making goal. However these benefits might be perceived, they usually are not thought of as goodwill.

Closely associated with the foregoing is the characteristic that goodwill represents an above-average ability to make a profit. Whatever may be said of a firm's contribution to a stable livelihood or serviceability of its product, its dominant goal must be profitability measured in terms of money values.[3] Thus goodwill ultimately is not perceived in terms of livelihood or serviceability but in terms of profit, although of course serviceability may affect profitability and, therefore, goodwill as well.

Because goodwill is commercially valuable, it is commonly regarded as an asset. There may be specific factors, such as a good location, that contribute to the ability to generate excess profits, or the presence of excess profits may be inferred as indicating goodwill. Whatever the reason, goodwill, like all assets, is capitalized according to its assumed ability to contribute to profitability.

Representing an ability to succeed in a relative sense, goodwill has no physical substance. It is, therefore, an intangible asset, and it differs from other intangibles (such as franchises or patents) in that it is not protected by special legislation or by legal instrument.[4]

Viewed in this way, goodwill is a product of its environment. As profit-making businesses began to arise—an evolutionary process which took several centuries—goodwill as it is currently and commonly perceived began to arise, also. Even so subjective an evaluation as the importance of goodwill may be viewed in a similar vein. If, as Veblen wrote in 1904, "the material framework of modern civilization is the industrial system, and the directing force which animates this framework is business enterprise,"[5] then the significance of goodwill is evident.

One last characteristic merits explicit consideration at this point. The "directing force" just spoken of is possible only to the extent that full discretionary control can be exercised by business. Such control is achieved through ownership, which must be relatively free of restrictions.[6] Where ownership has been more restricted than at present, goodwill has been more difficult to foster and sustain.

The Environment

Thus the history which follows is not the history of the essence of some phenomenon called goodwill; goodwill is viewed herein as an abstract term used to describe a particular combination and interaction of the characteristics described previously. Therefore, the history is really an evolutionary sketch of the characteristics or ingredients that comprise goodwill.

Although the 500-year period preceding the eleventh century might be described as "static," with somewhat unfavorable undertones, it also might be described as "stable." A way of life developed in which man's relation to his cultural setting was defined and remained fixed. One's relationships to his village, church, and other classes in the community were known precisely. During and after the eleventh century this cultural setting began to change, but through the fourteenth century the broad outlines of the social and economic environment remained intact.

Manorial Life: The basic unit for obtaining a livelihood was the manor, and all of its inhabitants usually lived in a village. The lord of the manor owned all of the land, which was divided into tracts, some of which were reserved for the benefit of the lord and some for the villagers.[7] The villagers cultivated the soil of the manor, working so many days of the week for their own livelihood and so many days for the lord. The villagers also were required to put in additional time for the lord at harvest and to make periodic payments in money and in kind.[8] The result was economic domination of the villagers by the lords.[9]

If the villagers wished to move from the community, they were not free to take their possessions. Before they could leave, they had to pay a large fine to the lord—so large in fact that their position in any community to which they might go would be substantially lowered.

> He could not gain if he went empty-handed; and that he should go empty-handed was secured by the universal rule of all manors that villeins [villagers] should not sell ox or horse without license.[10]

The manorial community was virtually self-sufficient, as the villagers provided all that was necessary for their own sustenance. This self-sufficiency forced individual members to work for the group as a whole, however, and the people were very dependent on each other.[11] When manors produced more than was required for their own sustenance, the excess was sent to towns for trade or for money. The origins of these towns are obscure, but their existence seems to have depended on excess agricultural goods from the manor.[12]

Town Life and Guild Regulation: The towns, like the manors, showed tendencies of self-sufficiency and of mutual interdependence among inhabitants. For the common good of the townspeople, municipal authorities attempted to regulate the quality of the goods made. Much of this regulation was accomplished by control of the guilds.[13] The merchant guild, arising in the eleventh century "was a society formed primarily for the purpose of obtaining and maintaining the privilege of carrying on trade."[14] Craft guilds began to appear in the twelfth century and were organizations of "artisans engaged in a particular industry in a particular town."[15] The local nature of trade was a dominant factor in this mutual interdependence and the resultant strict regulation. What trade there was existed in towns between townspeople. "Consumer and producer stood in direct relation with one another."[16] Virtually no alternatives for trade existed; each villager knew those with whom he traded and needed their goods as they needed his. The need for such control thus was apparent, and the environment of local markets made such controls feasible as well.[17]

Regulation of the quality of goods produced had two facets—protection of consumers and protection of producers. If goods were of inferior or unacceptable quality, the consumer was not getting the full benefit of the product he bought, and the producers, collectively as a craft guild, found their image damaged by the act of one member. Producers therefore had an interest in regulating the quality of goods, both for their own protection and for that of the consumer.[18]

The motivating force behind such an interest in regulation is indicated in the following:

> The spirit of the medieval western guild is most simply expressed in the proposition, guild policy is livelihood policy. It signifies the maintenance of a substantial burgherly prosperity for the members of the guild, in spite of increased competition in consequence of the narrowness of the opportunities of life; the individual guild member must obtain the traditional standard of life and be made secure in it.[19]

The permanence of the environment was a factor to be reckoned with in pursuing a policy of livelihood. As indicated by reference to workers striving for a traditional standard and its security, the policy was one of maintenance rather than of increase.

In following this policy of livelihood, measures were required to establish and maintain equality of opportunity for guild members.

> To realize this equality the development of capitalistic power must be opposed, especially by preventing the unequal growth of capital in the hands of individual masters and consequent differentiation among them; one master must not progress beyond another.[20]

The guilds purchased the raw materials, parcelled them to the masters, regulated how the work was done, determined the acceptable number of apprentices, limited the amount of capital employed, prescribed the form of tools, and forbade masters from working for other masters.[21] "Each hoped to get a fair share of existing trade rather than to extend it; the regulations of their craft guilds were not favorable to the formation or application of capital."[22]

The price mechanism was employed to accomplish these regulations. Like most other features of the economy, prices were subject to control, and these controls had as their foundation the then extant doctrine of just price. The just price doctrine was a question of ethics, and at that time ethics were rooted in theology.[23] One objective of this doctrine was to prevent "material gain from becoming the sole motive of economic activity," and it recognized no valid existence "for economic activity as such."[24] The result was that the regulation of what today might be termed economic activity became virtually complete with the inclusion of price controls.

Because economic activity was not regarded as a separate phase of community life, the regulations were not strictly economic in nature. Rather, these regulations of community livelihood were extended to the inhabitants collectively and individually in all phases of life. In any analysis of the economic implications of such a style of living, it must be kept in mind that no economic phase existed separately in such a close-knit state of affairs. Therefore, any purely economic distinction is somewhat artificial.

Environmental Effects on Goodwill

The implications of such an environment upon the development of goodwill are significant. Although certain vital characteristics were present that would be necessary to its development, certain other characteristics were not. For example, one necessary constituent of goodwill is the existence of a preferential advantage of one person or group over that of another person or group. Such advantage may arise from custom, such as the traditional prerogatives of one's social class over another, or may be attributable to ability or inherited traits.

Such preferential advantages did exist—most obviously in the manor where the lord held control over the villagers and in towns where gifted craftsmen exhibited superior skills and workmanship. Given these advantages, the issue of whether goodwill could exist depended on the manner and use, if any, to which the advantages could benefit the individual.

Implications of the Manorial System: "Under the agrarian-manorial régime of the Middle Ages it was not felt that the wealth of the large owners must, as a matter of course, increase by virtue of what they already had in hand—whatever may be the historical fact as regards the increase of wealth in their hands."[25] The lord exercised and maintained his advantage by following the customs and traditions that had been in existence for centuries. He followed a policy of maintenance—both of the existing social differentiation and of the manor in its existing condition. Stated differently, he followed a policy of livelihood regarding the various phases of the manor. Although his livelihood might be substantially above that of the villagers, it was still a livelihood in the traditional sense.

In contrast to the manorial system, business enterprise follows a policy of seeking an increase in wealth rather than merely its maintenance, and the asset goodwill exists only because one business is more successful in this endeavor than its competitors. Because production of goods and services in the manor was primarily for internal consumption, no economic competition as is presently known existed; there was no vying for the customers of another business or marketplace. Thus, even where a lord sought an increase in his own power or wealth at the expense of neighboring manors and/or his serfs, such an increase would not take place with a profit motive or "orderly rate of return" in mind.

With no profit motive, the possessions of the manor were not assets, if that term is understood to mean the capitalization of some object based on its profit-making capability. In short, there was no profit motive, no basis for perceiving (let alone measuring) differential profits, no assets, and no goodwill.

Implications of Town and Guild Controls: In the towns it would appear likely that certain ambitious or gifted individuals might have attempted to turn this ambition or skill to their own advantage and increased their wealth and position relative to fellow guildsmen. But when the guilds so strictly regulated their lives, they were unable to take advantage of the situation. Those policies that worked to provide equality for members also worked to limit the acquisition and use of differential advantages. Superior skill could not be used for individual profit where the quality of goods was controlled, the form of tools prescribed, and the exact techniques of production defined.

Further, because the number of workers or apprentices in the service of any given master was fixed, capitalistic ambitions were thwarted. The saying, "the touch of the master's hand," might be interpreted as the application of superior knowledge to some situation and the reaping of superior returns, but during this period of time the master was not allowed to exercise his touch.

Factors restricting the development of goodwill could exist only so long as the environment retained its relatively stable character. Toward the end of the Middle Ages, important implications for economic organization and for goodwill arose from changes that contributed to the evolution of a more dynamic environment.

The End of the Middle Ages—Early Modern Times

The Environment

> It must not be understood that old things altogether passed away, and all things became new; that one system followed another like dissolving views upon a screen. The relation to one another of stages in social evolution is far more complex. While in each successive period there is much that is altogether new, there is also much that is but an enlargement or wider application of the old. Much, again, that is old continues to survive, although no longer in complete harmony with the prevailing tendencies of the time, because it has some use in a subordinate sphere; or even from the mere force of inertia, because economic forces are not strong enough to sweep it away.[26]

Such should be the interpretation of events from roughly the fourteenth century through the eighteenth century. The environment was no longer stable; it was changing in many ways—though very slowly at first.

Breakdown of the Manorial System: The manorial system began to give way in the fourteenth century. As early as the eleventh century, a money economy was developing in the Italian cities and slowly spreading throughout Europe.[27] By the thirteenth century this increased reliance on money began affecting manorial life. Money payments to the lord replaced the former tradition of paying in kind. Before this time some pecuniary payments had been made, but now the lord received a predominance of money. Commutation of payments in kind worked for the benefit of both lord and peasant. The lord now had a form of wealth he could utilize in a number of ways—a form of wealth he could capitalize and thereby make a profit.[28] Commutation also worked to the benefit of the villager, as he was allowed to devote full time to his own interests and could sell his agricultural produce where he wanted.[29] The villagers began rising from the status of serfs to that of tenants and eventually were able to leave the land to which they once were bound.

Commutation also meant that the lord was now interested in money, however, and he did not care from whom or how many he received his due. That he should receive his money from a few tenants with large land holdings rather than a large number of tenants with small holdings was sometimes preferable. The result was a concentration of the land and an inequality of holdings, which would lay the foundation for the emergence of capitalistic farming in the seventeenth and eighteenth centuries.[30]

Peasants were freed from the land in other, less favorable, involuntary ways, also. When land was enclosed by some ambitious lord, the peasant lost a vital portion of his means of subsistence. "In accordance with the principle fitting the situation, the peasants were expropriated in favor of the proprietors. The peasants became free but without land."[31]

With emphasis on money rather than livelihood, there was no longer concern for equality, as it was useful only to promote the cohesiveness of the community. The cohesiveness and well-being of the community was no longer the issue at stake.

Decline of Towns and Guilds: No less important changes were occurring in the towns. In the fifteenth century, the towns had reached the peak of their development.[32]

> The more or less complete independence of the towns in matters commercial and industrial, the mutual alliance of the members of each civic body for the pursuit of the common advantage of the town, are distinguishing features of this period of economic development in every part of Central and Western Europe.[33]

Trade had developed within the towns, but the extension of trade to new horizons resulted in the growth of national interests. Finally, in the sixteenth century, the towns gave way to the state.[34] The rise of capitalism added further to the aura of change. From the viewpoint of the practical man during this time, one commentator noted that,

> A century before, he had practised extortion and been told that it was wrong; for it was contrary to the law of God. A century later he was to practise it and be told that he was right; for it was in accordance with the law of nature.[35]

Although changes and deterioration were evident in earlier times, the sixteenth century brought the guild system into an advanced state of decay. Compared to its peak, conditions of the sixteenth century presented a view of imbalance: (1) an equality of status no longer prevailed among members, (2) some members acquired large amounts of capital and employed workers or other masters, and (3) older and economically stronger members gradually gained power in the guild, taking over guild offices and the right to vote.[36] External problems existed as well as internal ones. Capitalism was applied to industrial pursuits, and the guild system rested on a municipal trade basis, which gave way to a nationalistic trade basis. Furthermore, the guilds became dependent on importers of raw materials and on exporters who sold their finished wares.[37]

The guild regulations functioned well under the local system, but a growing national trade undermined the strict local surveillance for the common good. With the power of the cities and guilds sapped, maintenance of a stable livelihood policy became impossible. Distant locations were more dependent on one another, and municipal regulation proved ineffective in controlling trade on a national basis. In order to survive, the individual was forced to work for his own benefit—which no longer necessarily coincided with that of the common good. The effects of these changes on life were illustrated by a contemporary (1550) writer, Robert Crowley, in the following verse:

> And this is a Citye
>   in name, but, indede,
> It is a pack of people
>   that seke after meede;
> For officers and al
>   do seke their owne gaine,
> But for the wealth of the commons
>   not one taketh paine.
> An hell with out order,
>   I maye it well call,
> Were euerye man is for him selfe,
>   And no manne for all.[38]

Livelihood was no longer the crucial point; gain now dominated men's considerations. The gain was obtained by whatever means the individual could turn to account, including a friendly disposition or a good location, both elementary forms of goodwill. The basis of determining fairness or equity shifted from what was necessary to maintain a livelihood to what was necessary to maintain rights of property.

Environmental Effects on Goodwill

Initial Development of Goodwill and Restraint of Trade Doctrines: With the rise of this "early capitalism," the differential attributes spoken of earlier (such as superior skill or ambition) now might be turned to one's advantage and possibly could be sustained. Before this time all members of a given craft had to live on the same street or in the same area, but the demise of the guild system meant they were no longer bound by such restrictions. An individual might find a superior location for operating his business and therefore would make—and be entitled to—the superior returns that would result. He might have an older business with a number of regular customers, which newer businesses would need years to establish. The guild system prevented these situations from developing, but the new system enabled people to take advantage of such opportunities. Those various factors had value, for they were differential advantages capable of being developed and maintained for the benefit of the businessman.

Although these factors were goodwill, they were not yet thought of as assets and the benefits derived therefrom were severely restricted. If a merchant attempted to sell his business—and the goodwill that went with it—he frequently ran afoul of rather formidable restraint of trade laws. Of the various types of contracts held to be in restraint of trade, a promise by a worker not to compete with his employer after the termination of the employment and an agreement by the seller of a business not to compete with his buyer are of immediate interest.[39] The former was the earliest known of contracts not to compete and usually involved apprentices or craftsmen agreeing to refrain from their trade. These contracts were regarded with hostility by the courts because

> In a society of restricted opportunity in which men were trained for
> a definite occupation such covenants either deprived the worker of
> the means of livelihood, reducing him to a state of idleness, . . . or
> promoted change, which was equally abhorred.[40]

In essence, the emerging capitalistic organization of industry in the fifteenth century, based on property rights and profit capabilities, was coming into conflict with the earlier restraint of trade objectives based on livelihood.

When the purchaser of a business secured the seller's promise not to compete, the agreement was illegal and the parties were subject to fine or imprisonment or both.[41] The practice continued, however, even though the law retained the concept of livelihood in the traditional sense and therefore was not in tune with the emerging system built on property rights. The purchaser thus had no legal means of protecting himself, and he suffered serious consequences when the agreement was heard in court. He was in the predicament of purchasing property without being able to protect the right of beneficial use thereof. Furthermore, the property could not be used for personal consumption—production was for a market and the producer needed protection in delivering the wares to market. An individual's possession of physical property was not disputed, but the uses of property were limited to production for a market. The right of possession was protected, but the use of it was not.

The change in the policy of restraint of trade came in 1620 when an individual sold his wares and agreed not to compete with the purchaser. Upon violation of the agreement, the purchaser sued the seller, and the court decided in the purchaser's favor.[42] For the first time, the courts decided that an individual could sell his liberty as well as his property,[43] and goodwill was accorded legal protection.

Types of Goodwill: The ideas concerning goodwill in the sixteenth and seventeenth centuries were products of the form of business dominant at the time. The business concern was usually small and the proprietor was confined to dealings on a local scale, necessitating personal contact with his customers. In such circumstances, goodwill was defined roughly as the good feeling of customers of the business toward the proprietor because of the cordial and friendly relationship or because of a favorable location for business.

These types of goodwill required a relatively long period of time to develop; and they probably account for what has been termed the momentum theory of goodwill—i.e., goodwill as the value attaching to an old or existing firm over that of a similar but new firm. In an age when communication and transportation were relatively slow, it took time for the community to establish the habit of trading with a concern and to accept a new business. Therefore, the purchase of an established enterprise required a larger investment than the purchase of property and other assets necessary to start a new enterprise.

The foregoing considerations also illustrate the dependence of goodwill upon its environment. Because goodwill is a phenomenon of business, the business structure affects the form in which goodwill may appear, the methods in which it may be acquired, and the methods in which it may be maintained. When the nature of business changes, so does goodwill.

Early Modern Developments

The Environment

Technological and Institutional Change: The period from the middle of the eighteenth century to nearly the end of the nineteenth century was marked by great technological development and institutional change. Although much technological change necessarily preceded the industrial revolution that began to develop in the 1750s, the particular surge and direction of this phenomenon within the institutional framework of business enterprise and the framework's subsequent modification were unique in modern times. Technological developments in the last half of the eighteenth century and first quarter of the nineteenth brought about the factory system, which took advantage of greater efficiency and speed in manufacturing, plentiful fuel, and more rapid transportation.[44] An effect of these developments was an increase in the sheer size of industrial equipment and the use of a substantial number of people to set the equipment in motion. Large organizations were established to provide goods and services on a regional, national, or even international basis.

The force motivating these establishments continued to be business enterprise—but on an unprecedented scale. Individual entrepreneurs were less able to gather the capital necessary to handle the larger concerns, and the corporate form was utilized more extensively. However, the sizable corporate organizations were unable to retain the same personal relationship that had developed from localized enterprise between producer and consumer. Furthermore, the idea of a good location from which to do business was superseded to the extent that business was maintained on a regional or larger basis.[4][5]

The newer situation forced a different viewpoint regarding profits and the factors that caused profits. In the earlier environment, a readily observable and causal relationship appeared to exist between assets and the resulting profits. In a small enterprise, a close relationship between patronage and profitability could be expected, and these factors could be delineated in a relatively clear fashion.[4][6] As the enterprise grew in size and complexity, the close relationships between the business and consumers and between specific assets and profits disappeared. As before, earnings were assumed to be a function of assets, but the old method of looking first to the assets and then to the resulting profits no longer applied. It was necessary in many instances to look first to earnings and then to assets. The earning power of the firm rather than the individual assets became the central issue, with the valuation of specific assets of that firm of secondary interest.[4][7]

Legal Aspects of Goodwill: Implications for the evolving concepts of goodwill were evident in early nineteenth century legal definitions of goodwill in Great Britain. In 1810, in what appears to be the first definition on goodwill, Lord Eldon stated that "the good-will, which has been the subject of sale is nothing more than the probability that the old customers will resort to the old place."[4][8] This definition pertained to beneficial location and referred only to the facts of the case. Beneficial location formed the basis for location goodwill discussed earlier and was adequate to describe the goodwill of the country wagon driver involved in the case.[4][9] Although the definition may be criticized for being narrow, in most cases a comprehensive definition of the term was not the main object of discussion. Goodwill was interpreted only within the facts of a given case, and the chief point of concern was the true intent of the parties involved.[5][0]

In 1859 a much broader definition was given in the case of *Churton* v. *Douglas*. For many years, Douglas conducted a partnership with Churton and others under the name of "John Douglas & Company" in the town of Bradford. Douglas sold his share of the business and his goodwill and moved to a different city. Over a period of approximately eighteen months, Douglas moved his business back to Bradford (next door to the old business which was still in existence), placarded the location with the John Douglas & Company name, enticed several trusted employees of the old firm to enter into partnership with him, and held his new firm out to the old firm's customers and to the public as a continuation of and as identical with the old firm. Churton and his partners then sought an injunction restraining Douglas from carrying on business representing himself as a successor to or continuation of the old dissolved firm of John Douglas & Company. The injunction was granted. Vice-Chancellor Wood argued that the defendant had every right to set up business after the sale of his partnership interest and goodwill; he even had the right to set up business next door to the old business in the absence of an agreement stipulating the contrary. When Douglas sold his goodwill, however, he sold the benefits that result from being identified with the old firm. Although he could set up business next door, he could not hold himself out as the successor of the old firm, for that privilege was sold with the goodwill which Vice-Chancellor Wood defined as

> every advantage ... that has been acquired by the old firm in carrying on its business, whether connected with the premises in which the business was previously carried on, or with the name of the late firm, or with any other matter carrying with it the benefit of the business.[51]

Although legal recognition of goodwill as an asset appeared in Great Britain as early as 1743,[52] American recognition evolved in a series of decisions from 1872 to 1897.[53] Originally, property was held to be physical things in accordance with the common-law meaning in the United States.[54] With the change of the definition from the use-value of physical property to the exchange-value of anything, "it was an easy step to change the definition of goodwill from 'fair competition' to 'property.' "[55]

Environmental Effects on Goodwill

Technological and legal developments in the nineteenth century changed the form in which goodwill appeared, the methods of acquiring it, and the methods of its maintenance. In contrasting the earlier situation with the developing one, Veblen observed that

> In the earlier days of the concept, in the period of growth to which it owes its name, when good-will was coming into recognition as a factor affecting assets, it was apparently looked on habitually as an advantitious differential advantage accruing spontaneously to the business concern to which it appertained; an immaterial by-product of the concern's conduct of business—commonly presumed to be an advantitious blessing incident to an upright and humane course of business life.[56]

The goodwill so generated was not necessarily the result of deliberate action on its behalf, and the form of goodwill was of a personal and local character. As business broadened in scope, so did the concept of goodwill. Its acquisition was no longer incidental to business operation and it was deliberately pursued. The time element was not as important because it was no longer necessary to rely on personal integrity or custom built up slowly in a local community.[57] Deliberate attempts to secure goodwill were concerned with differential advantages, and anything giving rise to a differential advantage was considered goodwill.

> Goods would be given a more elegant finish for the sake of a readier sale, beyond what would conduce to their brute serviceability simply; smooth-spoken and obsequious salesmen and solicitors, gifted with a tactful effrontery, have come to be preferred to others,

who, without these merits, may be possessed of all diligence, dexterity, and muscular force required in their trade; . . . much thought and substance is spent on advertising of many kinds.[58]

This view of goodwill is consonant with the most common method of valuing goodwill. With the issue turning on the firm's earning power, all of the various instruments of production are assumed to earn some normal rate of return. The normal amount of income generated by these assets is subtracted from the total income of the firm, and the residue is considered to be due to a complex variety of factors and is capitalized at some percent to determine an approximate value for goodwill.[59] Goodwill of this type would be maintained by continuing the efforts spoken of previously, particularly as regards expenditures for advertising.

Summary

The development of goodwill paralleled the development of business enterprise. With the change from a pursuit of livelihood to a pursuit of profit, differential advantages in the form of local and personal goodwill were sustained. By approximately 1884, goodwill was legally considered a valuable property right in Great Britain and was evolving toward being considered such by courts in the United States. With the development of large corporate business, the concept of goodwill broadened to include virtually every differential advantage a concern might obtain. It was no longer considered an incidental by-product, but a valuable asset resulting from deliberate action.

The earlier ideas concerning goodwill had not vanished but were applicable mainly to concerns that operated on a limited basis. The relative importance of earlier concepts declined, therefore, as the corporate form of business gained ascendancy.

---

1. John R. Commons, *Legal Foundations of Capitalism* (New York: MacMillan Company, 1924), p. 264.

2. P.D. Leake, *Commercial Goodwill: Its History, Value and Treatment in Accounts*, 3rd ed. (London: Sir Isaac Pitman & Sons, Ltd., 1938), p. 1.

3. Thorstein Veblen, *The Theory of Business Enterprise* (New York: Charles Scribner's Sons, 1915), Chapter 4. (Hereinafter referred to as *Business Enterprise*.)

4. Thorstein Veblen, "On the Nature of Capital: Investment, Intangible Assets, and the Pecuniary Magnate," *The Quarterly Journal of Economics*, November 1908, p. 115. (Hereinafter referred to as "Capital: Investment, Intangible Assets, and the Pecuniary Magnate.") For later sources where this article may be found, see the Bibliography.

5. Veblen, *Business Enterprise*, p. 1.

6. Ibid., Chapter 4.

7. William Ashley, *An Introduction to English Economic History and Theory, Pt. I: The Middle Ages*, 4th ed. (London: Longmans, Green and Co., 1919), pp. 6-7. (Hereinafter referred to as *The Middle Ages*.)

8. Ibid., pp. 8-9.

9. Thorstein Veblen, "On the Nature of Capital: (The Productivity of Capital Goods)," *The Quarterly Journal of Economics*, August 1908, p. 528. For later sources where this article may be found, see the Bibliography.

10. Ashley, *The Middle Ages*, pp. 37-38.

11. Ibid., sec. 5.

12. Ibid., p. 35.

13. Ibid., pp. 94-95.

14. Ibid., p. 71.

15. Ibid., p. 76.

16. Ibid., p. 95.

17. William Ashley, *An Introduction to English History and Theory, Pt. II: The End of the Middle Ages*, 4th ed. (London: Longmans, Green and Co., 1925), p. 29. (Hereinafter referred to as *End of the Middle Ages*.)

18. Ashley, *The Middle Ages*, p. 95.

19. Max Weber, *General Economic History* (Glencoe, Illinois: Free Press, 1927), p. 138.

20. Ibid.

21. Ibid., pp. 138-140.

22. W. Cunningham, *An Essay on Western Civilization in Its Economic Aspects, Bk. V: Nationalities* (New York: G.P. Putnam's Sons, 1913), p. 165.

23. Edgar Salin, "Just Price," *Encyclopaedia of the Social Sciences*, Edwin R.A. Seligman, ed., VIII (1932), p. 504.

24. Ibid., pp. 505-506.

25. Veblen, *Business Enterprise*, pp. 85-86.

26. Ashley, *End of the Middle Ages*, p. 43.

27. Salin, "Just Price," p. 505.

28. Ashley, *The Middle Ages*, p. 43.

29. Frederic Austin Ogg, *Economic Development of Modern Europe* (New York: MacMillan Company, 1921), p. 26. (Hereinafter referred to as *Development of Europe*.)

30. Ibid., p. 30.

31. Weber, *General Economic History*, p. 98.

32. Ashley, *End of the Middle Ages*, p. 6.

33. Ibid., p. 7.

34. Ibid., p. 42.

35. R.H. Tawney, *Religion and the Rise of Capitalism* (New York: Harcourt, Brace and Company, 1926), p. 163.

36. Ogg, *Development of Europe*, pp. 34-35.

37. Weber, *General Economic History*, pp. 153-155.

38. Robert Crowley, *The Select Works of Robert Crowley*, J.M. Cowper, ed. (London: N. Truber & Co., 1872), p. 11.

39. Milton Handler, "Restraint of Trade," *Encyclopaedia of the Social Sciences*, Edwin R.A. Seligman, ed., XIII (1934), p. 339.

40. Ibid., pp. 339-340.

41. Commons, *Legal Foundations of Capitalism*, p. 22.

42. Broad v. Jollyfe, Cro. Jac. 596 (1620).

43. Commons, *Legal Foundations of Capitalism*, pp. 264-265.

44. Ogg, *Development of Europe*, p. 145.

45. Kemper Simpson, "Goodwill," *Encyclopaedia of the Social Sciences*, Edwin R.A. Seligman, ed., VI (1931), p. 699.

46. J.M. Yang, *Goodwill and Other Intangibles: Their Significance and Treatment in Accounts* (New York: Ronald Press Company, 1927), p. 90. (Hereinafter referred to as *Goodwill and Other Intangibles*.)

47. Ibid., pp. 90-91.

48. Cruttwell v. Lye, 17 Ves. 335 (1810).

49. Lawrence R. Dicksee and T.M. Stevens, *Goodwill and Its Treatment in Accounts* (London: Gee & Co., 1897), p. viii.

50. Ibid., p. vii.

51. Churton v. Douglas, Johns. 174 (1859).

52. Charles E. Allan, *The Law Relating to Goodwill* (London: Stevens and Sons, Limited, 1889), p. 3. Allan cites the case of Giblett v. Reade, 9 Mod. 459 as possibly being the first case to recognize goodwill as an asset.

53. Commons, *Legal Foundations of Capitalism*, pp. 11-28.

54. Ibid., p. 12.

55. Ibid., p. 18.

56. Veblen, "Capital: Investment, Intangible Assets, and the Pecuniary Magnate," pp. 117-118.

57. Simpson, "Goodwill," p. 699.

58. Veblen, "Capital: Investment, Intangible Assets, and the Pecuniary Magnate," p. 118.

59. Yang, *Goodwill and Other Intangibles*, p. 93.

Chapter III

History 1884-1909

The Business Environment

No single factor affected all facets of goodwill more then the rise of the modern business corporation. The 25 years of this period were marked by unparalleled growth of large corporate firms, a process that began years before and continued afterward. The legal foundations of the corporation were developed early in the nineteenth century and cleared the way for the corporation's dominance in economic affairs. However, the effects of corporate development upon concepts of and accounting for goodwill evolved mainly in this period. The position of the owners declined in importance, and concepts of goodwill changed as a result. Ideas regarding the permanence and transferability of goodwill arose, and financial statement presentation and disclosure became an issue of major importance as owners became separated from the affairs of the firm. Proprietorship and partnership forms of business were still relatively important, and accounting literature was devoted to their problems. After the turn of the century, however, emphasis was increasingly placed on corporate matters.

The Accounting Environment

Accounting literature on goodwill appeared in both Great Britain and the United States at about the time the accounting profession was beginning to make some progress in each country. Scottish and English societies were being formed in the mid-nineteenth century, and papers read at meetings of these societies were printed for the members and published in periodicals or newspapers, such as *The Accountant* started in 1874.[1] The first accounting article on goodwill appears to have been published in 1884.[2] The time was ripe for the appearance of an article on the subject. It was of great importance in business affairs, it was of ever increasing importance to accountants, and periodicals devoted to accounting subjects were available as a publication media.

The same conditions did not occur in the United States until around the turn of the century. The formation of associations of accountants began in the 1880s, and, after some initial faltering, periodical literature appeared in the first decade of the twentieth century.

The professional organizations were not yet strong enough to formulate accounting principles that would affect current practice. Their role in that respect was mainly to provide comments, criticisms, and recommendations concerning accounting practice, rather than to make deliberate efforts to change it. Criticism was needed, however, for some corporate reporting practices were deplorable and deliberately misleading. Such practices had their effect on the treatment of goodwill, and various methods were employed to use the caption "goodwill" for purposes of manipulation in financial statements.

Characteristics of the Literature

One striking feature of the literature of this period is the similarity of the topics and arguments discussed then and those discussed now. By 1907, for instance, the question of writing down goodwill had been raised so often and had settled into such a familiar pattern that two men were said to have "fairly well exhausted the *stock arguments* that have from time to time been put forward"[3] (italics mine). Basing the valuation of goodwill on superior or excess profits was mentioned as early as 1891 by Francis More.[4] Virtually the first writer to examine in detail the problem of goodwill valuation, his reasoning and approach have yet to be significantly improved.

As accounting literature was almost entirely British, discussion there dealt with problems encountered in British practice. Early writers on goodwill gave emphasis to partnership and proprietary forms of business (as opposed to the corporate form) and considered in detail the numerous legal implications occasioned by sale and transfer of those firms. One reason for this interest in proprietorships and partnerships might have been the sale of professional practices, which was more common in England than in the United States.[5] In neither country was the corporation yet as important relatively as it later came to be.

More emphasis was given to corporation problems around the turn of the century, when huge trusts virtually came to dominate the economic sphere of life. The early legal emphasis appears to be due to the importance of specifying in a contract the exact relationships, rights, and duties of all parties concerned in the sale or dissolution of a noncorporate entity. The law also represented the only systematic attempt to cope with goodwill and served as a foundation and point of departure for accounting writers.

Issues and Problems Concerning Goodwill

The Rise of the Corporation

The English concern with proprietorships, partnerships, and related legal considerations serves to illustrate some distinguishing features of corporate goodwill. Proprietorships and partnerships are usually thought of as personal businesses. Specific individuals may be identified as both owners and managers, and the owners' personal fortunes may be bound substantially to the enterprise. The firm, being so closely identified with its owner-manager, takes on personal characteristics, not the least of which is an ultimate mortality—that is unless the business can be carried on by a new proprietor or new partners.

The ultimate transferability of the firm, by a partner or proprietor, depends on the extent to which the owner leaving the firm is bound to the work. An extreme example might be that of an actor, whose talent might be considered to be the "business." Upon retirement, an actor could get nothing for his business because it is so inseparably a part of himself. What he would be trying to sell would be intangible—his voice or his wit, for instance, which brought the goodwill of his patrons—something on which he had capitalized but on which no one else could. His talent could have been an intangible asset (goodwill) except for its lack of transferability. Similarly, a professional man such as a surgeon or lawyer might die and his goodwill might lapse. But if the surgeon or lawyer retires, an opportunity of selling goodwill exists to a limited extent. Although talent is not transferable, another practitioner might be brought into the business, and the patients or clients would be introduced to him.

Although skill passes with the lawyer or surgeon, to some extent business connections may be sold. Discussing the transferability of such differential advantages, Veblen wrote that:

> They come to have a pecuniary value and rating, whether they are transferable or not; and if they are transferable, if they can be sold and delivered, they become assets in a fairly clear and full sense of that term.[6]

An ordinary business that makes or sells goods potentially has a great degree of transferability. Upon the retirement or death of an owner, the business might be passed substantially intact to someone else. The business may be less attached to its owner, and vendibility of the business certainly enhances the value of the goodwill. There still remains, however, the possibility of jeopardizing the value of goodwill when the business is sold.

And, although the Goodwill of a trading concern, after it has been fairly established, is not generally dependent, to any great extent at least, on the man, still there must always be more or less risk of the Goodwill going down on its being transferred to a new man, even though he should be in every way equal in energy and ability to the founder of the Goodwill.[7]

Various writers such as Stacey, More, Roby, and Guthrie referred to goodwill with the preceding examples.[8] The topic of commercial versus professional goodwill was relatively important, and the personal nature of businesses pervaded the discussion. Even as they wrote, however, the corporate form of organization was coming into a place of its own in business affairs. The corporation ceased to be a device useful only to a small group of individuals intent on conducting business in much the same fashion as a proprietorship or partnership. A corporate system was evolving—a system that was attracting to itself a combination of attributes and powers and was attaining a degree of prominence entitling it to be dealt with as a major social institution.[9] Berle and Means felt that the system had not yet reached its peak when they wrote in the 1930s, but the process was well under way at the turn of the century and thereafter became progressively more pronounced. The corporate structure permitted formation of huge concerns and the amassing of wealth by a multitude of owners. As a result, the owner ceased to be an active participant in corporate affairs. With some exceptions, the shareholder had possession but relinquished control of the business.

Although the corporation lost many of the individual and personal characteristics of its owners, it also was free of those characteristics. The question of ownership transferability no longer jeopardized the continuance of the business. Furthermore, goodwill of the business was no longer jeopardized when shares were sold. The business would not be concerned with losing goodwill built up by individual initiative of the owner because that type of goodwill was no longer important and had ceased to exist. The owner's concern shifted from management of the business to vendibility of the stock and the right to receive a dividend.

> Tersely, the shareholder has a piece of paper with an open market value, and as holder of this paper may receive from time to time, at the pleasure of the management, periodic distributions. He is forced to measure his participation, not in assets, but in a market quotation; and this market quotation "discounts" or appraises the expectation of distributions.[10]

This line of reasoning is consonant with the view expressed in Chapter 2. The earning power of the firm was becoming the central point of concern; the specific assets of the firm were of secondary interest at best. Because earning power had become so important, anything that enhanced it enhanced the owners' position, also. The concept of goodwill changed correspondingly to include any advantage, or—in the previously quoted words of Vice-Chancellor

Wood—every advantage, whether connected with the premises or the name of the firm or any other matter.

In summary, the owners' position in many firms changed from a dominant role to a much smaller one by comparison. As the corporate system developed, the individual initiative and personal goodwill of the owners diminished in importance. The position of the corporation changed from a legal device for its owner to a dominant institution in its own right, no longer subject to the perils of ownership transferability. The position of goodwill changed from incidental advantages depending on certain specific factors to any and every advantage benefiting the firm. Veblen alluded to the importance of goodwill by referring to it as "the nucleus of capitalization in modern corporation finance."[11]

Initial Valuation of Goodwill

First Accounting Discussion: "I am sorry I cannot refer you to any authorities on the subject, for I know of none."[12] Such was the position in which Francis More found himself when addressing the meeting of an accounting students' society in 1891. Prior to More's speech, valuation of goodwill had been discussed only incidentally in connection with court cases involved in setting a value for a specific dispute. After raising the issue, More then proceeded to deliver what appears to be the first lecture on goodwill valuation from the accountant's point of view.

More offered a short sketch of the development of goodwill valuation. At one time, goodwill was paid for by offering the seller a share of future profits. More preferred this method; it based the seller's receipts for goodwill on what actually took place when business was conducted in the new owner's hands. That method gave way to one in which tangible assets were valued at some figure, then goodwill was valued at so many years' purchase of the firm's profits, and cash was paid for the entire amount. This method provided a set sales price to the seller but offered greater opportunity for over-valuation of goodwill. More felt these valuation methods had been superseded by another, stating that "The plan however, which is at present in favour, is to regard the profits as the real basis of the valuation, the tangible assets being regarded merely as one of the means whereby the profits are earned."[13]

In any case, no price was to be paid for goodwill unless the firm was making in excess of an ordinary return. For those firms making superior returns, the excess should be divided into several layers. Each successive increment should be valued lower than the previous one because it became succeedingly harder to maintain higher and higher levels of excess income. Although a numerical example was given, no guidelines were offered for a specific business as to how the increments should be determined or how the increments should be valued. "His claim was simply that if a firm doubled the amount of its profits after deducting that required return on net tangible assets, the value of the goodwill should normally be less than doubled."[14]

More added one further refinement to his approach. He assumed that any given goodwill increment was assumed to be paid for in a predetermined number of equal annual installments. If one current payment was made for it instead, then each installment was discounted by a percentage representing a normal return to obtain the present value of future receipts or disbursements. This value became the valuation basis for goodwill.

The capitalization of excess profits to obtain a value for goodwill thus was affected in two ways: (1) higher increments of excess returns were valued less than previous ones due to risk and (2) the installments used to pay for these increments were discounted because of the time value of money.

Influence of Business Form on Goodwill Valuation: Lawrence Robert Dicksee delivered an extended lecture on goodwill in late November 1896.[15] The discussion was very comprehensive from an accounting point of view—so comprehensive, in fact, that it formed the core of the first book devoted entirely to the subject of goodwill in accounting.[16] (The wording of the lecture appears to have been altered only in a minor fashion to fit the occasion of a book. An introductory chapter on legal matters was placed before the main text, and a section explaining the entries required and the resulting financial statements was placed after it.)

Dicksee's discussion, although certainly paying attention to the treatment of goodwill in corporate situations, mainly emphasized noncorporate enterprises. Three circumstances needed to exist before goodwill could have a value: use of the old location, use of the old name, and a promise by the original owners not to compete. These circumstances, particularly the last, indicate concern with an enterprise in which the owner played a relatively major managerial role.

A valuation of goodwill became necessary upon sale of all or a portion of the enterprise. The attitude of the retiring owner became of paramount importance. Would he assist or oppose the new undertaking? If the owner had died, both were beyond his power. If he retired and assisted the new firm, the goodwill would be more valuable. But if he opposed it (for instance, if he had been expelled from a partnership), the goodwill might be worth less due to possible conflict.

With those factors in mind, the valuation was based on an excess-profits concept. From average net profits (usually the average of from three to four years) was deducted interest on capital and the cost of the time and skill of management. The remainder was multiplied by some factor to obtain a value for goodwill. The reasoning and assumption behind the managerial cost deduction warrant analysis. A business requiring a great deal of time and skill is worth less than one not requiring as much, assuming the new proprietor appears in the role of both owner and manager. In a corporation, management expense should already be provided for. It usually is handled through the drawing account in noncorporate firms, however, and does not appear in the income statement. In noncorporate firms, then, Dicksee was in effect calling for recognition of the cost of management in income computations for goodwill valuation purposes.

Where Dicksee discussed goodwill related to a corporation ("company" in his text), he mentioned that the goodwill would be valued higher because shareholders were investors and not "workers," and their liability was limited.[17] Another writer, Browne, came to the same conclusions because shareholders "need not, and generally are not, required to take an active part in the affairs of the undertaking."[18] The corporate form of business thus provided a basis for a higher valuation of goodwill due to separation of the ownership and management roles, the resulting inactive position of the shareholder, and his limited liability.

Reasons for higher corporate goodwill valuations also can be seen by using Dicksee's own framework sketched previously. Of Dicksee's three circumstances, the promise not to compete is of little use. When shares of stock of a large corporation are purchased on the open market, there is little need to secure a former shareholder's covenant to restrain from competition. Because the shareholder was not active in the first place, the covenant has no meaning in a continuing firm from the point of view of a corporate buyer and seller. Similarly, the attitude of the retiring owner of a corporation is of no consequence. The vendor has no power to hinder the new concern as he probably had no such power to begin with. A managerial cost deduction has already been provided for as an expense rather than as a withdrawal by an owner closely identified with the firm.

Over-capitalization and Watered Stock: Higher valuations of corporate goodwill did not justify the over-valuation and possible subsequent over-capitalization of the firm. Over-capitalization can have various meanings, but the meaning attributed to it in this discussion is primarily from the investor's viewpoint. A firm is over-capitalized in this sense when it is unable to pay an adequate return of interest or dividends to the bearers of its securities.[19] Browne noted that some private concerns conducted business profitably but reached a state of stagnation when converted to corporations.[20] Promoters, through optimism, ignorance, deceit, or some of each, had capitalized average net profits at the highest figure the firm might ever hope to make and set the purchase price accordingly. The difference between that figure and the value of tangible assets was called goodwill and was potentially a very inflated figure. The large capitalization of the company, with resulting goodwill over-valuation, caused investors to obtain a less than adequate return.

The issue of watered stock was closely related to that of over-capitalization, as watered stock frequently was the method whereby over-capitalization was achieved. The problems associated with watered stock centered on the importance attached to par value at the time. The law required that shares be issued or subscribed only if fully paid for. In the case of cash, no problem existed. If the property given was something other than cash, then a question of valuation arose. As it was assumed that stock was not issued unless fully paid for, the property, instead of being recorded at its market value, was recorded at the total par value of stock given for it. Either the property was grossly overstated, or an artificial asset *goodwill* was created for the difference between the asset's market value and the stock's par value. Henry Rand Hatfield condemned the latter practice and stated (concerning the inflated goodwill) that "such an item is not merely immaterial but also imaginary."[21] He argued that had the stock been issued for gold, no one would have calmly added to the list of assets an equal amount representing an imaginary asset *silver*. Although he admitted that a valuation would be very difficult in the case of a manufacturing plant,

> The claim is still made that to reject the standard of attempted accuracy is a confession of impotence, which, while it exhibits a commendable modesty on the part of professional accountants, seems, to the layman, to do scant justice to the ability of that profession.[22]

Initial Treatment in Accounts: Once some consideration had been given for goodwill, the problem arose as to what to do with it in the accounts. The question was partially resolved based on the form of the business acquiring the goodwill. In the case of proprietorships and partnerships, the general feeling was that the charge to goodwill should be written off immediately to the capital account(s) and never charged to revenue. Of course, the proprietor or partners were free to choose accounting procedures as no reporting responsibility existed outside the owners. However, at some future time the present owners might have occasion to open their accounts to a prospective purchaser—accounts that would show the price originally paid for goodwill. According to Dicksee,

> The chances are (at all events, if the business is an increasing one) that they will find it rather embarrassing to disclose this cost price at a subsequent date, and thus there is a very powerful argument in favour of the amount standing to the debit of Goodwill being written off with all due speed.[23]

In other words, the present owners would likely demand a much higher price for goodwill than the amount originally paid for it, and this fact was, from their point of view, better left undisclosed to the prospective purchaser.

The Companies Acts in Great Britain prohibited corporations, but not proprietorships and partnerships, from writing off goodwill through the capital account.[24] As a result, goodwill could be either left in the accounts permanently as an asset or dealt with in some relation to revenue—by writing it off to revenue or by setting up a reserve. This issue is discussed in more detail in the following subsection, "Subsequent Treatment in Accounts."

There appears to have been an aversion to including goodwill as an asset at this time. Accounting and reporting abuses resulted from manipulating the recorded amount and from the uncertainty of what the correct accounting procedure should be. The tendency to exclude the asset reached such a point that one writer felt a prejudice existed against goodwill as an asset, though it was an important factor in the economy. Although he realized that the greatest care was needed in dealing with goodwill, "the general denouncement and depreciation of the term as an asset is altogether unnecessary, and, at the same time, injudicious."[25]

Significance of the Subject of Goodwill Valuation: A Summary: The proper valuation of goodwill offered the accountant an opportunity to utilize his particular skills. Legal matters were important in the period from 1884 to 1909, yet they represented a point of departure from which the accountant was required to rely on his own area of expertise. The accountant first encountered goodwill in dealing with its appraisal and treatment in accounts. From the viewpoint of valuation, the literature at the time showed the influence of the form of business and the (British) legal requirements for corporations. Promoter abuses in connection with initial valuation led to criticism of questionable accounting practices and (along with other influences) a conservative view in favor of not recognizing goodwill at all. Other areas, for instance tax considerations, would command major attention in later years; but for the time, the subject of initial valuation was of primary importance.

Subsequent Treatment in Accounts

There can be no complete or clean division of areas studied where such topics as initial treatment, subsequent treatment, and statement presentation are under consideration. To a large extent, a stand on a given point implies the position taken in all three areas, so that necessarily there is some overlap in the issues discussed. The present division of the subject matter is utilized, however, because the issues tend to be separated in a general way along these lines.

Immediate Write-off: In the case of proprietorships and partnerships, the issue of subsequent treatment seems to have been resolved in favor of immediate write-off. This method offered a quick and easy way to deal with a potentially troublesome matter. If, for example, goodwill had been retained, what could be done with it subsequently? Here was an asset that did not always appear to behave like the others. Goodwill did not necessarily depreciate; quite possibly it might appreciate or aimlessly fluctuate. If these fluctuations were recorded—a rise in the value of goodwill in good times and a decline in bad times—the effect on the income statement would be to show even wider fluctuations in the net profit or loss than would otherwise be reported.

Dicksee called goodwill "an asset which it is undesirable to retain as such" and preferred immediate write-off to capital with the following logic.[26] The main motivation for getting it off the books of accounts was to avoid possible future embarrassment to present owners if they decided to sell. The suggested write-off method was based on a perception of goodwill as a permanent asset, much like land. To charge goodwill to revenue was just as erroneous as to do so with land. Goodwill therefore should be charged to capital at the earliest time, and in the case of a partnership to the various partners in the ratio in which they shared profits.

In other words, though the idea of goodwill as a permanent asset might suggest that it be treated like land, i.e., its cost be retained permanently on the books, this perception was coupled with other considerations, which led to an aversion against retaining it as an asset and suggested its removal from the accounts. The characteristic of permanence restricted the method of its removal by precluding charges to or allocations of revenue, so that the ultimate solution was to charge capital.

As noted, this approach was not available to corporations because of restrictions in the Companies Acts prohibiting the reduction of goodwill by a charge to capital. Several practices arose, as did arguments on how best to deal with goodwill from the corporate viewpoint.

Permanent Retention as an Asset: Proponents of immediate write-off followed through as closely as possible with their same reasoning (modified by law for corporate accounting) and decided that goodwill should be retained permanently as an asset in corporate accounts. They felt that goodwill was permanent but had an aversion to treating it as an asset. By their own logic they were against charging goodwill to revenue; by law they could not charge it to capital. The only thing left to do was to leave it on the books indefinitely as an asset. This solution had the advantage of recognizing goodwill as the permanent asset that it was assumed to be. Therefore, the proponents of immediate write-off had found a less desirable but reasonably acceptable method for dealing with corporate goodwill.

Accountants differed in the degree to which they believed the argument should be carried. One felt that only "ignorant prejudice" called for the gradual writing down of goodwill, and it should be valued at cost only.[27] Some felt goodwill should be valued at cost but, where profits permitted, could be written down gradually. The more faithful adherents of the view set forth earlier replied that "the very possibility of being able to apply current profits to the reduction or extinction of Goodwill, as it stands in the books, is one of the best proofs of its value."[28] They therefore reaffirmed its retention in the accounts. Other reasons advocated for this method are discussed in a following subsection, "Financial Presentation and Disclosure."

Gradual Reduction: The foregoing reasoning was stretched one step further, for even though permanent retention of goodwill was felt to be desirable, some support existed for gradually eliminating it from the books. As a practical possibility, a firm usually considered reducing goodwill only when it was doing well. As noted, however, the possibility of being able to write it down raised arguments against doing it, i.e., the desirability of reducing goodwill came under increasing attack in proportion to the ability to do so. The motivation for amortization or write-downs appears to have stemmed from those who wished the accounts and statements to be more conservative. Because of the reluctance to recognize it as an asset, uneasiness existed in seeing goodwill on the books. A prudent course would be to remove it when the firm was in a position to do so.

But how could the reduction be accomplished with the foregoing basic arguments still kept relatively intact? How could the gradual reduction of an asset be reconciled with its assumed permanent existence? Even granted some solution to that problem, how could the actual entries be accomplished, given the theoretical and legal arguments against the various methods of reduction already mentioned? What would happen to the plan of reduction in bad times?

Confronted with these and other problems, the arguments appear to have splintered in several directions. A general theme developed, however, though it was not espoused completely without individual variations. First of all, the basic assumption of the permanence of goodwill was allowed to stand intact. Thus the idea of a charge to revenue continued to be disavowed. Instead of a charge to profits, some recommended that a "reserve fund" be gradually accumulated out of current or accumulated profits up to the amount of goodwill shown on the books.[29] The reasoning developed that goodwill still was assumed to be a permanent asset—only its book figure was being dealt with. Use of the reserve method offered the advantages of allowing goodwill to appear at its original cost in financial statements as well as showing an appropriation of earnings for it. The emphasis was on the idea of an allocation of profits rather than as a charge against profits.[30] What conceivably would happen to the plan of reduction if the corporation fell on hard times does not appear to have been answered to anyone's satisfaction. Obviously, it was undesirable to continue adding to the reserve, but what justification existed for suspending the allocations? As one writer admitted in a presumed rejoinder to his own contentions,

> Surely what you propose is very illogical; . . . when by reason of large profits the goodwill must be worth more you would show it to be worth less, and by inference, when profits are small and the goodwill worth less, the charge for redemption of goodwill would be postponed.[31]

Aside from this dilemma, the possibility existed that some company would feel the time had arrived for the reserve to be useful and would begin allocating the reserve back to profit and loss, a practice not very highly regarded.

Some writers who favored gradual reduction of goodwill did not agree with the assumed permanence of the asset. Hatfield felt that "this doctrine of the permanence of Goodwill seems inconsistent with the theory of valuing it as the purchase of a temporary terminating annuity."[32] Guthrie similarly felt that no goodwill was eternal, and some provision, even though based on an arbitrary estimate of the life of goodwill, should be made.[33] Dropping this assumption left them free to advocate the depreciation (in their terms) of goodwill by charges to revenue, though Guthrie felt that the process of restricting retained earnings was acceptable as an option. This view of goodwill constituted an open break with the earlier view of its permanence and had ramifications from subsequent treatment through financial presentation. Although those who assumed goodwill's permanence might grumble at the allocation of profits as theoretically questionable, a charge to profits was simply wrong in their view.

The logic of either set of arguments appears to have been consistent—given the assumptions. Part of the problem was to be found not so much in the ultimate accounting practices advocated, therefore, as in the initial assumptions from which those accounting practices originated. But what is the point of subsequent argument if the grounds for that argument are not agreed upon? That problem is not new and appears yet to be adequately resolved.

Financial Presentation and Disclosure

Recommended Treatment: Of major significance to the preceding arguments was the ultimate effect obtained by presentation and disclosure of goodwill in financial statements and the resulting interpretations. Again, the issue was confined mainly to corporate reporting practices; noncorporate businesses supposedly were understood thoroughly by owners who knew exactly what the representations in their own financial statements meant. This issue arose when communication became a major factor as a result of the rise of corporations and the subsequent separation of owners from the businesses.

Those who advocated permanent retention of goodwill took the following position as to its interpretation and presentation. The amount stated in the balance sheet represented neither its maximum nor its minimum value.

> In short, the amount is absolutely meaningless, except as an indication of what the Goodwill may have *cost* in the first instance. Inasmuch, therefore, as nobody can be deceived by its retention, there is no *necessity* for the amount of Goodwill Account to be written down.[34]

The permanent retention testified to the asset's permanent existence, and although its value fluctuated, it was assumed that interested parties would understand that the figure represented only initial cost.

Evidently some writers felt that more significance was attached to goodwill in the balance sheet, or at least they had an aversion to stating the item unless some reserve was provided from profits. It was thought to be "injudicious and unsafe" to allow an item of such uncertain value to appear in financial statements; the sooner profits were allocated to a reserve for it, the better.[35] For anyone who cared, the original cost was still shown, as well as the reserve allotted from profits at a given date, and the income statement was still free of charges.

Those arguments for depreciation of goodwill due to its assumed indefiniteness were carried out by charges on the income statement and a reduction of its book value reported in the balance sheet. Although this treatment was logical, given their assumptions, it drew special criticism from those who viewed goodwill as permanent. Charging depreciation to profits necessarily meant that the income statement was affected. In their view, this brought extraneous profits or losses into the income statement.[36]

The problem, as before, was due to the different assumptions followed. From one point of view, for instance, the charge to profits was extraneous and obscured the meaning of financial statements. But if the charge was viewed as depreciation of an asset whose life was limited, it was not extraneous at all and no obscurity resulted. Thus, as noted earlier, the various recommended treatments of goodwill in financial statements were but the logical culmination of arguments based on different grounds.

Actual Practice: By the third edition of his work on goodwill in 1906, Dicksee disapproved of current reporting practices, noting that goodwill was "either lumped together with half-a-dozen other assets" or was "smuggled away in some far corner" where the investor "was not likely to discover it."[37] Dicksee condemned such practice as "sheer jugglery, for which there can be no excuse and no palliation."[38] Some explanation for these practices might be found in a discussion following a lecture on goodwill. One participant wondered how any auditor could certify a balance sheet as a "full and fair one" when goodwill had been "clubbed" with a number of assets. The chairman of the meeting agreed with him but noted that ulterior considerations frequently motivated directors to hide the asset. "And, as a rule, the point is not of sufficient practical importance to induce the auditor to take a hostile attitude, especially in those cases where he is virtually the appointee of the board."[39] Hatfield noted the same practice in America and cited specific examples where goodwill was shown under the following illustrative captions: Property, etc.; Goodwill, Patents, Leases, Trade Marks, etc.; Patent Rights and Goodwill.[40]

What was presented and disclosed both in Great Britain and the United States can be summed up under the caption "anything goes," and apparently it did. Problems in disclosure were not limited to matters concerning goodwill, however; the treatment accorded goodwill appears to have been symptomatic of the general absence of reporting standards at that time.

Auditing Considerations

The relation of goodwill to auditing did not receive much attention during this period. Questions of auditing usually arose at two points: (1) the valuation of goodwill for purposes of purchasing a business and (2) the presentation of goodwill in the balance sheet. If a business was changing hands, the valuation of goodwill might be based on so many years' purchase of average net profits or of average net profits reduced by a normal return. In this case, therefore, heavy reliance was placed on the validity of the profit computation, and the prospective purchasers might retain an auditor to ascertain the correctness of the figure. The auditor would be conducting an investigation—a special audit undertaken for a particular purpose—which would change his approach.[41]

A regular audit in Great Britain at this time usually had as a major goal the prevention of fraud. In the case of a special investigation, the auditor would not be so concerned with this matter. Instead he would be interested in those items that could materially affect profits—fictitious reductions of expenses or fictitious increases in revenue.[42] The auditor would look for such things as unreasonable reduction of expenses or a large number of sales at the end of the period in question. Attention also would be directed to the actual results of the past few years. The average net profits figure taken by itself would not reveal the possibility of declining profits or of greatly fluctuating profits; either condition would render the goodwill less valuable, regardless of the average.

It was agreed almost unanimously that goodwill should be stated separately in the balance sheet, and the auditor should see that this was accomplished. Where expenditures on advertising were incurred to produce goodwill, capitalization would be allowed, but only with caution. The auditor should see that no advertising had been capitalized under the heading of goodwill; the amounts represented as an asset needed to be stated separately. If directors of a corporation found it desirable to reduce goodwill, the auditor was not required to express his opinion on the desirability of doing so, although he might suggest a course of action.[43]

Although auditing aspects of goodwill may have been significant, other possible problems concerning goodwill simply overshadowed it. Valuing goodwill for purposes of purchasing a business was important, but once the method had been decided on, nothing was left to do but follow through with routine auditing procedures, which were not the subject of the immediate problem. Presentation of goodwill from the viewpoint of the auditor's duties similarly appears to have been a problem involving auditing questions more than questions directly bearing on goodwill.

Tax Considerations

Little which bore directly on goodwill had been done in the area of taxation during this period. Accounting discussions were almost void of any mention of goodwill in connection with taxes; only later would tax considerations come to have an important bearing on goodwill in accounting.

Summary

The development of the corporation, accompanied by separation of the owner from his business, had extensive ramifications on all aspects of goodwill. The effects of these changes were felt in the area of accounting, where members of the emerging professions in Great Britain and the United States began discussing the problem in the newly formed accounting journals. At first concerned with legal matters and personal and location aspects of goodwill associated mainly with proprietorships and partnerships, the literature subsequently was directed more and more to considerations of corporate goodwill and its effects on corporate accounting and reporting.

Initial valuation of goodwill was a subject of major importance and offered the accountant his first opportunity to utilize his skills with regard to the asset. Writing at the turn of the century, certain authors brought out virtually all of the major theoretical points associated with valuing goodwill on an excess or superior profits basis.

After goodwill was recorded in the accounts, most writers preferred that the asset be written off immediately to the capital account and never be charged to revenue. This treatment, open to proprietorships and partnerships, was closed to corporations in Great Britain due to various statutory requirements. Several alternatives arose for handling the asset on corporate books, including permanent retention as an asset, permanent retention coupled with an appropriation of accumulated earnings, and a "depreciation charge" against current income. Arguments for and against these alternatives carried over into the asset's financial presentation and disclosure—a subject of increasing importance in the case of corporations due to the separation of owners from the business.

1. Richard Brown, *A History of Accounting and Accountants* (New York: Augustus M. Kelly, 1968), p. 245.

2. William Harris, "Goodwill," *The Accountant*, March 29, 1884, pp. 9-13.

3. "The Treatment of Goodwill in Accounts," *The Accountant*, June 15, 1907, p. 801.

4. Francis More, "Goodwill," *The Accountant*, April 11, 1891, pp. 282-287.

5. Edward S. Rogers, *Good Will, Trade-Marks and Unfair Trading* (Chicago: A.W. Shaw Company, 1914), p. 23.

6. Thorstein Veblen, "On the Nature of Capital: Investment, Intangible Assets, and the Pecuniary Magnate," *The Quarterly Journal of Economics*, November 1908, p. 362. For later sources where this article may be found, see the Bibliography.

7. More, "Goodwill," p. 282.

8. Walter E. Stacey, "Goodwill," *The Accountant*, September 22, 1888, pp. 605-606; More, "Goodwill," pp, 282-287; A.G. Roby, "Goodwill," *The Accountant*, April 2, 1892, pp. 288-293; and Edwin Guthrie, "Goodwill," *The Accountant*, April 23, 1898, pp. 425-431.

9. Adolf A. Berle, Jr. and Gardiner C. Means, *The Modern Corporation and Private Property* (New York: MacMillan Company, 1934), p. 1.

10. Ibid., p. 287.

11. Thorstein Veblen, *The Theory of Business Enterprise* (New York: Charles Scribner's Sons, 1915), p. 117.

12. More, "Goodwill," p. 284.

13. Ibid.

14. Bryan V. Carsberg, "The Contribution of P.D. Leake to the Theory of Goodwill Valuation," *Journal of Accounting Research*, Spring 1966, p. 4.

15. Lawrence R. Dicksee, "Goodwill and Its Treatment in Accounts," *The Accountant*, January 9, 1897, pp. 40-48.

16. Lawrence R. Dicksee and T.M. Stevens, *Goodwill and Its Treatment in Accounts* (London: Gee & Co., 1897). (Hereinafter referred to as *Goodwill*.)

17. Ibid., p. 13.

18. E.A. Browne, "Goodwill: Its Ascertainment and Treatment in Accounts," *The Accountant*, December 20, 1902, pp. 1339-1344.

19. For further discussion of over-capitalization, see Victor Rosewater, "Over-Capitalization Injures the Public," *The Journal of Accountancy*, September 1907, pp. 330-332.

20. Browne, "Goodwill: Its Ascertainment and Treatment in Accounts," pp. 1339-1344.

21. Henry Rand Hatfield, *Modern Accounting* (New York: D. Appleton and Company, 1913), p. 115.

22. Ibid., pp. 170-171.

23. Dicksee and Stevens, *Goodwill*, p. 20.

24. Browne, "Goodwill: Its Ascertainment and Treatment in Accounts," p. 1342; and Sidney S. Dawson, "Goodwill," *Encyclopedia of Accounting*, vol. III, p. 204.

25. William H. Gundry, "Goodwill," *The Accountant*, June 28, 1902, p. 663.

26. Dicksee and Stevens, *Goodwill*, pp. 20-21.

27. Stanley G. Smith, "Depreciation of Assets and Goodwill of Limited Companies," *The Accountant*, January 9, 1904, p. 49. Smith attributed these remarks to a Mr. Welton.

28. Browne, "Goodwill," p. 1342.

29. Sidney S. Dawson, "Goodwill," pp. 205-207.

30. Ibid.

31. Guthrie, "Goodwill," p. 428.

32. Hatfield, *Modern Accounting*, p. 116.

33. Guthrie, "Goodwill," p. 429.

34. Lawrence R. Dicksee, *Auditing: A Practical Manual for Auditors*, 3rd ed. (London: Gee & Co., 1898), pp. 195-196. (Hereinafter referred to as *Auditing*.)

35. More, "Goodwill," p. 286.

36. Sidney S. Dawson, "Goodwill," p. 205.

37. Lawrence R. Dicksee and Frank Tillyard, *Goodwill and Its Treatment in Accounts*, 3rd ed. (London: Gee & Co., 1906), p. 73.

38. Ibid., p. 91.

39. Browne, "Goodwill," pp. 1342, 1344.

40. Hatfield, *Modern Accounting*, p. 117.

41. Dicksee, *Auditing*, p. 344.

42. W.J. Dawson, "Goodwill," *The Accountant*, January 12, 1901, p. 50.

43. Sidney S. Dawson, "Goodwill," pp. 206-207.

Chapter IV

History 1910-1929

The Business Environment

The period from 1910 to 1920 was generally characterized by great prosperity and continued development of the corporate institution. Accompanying this prosperity was a rise in price levels, which led to a serious questioning of the stability of the monetary unit—an assumption long held in business generally and accounting specifically. (Before and during this era, many considered that book value should continuously approximate fair market value.) Recorded asset cost no longer could be considered even to roughly approximate its fair market value except at the time of acquisition, and the effects of inflation on the interpretation of financial information based on historical cost had to be recognized.

The influence of the continued development of the corporation may be seen in the effects of the adoption of no-par stock laws. The first of these laws was passed in New York in 1912, and other states soon followed suit.[1] According to Berle and Means, these laws were part of a general movement to increase the powers of corporate boards of directors at the expense of traditional state regulation, protection of creditors, and direction by owners.[2] Accounting for goodwill was affected because the directors were now in a position to pursue their objectives without the necessity of watering stock and over-valuing assets, particularly goodwill.

An entirely new area of concern for accountants arose with the passage of the sixteenth amendment permitting taxation of income. Because goodwill constituted an important factor in the valuation of a firm, procedures for determining gain or loss treatment of goodwill had to be developed by tax authorities. With the passage of the prohibition amendment, firms involved in the sale of alcoholic beverages found their markets, and consequently their goodwill, wiped out. The proper tax treatment of goodwill that was destroyed in this manner required much consideration.

The effects of these developments were (1) an increased emphasis on corporate aspects of accounting for goodwill, (2) questioning of cost as the only basis for the asset, (3) a decline in the importance of watering stock and over-valuing goodwill, and (4) formulation of an appropriate treatment of goodwill for tax purposes.

The Accounting Environment

Although the accounting profession in the United States was developing, it still lacked the strength to formulate accounting principles. Due to the absence of any codification of accounting principles, a number of alternatives arose over the handling of numerous items, including goodwill. How an amount was determined for goodwill, how it was treated in the accounts, and how it was presented in financial statements were open to a variety of methods.

Another factor contributing to the increased number of alternatives was recognition of the instability of the monetary unit. As assets increased in monetary value at least partially due to monetary instability, some advocated recording unrealized appreciation in the accounts.[3] Although British law allowed considerable latitude in corporate accounting practice, it also placed heavy responsibility on corporate directors for proving that any recorded appreciation was realizable. As a result, British practice emphasized cost. No such laws existed in the United States, however, and writing up assets, though controversial, was more common in this country than in Great Britain.[4]

Much of the criticism concerning write-ups of asset values undoubtedly was justified. George O. May noted, however, that:

> Write-ups of fixed assets are in many quarters strongly disapproved. Not only is this so, but past write-ups are condemned, as if they had been originally violations of a fundamental principle instead of being merely something that is outmoded today.[5]

These comments by May should be considered in any evaluation of the following criticisms of the write-up of goodwill.

Characteristics of the Literature

Repetitive Nature of the Discussion

With most of the major points already discussed in the previous period, the large outpouring of articles on goodwill could hardly have been anything but repetitious. More journals were being established in Great Britain, Canada, and the United States, and the same issues were unremittingly reiterated in a consistently mediocre manner.

Some positive aspects existed in this outflow of mediocrity, however. If the major points had been decided, many fine points received more attention and some of the arguments were elaborated. Writers of the previous period now were referred to as authorities (for example, Dicksee). This fact, coupled with the similarity of views in the literature, indicated a growing acceptance of certain accounting practices to the exclusion of alternatives. Even though a variety of treatments of goodwill were discussed at this time, some were definitely preferred. ·

American Domination

American domination of the discussions on the subject came swiftly and decisively. This was probably due, at least in part, to the fact that British practice was regulated by law and somewhat settled; American accountants had no such legal framework to rely on and, as a result, were faced with several alternatives. With this American domination and the importance of the corporation increasing rapidly, matters of goodwill peculiar to proprietary and partnership businesses faded into the background, along with the related legal considerations.

Issues and Problems Concerning Goodwill

Initial Valuation of Goodwill

The subject of initial valuation was expanded during this period, and, as a result, some initial clarification and delimitation may prove helpful in following the discussion. As the environment changed, so did the relative importance and standing of the issues and problems of the previous period. These changes are brought out in the subsequent topic. Then the next topic is concerned with problems encountered in the purchase of a business where questions arose as to what items should be included in the valuation of goodwill.

Some individuals felt that certain items could be capitalized as goodwill at stages in a firm's life other than the date of the firm's purchase, and the relative merits of considering these items as goodwill and the timing of their capitalization forms the basis for discussion in the next three topics. These topics represent stages in the life of a firm which were used by W.A. Paton in a discourse on going value, an area closely related to goodwill.[6] For purposes of this discussion, initial valuation includes the valuation of goodwill upon purchase of a business, as well as the initial valuation of any item as goodwill at various stages of a firm's life.

Relationship of Previous Issues to This Period: Some of the older issues diminished in importance and passed out of the picture. However, one subject (initial treatment in accounts) was expanded and became much more important.

Influence of business form on goodwill valuation. The corporation obviously had become the dominant business form, and comparisons with proprietorship and partnership forms virtually ceased to concern writers. Hence the problem of transferability of goodwill did not warrant much further discussion. The influence of the form of business was pertinent to understanding the advantages, disadvantages, and uses of each structure, but as a practical matter involving the organization of business on a large scale, it ceased to be of importance. Writers became more concerned with goodwill built up from advertising than that from personal efforts of owners or locational advantages which required time to develop properly.

Over-capitalization and watered stock. The immediate reason for the passage of no-par stock laws was to protect investors from being misled when par value stock was issued for a group of tangible and intangible assets.[7] With the adoption of these laws, accounting for goodwill was improved to the extent that extraneous over-valuation from this source was no longer recorded in accounts. Whether or not the laws accomplished their objectives, the practice of stock watering was generally discarded and became mainly a topic of historic interest.

Initial treatment in accounts. The subject of initial accounting treatment did not share the fate of the issues mentioned previously. Writers detailed what items should be included in goodwill and devised methods of treating them in the accounts. This subject forms the core of the discussion that follows.

Purchase of a Going Concern: The mechanics of valuing goodwill in the purchase of a going concern had been settled to a great extent by this time. The favored method capitalized excess profits above some normal return to obtain a valuation for goodwill, and discussions in this era were more detailed as to its uses, computation, and problems.

Excess profits method—use and limitations. The excess profits method was useful in an important role in the actual valuation of goodwill as agreed on by both buyer and seller. In the computation of goodwill, the final valuation rests on the capitalization of excess profits. The excess profits are determined by subtracting normal profits from total average profits for a given number of years. Normal profits are determined by applying a given percentage to the average investment. In dealing with a related point, one writer pointed out the arbitrary factors necessary in the computation: the number of years used for the various averages, the percentage used for the capitalization of excess profits, and the rate applied to average investment to obtain normal profits.[8] With so many of the key aspects of the method based on arbitrary assumptions, the capitalization of excess profits gives only a rough approximation and can be readily manipulated to the advantage of either buyer or seller.

Excess profits method—elimination of extraordinary items. The treatment of extraneous or extraordinary items also presented a problem, and H.C. Freeman pointed out a number of situations to be considered. In the adjustment of profits, discontinued divisions of the business should be excluded while fixed charges distributed to them might have to be allocated back to divisions still in operation. The shrinkage of merchandise values, coupled with the effects of a recession on the average annual profits, presented a difficult problem. Freeman recommended that years such as 1920 and 1921, in which a significant recession had occurred, be excluded from the bases of calculation as entirely abnormal. Similarly, unproductive assets may be owned, but the reason for holding them should be examined before they are excluded for computational purposes. The cost of excess facilities representing equipment not currently in use but held for anticipated expansion should be excluded.[9] The object in all of these adjustments was to show profits as normal as possible, on the assumption that these normal profits more clearly represented the conditions that the future owner could expect. But, as one writer noted, "If so-called extraordinary expenses are all eliminated from statements of past operations, wherein is there room for improvement and what allowance is there for the mistakes of the future?"[10] Assumptions were made not only in the percentages and number of years used, but also in the average profits and investment to which those percentages pertained.

Goodwill determined. Whatever the problems in determining the value of goodwill, the figure finally decided on and paid established its validity for recognition in accounting records, and accountants agreed that the cost of goodwill so established could be entered in the books. Recording goodwill at cost seems to be the only point of agreement about the handling of goodwill in accounts, however. The determination of its value, the problem of what to do with it once it had been recorded, the issue of whether to write on a figure for self-generated goodwill, and the inclusion of various items such as advertising under the heading "goodwill" were all points of controversy. But if goodwill had been purchased, it could be recorded at cost with virtually no objections.

Arguments supporting exclusive recognition of purchased goodwill. Some writers, recommending a strict adherence to the cost principle, felt that the purchase of a going concern afforded the only time goodwill should be recorded. Hatfield felt that such a restriction was necessary to prevent harmful exaggeration, noting that, "Human nature is so incurably optimistic, especially when it comes to estimating one's own possessions."[11] Paton and Stevenson felt the rate of return on the actual investment was the significant fact for the owner, and this rate would be obscured if goodwill was capitalized at a figure other than cost.[12] In these and other arguments for the cost principle, however, "the justification of the cost basis rests, perhaps, more on the inherent defects of any suggested method of valuation than upon the abstract merits of the cost approach, itself."[13]

Initial Organization of a New Business: Rather than purchase an established business and pay for and inherit the goodwill already developed, potential investors might wish to start their own business and run the risks and perils of establishing their own connections. According to Paton, the first phase of the life of a new business begins with the activities necessary to organize and construct the firm and ends when the firm is capable of commencing regular operations and making its first sales. The second period extends from this time until the firm begins making a normal return. The third phase is attained when the firm is capable of maintaining this normal return.[14] Although these phases are somewhat arbitrary, they provide a useful framework for the analysis of various expenditures in terms of the merits of their being capitalized under the caption of goodwill. The first phase is discussed in this topic; the others follow in the next two topics.

In the first phase, large expenditures on advertising and for organizing and constructing the business would be necessary. Questions pertaining to the disposition of these items in the accounts concerned: (1) the capitalization or expensing of the items and (2) if capitalized, the account in which they should be placed. Usually there was no argument over the first question; the firm had not yet begun profit-seeking activities. No revenues yet existed to which such costs could be charged as expenses; these costs represented necessary costs of constructing the business in much the same manner as expenditures made on constructing the physical plant of the business. Therefore, they should be capitalized and charged eventually to the future periods that they were intended to benefit.

Where to place these capitalized costs posed a different question, however, and the usual amount of controversy that pervades most discussions of goodwill again appeared. Advocates of a strict application of the cost principle argued that goodwill was created only on the purchase of an existing business. Goodwill represented a part of the purchase price occasioned by superior earning power of the business, which could not be assigned to other specific assets. Although these expenditures should be capitalized, they should be capitalized under some heading other than goodwill. A reasonable approach would be to treat them as deferred charges under some descriptive caption, such as "Organizational Costs" or "Pioneering Costs."

Others might have agreed that the purchase of a going concern afforded a good opportunity for placing goodwill on the books, but they disagreed that it afforded the only opportunity. Advertising expenditures represented an example. For what other reason, they might ask, were advertising expenditures made than to build goodwill? The advertising expenditures served the same purpose in the construction of a new business as payment for goodwill did in the purchase of an old business. Why not call the expenditure what it was meant to develop?[15] The rejoinder to this argument rested on two points: the caption "goodwill" was not appropriate, and new businesses just could not have goodwill. These points, however, depended to some extent on the assumptions chosen. The environment had changed greatly since the time when goodwill was slowly cultivated by a good personality or a reputation for honesty. Advertising could create a demand for a product almost overnight, and a new firm could benefit from advertising in the same manner as an old firm. Where an established firm was acquired, the payment for goodwill probably was based on past earnings performance, giving the appearance of objectivity. However, the payment for goodwill, like that for advertising, was made only on the basis of what was expected to develop in the future. In short, payment for both was grounded on expectations or hope. In one instance, payment was made to acquire existing goodwill; in the other, payment was made to develop goodwill. In either case, though, the expenditures were, in substance, made for the same thing.

Other types of organization expenditures were not so closely connected to the development of goodwill and, therefore, could not be capitalized so readily under the goodwill heading. These expenditures were shown as goodwill in some instances, but at least one writer felt this was an abuse of the goodwill account.[16] The item was best treated as a deferred charge.

Developmental Phase of a New Business: Although there can be no clean break between this phase and the previous phase, the developmental stage generally may be characterized by initial increments of revenue, which are insufficient to produce a normal return on investment. Although substantial losses may be sustained, revenues, however small, are coming in to the firm. No longer is it strictly a matter of sinking resources into a stationary form; initial expenditures are finally beginning to be realized.

Expenditures on advertising again merited attention, as did substantial losses from initial profit-seeking operations. Again the two questions could be posed concerning the capitalization or expensing of the items and the account in which they should be placed if capitalized. In moving from the first to the second phase, some of the theoretical justification for capitalization of advertising had been removed. One of the earlier arguments for the capitalization of advertising now worked in the opposite direction. If these expenditures tended to benefit a firm almost overnight, or in the short run anyway, then the usefulness of advertising usually would be obtained in the period in which the expenditure was made, which would dictate expensing the item in most cases. Only if the expenditure would clearly benefit future periods could it be capitalized—and then only as a deferred charge to be assigned to the revenue of future periods. R.H. Montgomery preferred to be even more stringent by adding one slight refinement to advertising treated as a deferred charge. Instead of deferring advertising to the period that it *did* benefit, he felt that advertising should be deferred to the earliest period it *might* benefit.[17]

Some writers felt that there was sufficient justification for capitalizing at least some advertising expenditures. The foregoing arguments might be conceded for normal amounts of advertising, and a continuing effort might be deemed necessary to sustain a normal sales volume. This effort was correctly treated as an expense of the current period. Situations occurred in which more than a normal advertising effort was necessary, however, as when a new firm was trying to secure a given amount of trade for its recently introduced product or when an old firm was introducing a new product line. Some of the expenditure clearly could benefit only the current period, but a significant portion was aimed at creating demand for the product to enhance future sales—which was the same thing as creating goodwill.[18] Kester felt that the difference between what was necessary to create a demand and what was necessary to sustain it should be treated as goodwill.[19] Theoretical considerations were one thing but practical considerations were another, and the difficulty of applying this valuation technique was admitted. Still, Kester felt that it could be done, though as he and another writer pointed out in this and related matters, with the utmost conservatism.[20]

Other items also were capitalized in the developmental phase of a business. What was variously called "going value," "pioneering value," or "missionary work" might be charged to accounts bearing those names, but it also might be charged to goodwill. These items usually referred to "the capitalized value of early losses and unrealized income" and had very little reason for being in a balance sheet—much less in the goodwill account.[21]

Instead of capitalizing only extraordinary expenditures that could be expected to benefit future periods, all expenses in excess of revenues might be capitalized on the basis that there was a developmental or going value representing the capitalized early losses and income deficiencies.[22] The argument is somewhat similar to the reasons for capitalizing extraordinary advertising expenditures, but it rests on less solid grounds. Most, if not all, of the items composing going value clearly could benefit only the current period, with the result that items were shown as assets on the balance sheet that had no future usefulness and simply were not assets. Finney felt that in such cases the goodwill account was being abused and served as "a device for effecting an eventual inflation of the Surplus account by relieving it of charges for expenses and losses."[23]

Attainment of Normal Operating Conditions: When a firm survives the construction and developmental stages, it is at least making and maintaining a normal return on invested capital and may be making an extraordinary profit. Because by definition of this third phase, revenues exceed expenses, one of the problems of the second phase is no longer under consideration: no losses exist that might be capitalized as goodwill. The problem concerning advertising expenditures remains the same as that of the previous period. Ordinary amounts of advertising should be charged to profit and loss; only that portion which might benefit future periods should be carried forward as an asset, to be written off quickly in the earliest period that might benefit. If this firm chose to expand its market and had to incur extraordinary advertising expenditures, the problems concerning their treatment would be identical to those discussed earlier.

But while one problem disappeared and another stayed the same, yet another problem arose that brought about a good deal of controversy. In the previous discussion, where some item was capitalized under the caption of goodwill (whether the caption was appropriate or not), some consideration had been given, and the amount capitalized as goodwill, rightly or wrongly, had been limited to the fair value of the consideration given. The practice of writing up goodwill departed from this one common thread. It might be thought of as the opposite of the cost principle, with other items (such as the capitalization of certain advertising expenditures) falling in varying degrees between these two extremes. Justification for the practice seems to have relied on an attempt to record the value of goodwill in the accounts. A firm might be experiencing extraordinary returns, and its management might feel that this good fortune was due to the goodwill built up from advertising. Instead of possibly capitalizing the advertising costs in the goodwill account, a practice itself that was open to controversy, the firm might appraise the goodwill. Goodwill would be debited for this amount, and some surplus account would be credited.

Part of the impetus for this practice stems from the fact that the cost principle was not nearly so accepted at this time as it later came to be.[24] An article in *Printers' Ink* noted that "many financiers . . . believe that the value of good will should be capitalized and that it is readily ascertainable."[25] The value of goodwill would be appraised so that return on investment would be normal for the year. As an instance of the practice, one writer mentioned that:

> Just the other day a great corporation added $2,000,000 to its statement under the head of good will, and most conservative bankers and investors agreed that the new asset was fully worth that figure.[26]

Carrying the practice one step further, a goodwill account and a special surplus account might be opened, and a stock dividend would be issued for the same amount. Although feeling that the cost principle should be followed generally, Bell and Powelson felt that little harm resulted from the foregoing practice.[27]

The write-up of goodwill met criticism from all quarters. Virtually no phase of the process from appraisal to presentation was left unscathed. How was the initial appraisal to be objectively done? How could the figure be made subject to verification? Once the figure was on the books, what did it mean? As noted in *The Accountant*, "it is difficult to see what one would gain for one's pains."[28] The credit portion of the entry was not held in any higher esteem. Where could it go? Probably the least undesirable alternative was to create a special reserve account which, when clearly described, revealed that capital had been inflated.[29] The worst thing that could be done would be to credit the surplus account and pay cash dividends from it. This solution would result in the payment of a fictitious dividend.[30] The effects of writing up goodwill on the balance sheet are discussed in the subsequent section on financial presentation.[31]

The implications of such a procedure were significant. If goodwill were written up to its supposed value, what would prevent the write-up of other fixed assets so that the balance sheet would show their current value, also?[32] To depart from the cost basis "would be to throw open the entire accounting system to a maze of conjecture and uncertainty."[33] Although the cost principle may not have been well established, it was at least well represented in discussions on this subject.

Subsequent Treatment in Accounts

The arguments for and against the various alternatives were by now well established and continuously reiterated. Although the discussion on these points was by now chronic, some important shifts of emphasis occurred. As with some of the topics concerning initial valuation of goodwill, the discussion was in greater detail than in the previous period. Because proprietorship and partnership matters in general had ceased to be of as much concern in contrast to the increased emphasis on corporations, the alternative of immediate write-off slipped into the background and generally was not discussed in the literature in the United States. This declining emphasis was not due to the desirability or undesirability of the alternative; from the corporate viewpoint, immediate write-off did not appear to be a relevant choice.

The other alternatives—permanent retention as an asset or gradual reduction—suffered no such fate. If not original, those discussing the merits of each choice were at least vociferous. The only thing that changed concerning the main points in each argument were the names of those who espoused them in books and articles. Some writers did get beyond a mere restatement to consider fine points that were possibly implied earlier but not explicitly brought out. Although the main arguments need not be repeated, the detailed considerations brought out since the previous period are discussed here.

Permanent Retention as an Asset: One reason for the permanent retention of goodwill as an asset was its assumed permanence. It was believed that in this respect goodwill was like another fixed asset, land. This similarity could be debated, however, and in the previous period it was. There was another reason for believing goodwill to be permanent, which did not rest on its assumed similarity to land. The perpetuation and continuing existence of businesses organized in the corporate form added strength to the contention that though goodwill might fluctuate with the fortunes of a business, it still remained a permanent factor as long as a business existed. Goodwill seemed to take on the characteristics of the entity of which it was a part. In small, local businesses, as noted earlier, goodwill was of a similar (local and personal) nature. With the development of a business whose existence could be assumed to be permanent, did not goodwill appear permanent as well? With this permanence, was not a degree of stability implied, which might also be reflected in goodwill? With the assumed permanence and higher degree of stability, goodwill might be valued higher, and this higher valuation would be further justified, considering the greater stability of excess profits on which valuation was based.[34]

This reasoning also could be used to criticize amortization of goodwill based on a number of years' purchase of excess profits. How could one justify the writing off of an asset that was becoming more stable as the business got older?[35] In the past, goodwill was recognized to be inseparably bound up with the business of which it was a part, but the businesses discussed were usually proprietorships or partnerships. These enterprises, although possibly existing many years, were not thought of as being permanent. The rise of the corporation and its increasingly obvious trait of longevity, coupled with the asset's inseparability from the firm, caused a more powerful argument to be developed for assuming goodwill's perpetual existence. This argument could not be ignored, and attempts made to refute it are presented in the next topic.

But, even if permanence was conceded as a characteristic of goodwill, some argued that the asset should be written off on the grounds of conservatism. To this, Esquerre' replied:

> If a concern has paid a large sum to acquire the goodwill of another, and has not only retained it, but even increased it, there is no apparent reason why so-called conservatism should demand the writing off of the asset, to the detriment of the very profits which its purchase gave the right to expect.[36]

Gradual Reduction: One practice of writing down goodwill seems to have been convincingly discredited—the practice of writing it down during good times and suspending the practice when the firm fell on bad times. The implications of such a policy were to write down goodwill when it was known to exist and to keep it on the books when it was known to have diminished or disappeared. This paradox tempted some writers to attempt a play on words, which afforded a pleasant departure from the usual dry and sober discussions on goodwill while effectively dispatching the argument. As Couchman said, "To put it briefly, if you can write it down, you need not; if you cannot, you should!"[37] Or, as noted in *The Accountant*,

> After once placing a value upon your books, if you actually have it, write it off; if not, then continue it and make a show of having it. If you have a thing, you haven't; if you haven't, you have![38]

In justifying the policy of gradually reducing goodwill in the accounts, arguments resting on its assumed permanence could be sidestepped. Whether or not it was permanent, if it was valued as the purchase of a temporary terminating annuity, then it should be reduced accordingly. This argument is a slight modification of Hatfield's statement written in 1909[39] and reiterated in 1927.[40] But, in either case, the argument is based mainly on the method of valuation rather than the question of durability. In the same manner, conservatism-based arguments for writing off goodwill were grounded more on the virtues of conservatism than on the life of the asset. Although these reasons might form some justification for reducing goodwill, further support could be gained if the assumed perpetual life could be questioned convincingly.

P.D. Leake offered at least two reasons why goodwill was not permanent and felt these reasons held true in all situations. The economic forces of competition were ever present and constantly at work to reduce excess profits. Excess profits earned by any firm tend to attract others who see an opportunity to gain similar returns, but the addition of these newcomers lowers the rate of profits to the point where *all* are making only a normal return. Furthermore, demand might slacken due to changing conditions, such as new inventions.[41]

Leake's argument concerning competition might be logically correct, but the implied assumptions were open to question. Those forces of competition might be present in the case of numerous, small enterprises dealing in some standardized product. But in the case of large corporations controlling significant segments of a national or world market, the entrance of competitors into the market to drive down the rate of return to some normal figure might not be in accordance with reality.

Leake, however, believed goodwill to be a temporary asset for a second reason, which could not be so easily discounted. He conceded that some firms who purchased goodwill not only had retained it but had increased it over ten or twenty years. This situation certainly looked as if goodwill was perpetual. His answer was that the goodwill presently owned was not the same goodwill as that purchased ten or twenty years ago, for the current goodwill was largely the work of the owners and managers in the intervening period. This was as true in the case of an old firm as of a relatively new one established in the past twenty years.[42]

This theory worked nicely for those who espoused strict adherence to the cost principle and a policy of gradual reduction. Goodwill should appear on the books only when something had been paid for it. The old goodwill, purchased two decades ago, had been paid for but had to be extinguished from the books as its usefulness declined. Meanwhile, new goodwill was being built up by current efforts and was taking the place of the old goodwill. Because it had not been paid for, it should not be placed on the books.

Some cause for uneasiness might exist, however, because human institutions once firmly entrenched tend to perpetuate themselves. (The word "institution" is used here very broadly to include habits, laws, and customs. Therefore, it may be generally used to describe such subjects as private property or patriotism or specifically used to describe a certain corporation.) Certain ways of doing things, attitudes, traditions, or philosophies were passed on to select individuals to continue the common theme. The human element still existed, however, and these people changed over an extended period of time. If the older traits were to continue and become permanent, the efforts of ever-changing people would be necessary. As always, more questions could be asked, more points raised, more reasons given. The point had been made, however; some reasonable grounds still existed for doubting goodwill's permanence. Enough doubt existed, in fact, that once again a deadlock had been reached on the question: should goodwill be permanently retained in or gradually expelled from the accounts?

Others had varying reasons for seeing goodwill amortized, and some peculiar twists developed in the arguments going back and forth. In an unsigned article in *The Accountant*, opposition was expressed to writing down goodwill because of its perpetual nature and because the practice created a secret reserve.[43] Although additional working capital would be secured by the directors, this fact would not appear in the accounts. A better procedure would be to create a "General Reserve Fund," which would let all concerned know that profits were being withheld for use in the business. Another writer, an Englishman came to the opposite conclusion for exactly the same reasons five years earlier. He felt that there was no theoretical necessity requiring a write-down because in theory a company was undying. A practical desirability did exist, however, because profits were being kept in the business for future use. He felt it was "easier to get shareholders to apply profit to writing off goodwill than to get them to keep on the debit side of the Balance Sheet a large amount of undistributed profit."[44]

The "secret reserve" argument could be attacked on other grounds as well. Seymour Walton felt that no secret reserve had been created, because "the dropping of the goodwill from the balance-sheet is no secret, as any one can see that it is not there."[45] Walton also contrasted the write-off of a tangible asset, such as a building, with that of goodwill. If a building was charged off and was still being used, a secret reserve would be established. Furthermore, the absence of a building in the accounts would infer that the business did not own one. This was not true of goodwill, for the possession of goodwill is inherent in the very nature of a business in proportion to its prosperity. . . . It cannot be inferred that it does not exist because it does not appear on the balance-sheet.[46]

Relative Standing of the Alternatives: The effect of the added refinements and details was to leave the two alternatives equally acceptable. The stability of the corporate form was a strong factor in supporting goodwill's permanence, but doubts of its perpetual usefulness and considerations of valuation and conservatism raised questions of the desirability of retaining goodwill in the accounts.

Items Other Than Purchased Goodwill: The foregoing discussion concerning subsequent treatment was aimed primarily at goodwill acquired in the purchase of an established business. As noted in the section on initial valuation, this was not the only item treated as goodwill—some advertising expenditures, operating losses, and estimates of the value of goodwill were capitalized under that heading.

Writers closely adhering to the cost principle usually did not concern themselves with this problem, because they felt these items should not be capitalized as goodwill in the first place. Others, who advocated placing them on the books, would have to deal with the matter of subsequent treatment.

Normal expenditures on advertising during the accounting period were treated as expenses; only those expenditures that clearly would benefit future periods could be capitalized, and then not as goodwill but as deferred charges. Large expenditures in excess of normal amounts might be capitalized as goodwill, and the treatment usually recommended in this case was an allocation to the earliest periods that might benefit.[47] But, permanent retention as an asset was not completely out of the question, and the argument could be advanced that goodwill created in this manner was just as permanent as purchased goodwill was assumed to be. Permanent retention was not likely, however, for it appeared dangerous to capitalize large amounts of extraordinary advertising expenditure indefinitely. Conservatism was a strong factor to contend with, and even if two alternatives could be said to exist, one of them was strongly favored.

In the previous section on initial valuation, reference was made to the division of a firm's life into three phases. The advertising expenditures discussed in the preceding paragraph could be placed in the last two phases: a period when initial sales were being made or a period when normal profits had been attained. But what of advertising or promotional expenditures made in the first phase when a firm is being organized and no sales have yet been made? Some argument could still be made to support capitalization of these expenditures as goodwill, but assuming they were capitalized under that caption, what should be done with them? These expenditures truly might benefit a firm throughout its entire life and appear to be a permanent asset.

The argument for permanent retention of initial advertising and promotional expenditures was definitely stronger than the same argument concerning expenditures made during operative phases of a firm's life. Much the same controversy over retention or reduction surrounded it as surrounded goodwill acquired upon the purchase of a going concern, and neither alternative was clearly favored.

Even if the subsequent treatment of various sorts of advertising expenditures could not be resolved completely, certain definite alternatives did emerge following some reasoned argument. No such situation existed concerning subsequent treatment of capitalized operating losses or arbitrary write-ups of goodwill to its estimated value. Occasional references were made to the reduction of capitalized losses at a time when the firm could absorb them, but no consideration was given to establishing a systematic plan or program to govern the rate or amount of the reduction. Similarly, some might advocate periodic adjustment of goodwill arbitrarily written up to its supposed current value, but this was by no means a general trend, and no thought appears to have been given to the procedure by which the adjustment would be accomplished. The procedure of capitalizing these items had departed so greatly from most contemporary accounting practice that accounting writers generally ignored the question of their disposition. The accountants might ask: what possible grounds exist for considering the subsequent treatment of items that never should have appeared in the accounts in the first place?

Financial Presentation and Disclosure

Compared to the attention given to initial valuation and subsequent treatment of goodwill, its financial presentation and disclosure were slighted. Although valuation and subsequent treatment might be used as a factor in determining financial presentation and disclosure, they by no means completely governed how goodwill was to appear in accounting statements.

Aside from the reasons given earlier for including items such as advertising expenditures as goodwill, advantages and disadvantages connected mainly with aspects of presentation and disclosure also existed and are discussed in the next topic. Once a figure for goodwill was obtained, the matter of what to do with it in the statements had to be settled; the disposition of the figure in the balance sheet is discussed in the second topic. Another item, not closely related to these topics, was by this time being treated as goodwill—the excess of cost over book value in consolidated statements of a parent or holding company and its subsidiaries. The assumptions and problems involved in treating this item as goodwill are considered in the third topic.

Inclusion of Various Items as Goodwill: The inclusion of goodwill acquired upon the purchase of a going concern was not questioned. Thus goodwill could appear at cost, and virtually no one concluded that the item confused or deluded users of financial statements. Controversy still existed concerning the effects of subsequent treatment upon financial disclosure and ran along much the same lines as the discussion in the previous period, but the inclusion of initial cost was not disputed.

Other items treated as goodwill did raise some questions, however, and the possibility of statement users being misled became apparent. Various advertising expenditures discussed previously, which warranted capitalization, posed problems of interpretation when capitalized as goodwill. The argument that extraordinary advertising expenditures were made to create goodwill was conceded. An attempt was being made to construct goodwill of a business just as a similar effort was needed to construct physical items, such as its plant and equipment. The argument, however, contained an element that could be used in its rebuttal. These expenditures were made to create something that previously did not exist. Although effort could be made to develop goodwill, there was no assurance that goodwill would result automatically. In other words, expenditures were made in hopes of creating an asset, and doubtless these expenditures were necessary before the asset could exist, but whether the asset actually did exist after the expenditure was a different matter. A hint of pretentiousness existed concerning the capitalization of an item as goodwill, which only future events could prove to be valid. As Hatfield noted, "Like the expense of experimentation, advertising may fail to bring forth fruit and instead of creating goodwill it may cause only a deficit."[48] A more conservative approach, which might not be so potentially misleading, would be to capitalize these expenditures as "Prepaid Advertising" and allow the investor to make his own assessment of the existence of goodwill.

At least one author changed his proposed treatment of advertising to the more conservative approach in a following edition of his text. R.B. Kester, in the first edition of his *Accounting—Theory and Practice*, recognized that goodwill could be created by advertising and felt that, with careful handling and conservatism, certain amounts of advertising could be brought on the books as goodwill.[49] In 1925, seven years later, Kester again recognized that goodwill could be created by advertising and felt that the expenditures could be capitalized. This time, however, he recommended that the expenditures be capitalized separately as prepaid advertising and that they be written off rapidly.[50]

A main point of contention concerning certain advertising expenditures had been one of classification, not of capitalization. Balance sheet categories were affected, but not the total sum of assets or equities. The income statement was not affected by the problem; the rate of return was the same no matter how the expenditures were classified. The capitalization of early losses and the arbitrary write-ups of goodwill, however, affected both statements and conclusions that might be drawn from them.

The capitalization of early losses was subject to question at several points.[51] The losses were not assets, because no more benefit could be expected from the expenditures. As a result, total assets and owners' equity on the balance sheet were overstated to the extent of their capitalization. In the income statement, expenses were understated and net income was overstated; various important measures, such as the rate of return, would be affected as well. The losses probably would be charged to profits in later, more prosperous years, and the effects in the income statement would be reversed. Because in lean years profits would be exaggerated and in good years they would be understated, fluctuations in net income and in the rate of return would tend to be eliminated, and the actual situation would be obscured.[52]

A simple way of writing up goodwill would be to charge goodwill and credit an appraisal surplus account. The objective of such a policy would be to state correctly the value of goodwill so that the rate of return on assets would be normal.

In the balance sheet, total assets would no longer be shown at cost but at some estimated value. The point might be made that because the asset does exist, the statement user should be made aware of its existence regardless of whether or not it was purchased. The balance sheet would now show the value of the entire firm and the value of the owners' share in it. The income statement would not be affected; revenue and expense accounts would not be changed, assuming some surplus account was credited upon recording the appraisal increment. Although reported net income would be the same, the rate of return on total assets would not. An extraordinary rate of return would no longer be shown; the rate would be reduced to a more normal one because the denominator, total assets, would be enlarged.

Write-ups were objected to at several points, one of which concerned the function of the balance sheet.

> A Balance Sheet does not pretend to be an index of values. What it does purport to do is to record actual expenditure not hitherto charged against profits, because in the circumstances it is thought more equitable to carry the expenditure forward with a view to charging it gradually against the profits of future years.[53]

The effect of this practice on the rate of return was also a point of contention. For the sake of analysis, Paton considered the effects of a general adoption of adjusting asset values among enterprises of a particular field. He felt that the rate of return on actual invested capital was the significant percentage for the owner, and if all firms showed a rate of return equal to or less than some normal or representative return, an important basis for comparison would be destroyed.

> It would result in an apparent uniformity of earning power when actually no such uniformity existed. Thus it would involve an obscuring of the very facts that the plan would be supposed to be emphasizing.[54]

The accumulation of problems concerning the treatment of these various items as goodwill is significant. Enough problems surrounded goodwill acquired upon the purchase of a business; and advertising, capitalized losses, and write-ups were causes of yet more controversy. The last three items particularly were vulnerable to the charge of subjectivity, and regardless of any theoretical reasons for their capitalization, they were readily open to manipulation. Because of the subjectivity and the resulting opportunity for manipulation, the significance and usefulness of the figure obtained and presented were open to serious question.

Disposition in the Balance Sheet: As with almost every other matter concerning goodwill and its relation to some aspect of accounting, several disposition alternatives were discussed. The alternative that probably was used most and accepted least was the practice of lumping goodwill with other assets.[55] One writer felt that the practice was used to avoid any question of the amount of goodwill because it was frequently out of all proportion to a fair value. He also noted that where a firm had written goodwill down to a nominal figure, such as $1, goodwill was always shown clearly.[56]

Whatever the reason for the practice, it apparently was adhered to with some degree of stubbornness. In Great Britain, the Companies Act of 1908 provided for the separate statement of goodwill, but an article in *The Accountant* noted that "for some obscure reason custom appears in this respect to overrule the provisions of Section 113 of the Companies (Consolidation) Act of 1908."[57]

In 1909, Hatfield mentioned that American companies followed the same practice.[58] In 1927, he reiterated the point but noted some improvement had recently taken place. "A large number of the more important corporations have in recent years adopted the policy of showing it as a separate item."[59]

Even if goodwill was separately disclosed, the questions of what to do with it and how to classify it remained. *Uniform Accounting*, a memorandum prepared in 1917 by the American Institute of Accountants and accepted by the Federal Trade Commission and the Federal Reserve Board, was a "tentative proposal for a uniform system of accounting" to be used by firms for obtaining credit from banks. It recommended that the book value of goodwill be shown as a deduction from net worth.[60] The apparent reason for this treatment, according to Yang, was the considerable disfavor by bankers for intangibles,

> because ... [intangibles] ... have been subject to manipulations of value to such a degree that they have become more or less of a nuisance, and fail to possess any significance in the eyes of the ordinary reader.[61]

If financial statements were not being prepared particularly for credit purposes, the foregoing treatment did not necessarily apply. Goodwill was a fixed asset and could be classified accordingly, and an improvement on this practice would be to further classify fixed assets as tangible and intangible so that various ratios on tangible property could be computed.[62] This treatment might be imputed to *Verification of Financial Statements*, the 1929 revision of *Uniform Accounting*.[63] No mention was made of intangible assets in the proposed balance sheet form. Presumably, goodwill would be listed under the category "Other fixed assets" or under "Other assets."

Although several alternatives were mentioned, there was no controversy as to which treatment was the best in all situations. Offsetting net worth with goodwill might be a sound practice for credit purposes, and listing goodwill as an asset might better serve general reporting needs. In any case, goodwill and other intangibles should be stated separately. As a result, the balance sheet presentation of goodwill afforded one of those rare instances in which broad areas of agreement existed concerning recommended treatment.

Goodwill in Consolidated Statements: With the large number of business combinations occurring in the early part of the twentieth century, the preparation of consolidated statements became important. Several approaches had arisen for bringing companies together, but the use of holding companies, which gave rise to consolidated financial presentation, had become very popular by this time.[64]

If one company purchased a small portion of another company's shares, it could record the investment as "Investment in 'A' Company." This was deemed to reflect correctly the purchasing company's financial condition concerning this one item. If controlling interest was obtained instead, the investor (now either a holding or parent company) would not present its true financial condition only in its own balance sheet. The investment account represented the assets and liabilities of the subsidiary and should be replaced by them.

> For while it is true from a legal standpoint that the holding company owns merely the stock, it is also true from a business standpoint that the holding company virtually owns and actually controls the subsidiary's net assets which the stock represents. . . .
>
> If we look past the legal fiction of separate corporate entities and view the related companies as a single organization, we find that no single balance sheet shows the total assets and liabilities of the organization, and the total stock of the organization in the hands of the public.[65]

The consolidated balance sheet avoided the disadvantages of presenting separate statements and attained the advantage of showing the related companies as an economic entity by combining all assets and liabilities of the corporations involved except intercompany items.

When the investment account was eliminated against the applicable portion of the subsidiary's net worth, a difference between the cost of the investment and its book value could occur and necessitated explanation in the consolidated balance sheet.

Excess of cost over book value. If cost was greater than book value, most accounting writers recommended treating the item as goodwill. Of 67 references dated before 1930 and analyzed by G.H. Newlove, 58 advocated this treatment solely or infrequently combined it with another approach. Only 5 references called for analysis of the positive excess element, and 3 of those were in works by 1 author, R.H. Montgomery.[66]

An assumption was involved that tended to make the caption "goodwill" inapplicable to the entire excess of cost over book value. The assets of the subsidiary company were consolidated with those of the parent company at their book values, as if the book values were the true cost to the parent. In a period of rising prices, the current valuation of assets using book values established in the past would tend to understate those assets. The company presumably would be paying a price at least equal to current market value of the net assets purchased but would be reporting those net assets at the lesser book figures. Although the entire excess of cost over book value was called goodwill, part of it might be due to other assets, the values of which were understated.

Those who advocated analysis of the positive excess element did not exclude an allocation of part or even all of the excess to goodwill; they felt it should be allocated to any assets (goodwill included) that were undervalued.

> The payment of more than book value means that book values are understated and should be adjusted, or (as is usually the case) there has been a payment for goodwill; in such cases the consolidated balance sheet should show the facts.[67]

The positive element could be added to a nondepreciating intangible asset account other than goodwill—Excess of Cost over Book Value of Subsidiary, for example. A noncommittal account, it allowed anyone analyzing the balance sheet to handle it as they desired, though it was subject to the same disadvantages as calling the excess "goodwill," because no attempt was made to state correctly the undervalued assets.

The excess might be subtracted from earned surplus, a treatment appearing to be a carry-over of conservative tendencies in writing off goodwill in other situations. (In the six sources Newlove cited before 1930 which advocated this alternative, all called for the deduction of the excess of cost over par value of subsidiary stock, usually a potentially larger figure than if the stock's book value were used.) If the excess was assumed to be goodwill in accordance with the first treatment mentioned previously, the amount might be written off in accordance with the popular disdain for the asset.

> Admittedly there is no valid reason for the reduction of the cost of an investment to the par value of the stocks which it contains. . . . But in some mysterious way the intangible asset goodwill has become very objectionable to business people. To them it is symptomatic of insufficiency of real values, and therefore, of inflation of assets.[68]

In eliminating an undesirable asset from the accounts, various financial ratios, such as rate of return on total assets and on net worth, subsequently would be affected because part of a commitment of resources contributing to profits would no longer be shown on the balance sheet. Utilizing Montgomery's phrase, the consolidated balance sheet might not show the facts. At any rate, he felt it was "not proper nor necessary to deduct the excess from surplus."[69]

Excess of book value over cost. In the elimination of the investment account against the subsidiary's net worth, book value could be greater than cost, and the reversed position in the size called for the reverse treatment for each of the previously mentioned alternatives—for instance, a subtraction of the amount from goodwill in place of an addition to existing goodwill. Because the occurrence of an excess of book value over cost was not considered ordinary, more attention was given to analysis of the element. Although the alternatives were still chosen on the intrinsic merits of the various practices, more emphasis was now given to circumstances surrounding a given situation than in cases where cost exceeded book value.

If all of the subsidiary's assets other than goodwill appeared or were assumed to be properly valued, then the excess might be deducted from goodwill appearing in the subsidiary's accounts. Presumably the holding company or parent company did not consider the subsidiary's goodwill conservatively valued.[70]

A problem arose if the subsidiary either had no recorded goodwill or had an insufficient amount to absorb the negative goodwill. Where positive goodwill existed in other companies being consolidated, some authorities advocated writing off the subsidiary's unabsorbable portion of negative goodwill to any positive goodwill found elsewhere in the consolidation. Consolidated statements presented all companies as one entity, emphasizing the total effort and contribution of all instead of the individual effort of each. Therefore, all goodwill elements, both positive and negative, should be combined in the consolidated balance sheet to present the total goodwill of the economic entity.

Finney felt the practice, though customary, was not theoretically correct. Only in cases where the subsidiary's assets were properly valued and the subsidiary was not making a reasonable return should be unabsorbable negative goodwill be applied against other goodwill in the consolidation.[71] Finney's position appears sufficiently reasonable to suggest the question of why he emphasized the obvious. In the early twenties, however, there appears to have been no great emphasis on scrutinizing asset valuations for consolidated statements—the apparent assumption being that they were properly valued whether they really were or not. Hatfield posed an analogous situation by supposing that a corporation acquired a plant worth $200,000 for $200,000, but it was recorded on the vendor's books for $100,000. The corporation further acquired a mine whose book value was $200,000 for $100,000. Hatfield concluded that obviously the plant should be recorded at $200,000 and the mine at $100,000, and that "there would be no argument in favor of subtracting from the actual value of the plant the amount which should be subtracted from the book value of the mine."[72]

The two points of view—subtracting negative goodwill only from goodwill of the subsidiary in question or from positive goodwill found anywhere in the consolidation—appear to have been reconcilable if overstated assets were first written down to reflect their market value. Whatever remained of negative goodwill might be applied to any positive goodwill. A problem that might be encountered in writing down assets was that of the difficulty of determining which assets were overstated. In order to properly state assets while avoiding the problems of attempting specific reductions, an account titled Allowance Representing Overvaluation of Assets of Subsidiaries could be created and handled in the balance sheet in the same manner as allowances for depreciation or bad debts.[73] The ultimate effect of either specific or general reduction of assets would be the same on the excess of book value over cost—the residual excess would be more clearly identifiable with a deficiency in earning power of the firm or negative goodwill, just as the reverse situation would reveal positive goodwill more clearly.

After deciding what amount of the excess, if any, should be used to specifically or generally reduce various fixed assets and what amount, if any, was applicable to positive goodwill of either the subsidiary or the entire consolidation, some residual excess might yet remain. Some authorities advocated crediting the differential to capital surplus on the assumption that a bargain purchase had been made, though usually after some analysis or allocation of the excess to goodwill or other assets.[74] This approach implied that, far from obtaining a firm with deficient earning power, the purchaser felt the consideration given did not properly reflect the acquired firm's profit capabilities, and an element of capital surplus was a necessary addition so that the assets and equity would be stated properly.

A factor that appears to have caused much of the concern (and so many alternatives to develop) was strong reliance on subsidiary book values and attempts to adjust book values to market values. Neither of these figures necessarily corresponded with the cost of the investment. Therefore, adjustments of book values to market values in an attempt to explain differences between book and cost figures resulted in only partial or approximate explanations of the differential. If, in the analysis of excess of book value over cost, the investment's cost would have been considered the truly significant figure, then all assets would have been reduced to a cost basis, regardless of any value figure, and the alternative involving a credit to capital surplus would cease to exist. For that matter, negative goodwill would cease to exist—only situations involving an excess of cost over book value would present questions of goodwill, and then only positive aspects would be considered. The effect of the current situation was to add a number of practices involving items named or misnamed as goodwill, with the result that whatever meaning and significance the caption goodwill had left in accounting was further obscured.

Significance of Financial Presentation and Disclosure: Virtually all of the problems connected with goodwill, whether discussed in the areas of initial valuation or subsequent treatment or in any other area, gradually accumulated and finally came to rest in the financial statements. Anyone attempting to understand the significance of goodwill in a balance sheet (if it was disclosed separately) might wonder if the goodwill appeared as a result of (1) the acquisition of another firm (complete or controlling interest), (2) its creation from extensive advertising, (3) the capitalization of early losses, or (4) estimates written on the books. With each of these sources came an assortment of treatments held in varying degrees of esteem. Even if the source and subsequent treatment could be ascertained, the statement user still had to be on his guard, because what appeared as goodwill might be subject to manipulation. The caption "goodwill" had been used to describe something that could originate almost anywhere, be almost anything, and was treated in almost every way imaginable. The significance of any amount shown as goodwill thus was open to serious question, with the result that the treatment recommended in *Uniform Accounting* rested on strong ground.

Auditing Considerations

In the early years of the twentieth century, significant changes in the role and work of the auditor occurred in the United States, which affected auditing aspects of goodwill. The changes may be seen by comparing certain points in the auditing texts of L.R. Dicksee and R.H. Montgomery. Dicksee was a leading British auditor around the turn of the century, and his text was considered an authority in America at this time, as well.[75] He said that the object of an audit was the detection of fraud and error; the auditor was not responsible simply for the correctness of the balance sheet.[76] This position implied little, if any, consideration by the auditor for the fairness of financial reports, and coupled with Dicksee's views of the insignificance of the stated amount of goodwill in the balance sheet, little consideration of its subsequent treatment was warranted. Because goodwill did not depreciate, but did fluctuate, the auditor should recommend that it be permanently and separately stated at cost—a meaningless figure except to indicate what it was originally acquired for.[77] Although Dicksee might have preferred that treatment, he did not require it, for he noted the common practice of writing down goodwill when profits existed. Possibly due to auditing objectives not emphasizing balance sheet presentation, the assumed insignificance of the statement figure for goodwill, and the lack of British legal requirements to periodically reduce the asset, Dicksee felt that writing down goodwill was optional, stating:

> The question is not, however, one upon which the Auditor is required to express an opinion; and, so long as the item is separately stated on the Balance Sheet, it is scarcely desirable that he should interfere with the discretion of the management.[78]

Although Dicksee's *Auditing* was available for use in the United States, it contained many pages applicable solely to British practice. R.H. Montgomery brought out an American edition of Dicksee's work in 1905, and again in 1909, omitting strictly British matters.[79] In 1912, however, Montgomery brought out his own text because he had noted "a radical departure from the principles and procedure enunciated by Mr. Dicksee. More is now expected of the auditor."[80] The objectives of an audit had changed; the primary objective now was the ascertainment of the actual financial condition and earnings of an enterprise, and the former objects of fraud and error detection were relegated to a subordinate position.[81] As a result, Montgomery felt that

> the question of the amount at which it [goodwill] shall stand in the balance sheet was not formerly deemed to be within the scope of the auditor's work, but the present range of an auditor's duties compels him to give serious thought to this item.[82]

Like Dicksee, he believed goodwill should be stated separately at cost and should not be depreciated. Unlike Dicksee, he evidently believed the auditor could no longer consider the figure to be meaningless; ascertaining the actual financial condition of the enterprise added a new dimension to goodwill's proper treatment not implied by mere search for fraud and error.[83]

In the fourth edition of his text, in 1927, Montgomery discussed the auditor's increased responsibility concerning goodwill. He noted that accountants previously had stated goodwill as shown on the books without assuming any responsibility for it—the public had to accept it for what it was worth. Anyone not familiar with this concept might be justified in believing the figure represented the auditor's opinion of the asset's true worth. To avoid either misrepresentation or misunderstanding, goodwill therefore should be explained fully in the balance sheet or certificate. The absence of uniform practice at the time concerning goodwill's initial valuation and subsequent treatment made such explanation highly desirable as well.[84]

> To summarize, the accountant should take the responsibility of valuing purchased goodwill and, if it is not assumed, the accountant should disclaim responsibility in the certificate. When goodwill is not purchased, but is set up by the company or computed by the auditor, full disclosure should be made on the balance-sheet, or the certificate should be qualified accordingly.[85]

Montgomery's *Auditing Theory and Practice* was the first American text on auditing and has taken a prominent, if not leading, role in auditing literature throughout its subsequent editions in this country. Except for Montgomery's work, auditing aspects of goodwill rarely were discussed either in textbooks or in the accounting literature. Eggleston considered the subject and recommended the same treatment as Montgomery,[86] though Bell and Powelson's text noted that amortization was optional.[87] Bell and Powelson also differed by allowing the write-up of goodwill and the payment of a stock dividend of the same amount. Although generally recommending a cost basis for the asset, they felt "little harm can be done, however, even if no good is accomplished."[88] What might account for the divergent views among the auditing writers was the amount of disagreement at this time among accountants generally concerning the treatment of goodwill.

Tax Considerations

In 1913, when the federal income tax came into being in the United States, provision had to be made for treatment of many items that would prove difficult to handle. One of these items was goodwill. Most of the major points concerning the treatment of goodwill had been settled by the late 1920s, and compared with methods recommended or in use in accounting generally, tax procedures were conservative.

In order that tax procedures might be understood in the proper context of tax law, the place of goodwill in the tax structure is outlined in the next topic. Not only did goodwill's valuation and subsequent treatment present accounting problems, they presented tax problems as well, and tax procedures adopted to deal with valuation and subsequent treatment are discussed in the second and third topics, respectively. The fourth topic compares tax treatment of goodwill with its accounting treatment.

The Place of Goodwill in the Tax Structure: Goodwill is considered to be property under the federal income tax law; when it is sold, a gain or loss must be realized for tax purposes. Furthermore, goodwill is considered to be a capital asset, making the proceeds taxable as capital gain instead of as ordinary income. For the first nine years of the tax law, the distinction was of no consequence in computing tax liability because rates on ordinary net income and capital gains were the same.[89] The Revenue Act of 1921 placed a ceiling on the capital gains taxation rates, however, and thereafter the distinction has been important.[90]

The tax authorities also recognized that goodwill attached to a specific business. Recognition of this characteristic had significant implications on when goodwill would be considered sold.

> Any profit or loss resulting from a sale of good will can be taken only when the business, or a part of it, to which the good will attaches is sold, in which case the profit or loss will be determined upon the basis of the cost of the assets, including good will.[91]

Valuation of Goodwill: Two valuations were necessary when goodwill was sold: value at date of sale and its initial value. Value at date of sale did not present as much of a problem as determination of its initial value, and either of two figures for initial valuation might be used depending on the circumstances.

The federal income tax law went into effect on March 1, 1913. Because gains or losses accruing prior to that date generally were not recognized for tax purposes, determination of taxable income of a business purchased before March 1, 1913 and sold afterwards could present a problem. The vendor of the business probably incurred a gain or loss on the sale, but part of the gain or loss might be due to the nontaxable portion of the vendor's period of ownership and thus should not be considered in computing tax liability. To eliminate as much as possible of the nontaxable gain or loss, either original cost of goodwill or its market value on March 1, 1913 was used to determine taxable income. For purposes of determining gain, the higher of original cost or market value was used; for purposes of determining loss, the lower. If the sales price fell between cost or market value, no gain or loss was recognized.

The computation of March 1, 1913 market value became an important matter, and the Committee on Appeals and Review formulated a method of establishing it.[93] Average earnings over (preferably) a period not shorter than five years prior to March 1, 1913 would be computed first. A return of ten percent then would be calculated on average tangible assets for the period, and this figure would be subtracted from average earnings to determine the earnings attributable to intangibles. The excessive earnings then would be multiplied by not more than five (capitalized at not less than 20 percent) to determine a value for goodwill. In businesses that were relatively stable, eight or nine percent might be used for tangible assets and fifteen percent used to capitalize intangibles.[94] The formula was not the only method that would be accepted or that was used; each case should be considered on its own merits.[95]

Subsequent Treatment: As in accounting, some method had to be devised for dealing with goodwill once it was recognized. Two alternatives were considered—gradual reduction and permanent retention. The Revenue Act of 1918 had allowed a deduction for "a reasonable allowance for the exhaustion, wear and tear of property used in the trade or business, including a reasonable allowance for obsolescence."[96] Goodwill might not be exhausted or worn down as time passed, however. As a result, its life was not definitely limited in duration, and no deduction for its depreciation was allowed.[97]

The question of a deduction for obsolescence of goodwill was not resolved immediately. At one time, deduction was permitted where the period of obsolescence could be determined with reasonable accuracy, no value existed at the end of a definite period, and the taxpayer was forced to discontinue his business and was unable to continue a similar one.[98] A similar provision was in effect from 1919 to 1927 concerning extraordinary obsolescence resulting from prohibition, when taxpayers might be forced to discontinue a business or discard its assets.[99] In *Red Wing Malting Co. v. Willcuts*, however, the obsolescence deduction was disallowed. Part of Red Wing's case rested on the previously quoted section of the Revenue Act of 1918 permitting a deduction for obsolescence. The district court held that goodwill was not property used in the trade or business.[100] Goodwill was not used; it was a result of the manner in which a business was conducted. In affirming the decision, the circuit court added that the phrase concerning obsolescence was only an enlargement of the earlier phrase concerning depreciation.[101] According to the court's interpretation, therefore, an obsolescence deduction was allowable only in the case of assets qualifying for a depreciation deduction.[102] After this decision, no deduction for obsolescence of goodwill was allowed.[103]

There was one other major attempt, however, to obtain an obsolescence deduction in the case of *Haberle Crystal Spring Brewing Co. v. Clarke*. This brewing company, in a similar position to Red Wing Malting Co., obtained the same treatment that Red Wing did in its district court proceedings, but the circuit court for the second circuit held that goodwill was property used in the trade or business and, therefore, an obsolescence deduction was allowable.[104] As a result of this decision, two circuit courts had taken opposite positions on the same point. In the *Haberle* case, the Commissioner carried the case to the Supreme Court, which ruled that no obsolescence deduction was allowable.[105]

> The Supreme Court pointed out that neither "exhaustion" nor "obsolescence" is an apt word to describe termination by law as an evil of a business otherwise flourishing, and that neither becomes more applicable because the death is lingering rather than instantaneous. When a business is extinguished as noxious under the Constitution the owners cannot demand partial compensation from the government in the form of an abatement of taxes otherwise due.[106]

With such reasoning, the decision appears to have been limited to the facts of the particular case—any other business not considered evil presumably might qualify for a deduction. Nevertheless, the disallowance was applied uniformly to all businesses thereafter.

The effect of policies disallowing deductions for depreciation or obsolescence was to retain goodwill permanently for tax purposes. Thus the only time expenditures for goodwill were used in computing tax liability was when the business to which the expenditures attached was sold.

Tax and Accounting Treatment of Goodwill Compared: Tax procedures for recognition, valuation, and subsequent treatment of goodwill were very similar to conservative accounting practices. Both treated goodwill as an asset attaching to a specific business or some segment thereof. The basic idea behind the procedure for finding March 1, 1913 value had been discussed in accounting literature for years, and theoretical as well as pragmatic arguments supported its use. Permanent retention, one of the oldest recommended accounting alternatives, was called for by tax law because of the unpredictability of the asset's life.

Although conservative accounting practice may have had an effect on tax procedures, the procedures once established appeared to influence accounting practice and were mentioned in accounting literature, usually in connection with the disallowed depreciation deduction. One writer felt the government's disallowance should be considered in accounting for goodwill, although he mentioned methods for handling its depreciation.[107] Another author was more committed to the permanent retention of goodwill and used the Treasury Department's ruling to support his contentions in his auditing text.[108]

Summary

The continued development of the corporation, accompanied by an era of prosperity, led to a major emphasis on discussing corporate aspects of goodwill. The arguments of the previous period were repeated, refined, and elaborated. Advertising expenditures were recognized as contributing significantly to the development of the asset, and methods were advocated for treating some of these expenditures as goodwill. A significant rise in price levels during this period led to the recording of unrealized appreciation in some asset accounts, including goodwill. Although controversy was always present in discussions of the subject, it was particularly noticeable in those discussions concerning capitalization of advertising expenditures and going value and in arbitrary write-ups of asset appraisals. The newly passed federal income tax laws came to deal with the subject, and through regulations and court decisions a treatment paralleling conservative accounting practice was developed.

---

1. Adolf A. Berle, Jr. and Gardiner C. Means, *The Modern Corporation and Private Property* (New York: MacMillan Company, 1934), p. 158.

2. Ibid., pp. 141-144, 158-159.

3. See pp. 48-49,

4. George O. May, *Financial Accounting: A Distillation of Experience* (New York: MacMillan Company, 1961), p. 90. (Hereinafter referred to as *Financial Accounting.*)

5. Ibid., p. 92.

6. William Andrew Paton, *Accounting Theory: With Special Reference to the Corporate Enterprise* (New York: Ronald Press Company, 1922), p. 326. (Hereinafter referred to as *Accounting Theory.*)

7. Herbert C. Freeman, "Some Considerations Involved in the Valuation of Goodwill," *The Journal of Accountancy*, October 1921, p. 249. (Hereinafter referred to as "Valuation of Goodwill.")

8. Charles B. Couchman, *The Balance-Sheet* (New York: Journal of Accountancy, Incorporated, 1924), p. 133.

9. Freeman, "Valuation of Goodwill," pp. 255-258.

10. Robert H. Montgomery, "The Appraisal of Good Will," *Bulletin. National Retail Dry Goods Association*, March 1926, p. 17.

11. Henry Rand Hatfield, *Modern Accounting* (New York: D. Appleton and Company, 1913), p. 113.

12. W.A. Paton and R.A. Stevenson, *Principles of Accounting* (New York: MacMillan Company, 1922), p. 531.

13. May, *Financial Accounting*, pp. 88-89.

14. Paton, *Accounting Theory*, p. 326.

15. Paul-Joseph Esquerre', "Goodwill, Patents, Trade-Marks, Copyrights and Franchises," *The Journal of Accountancy*, January 1913, p. 26. (Hereinafter referred to as "Goodwill.")

16. H.A. Finney, *Principles of Accounting*, II (New York: Prentice-Hall, Inc., 1927), Ch. 41, p. 11.

17. Montgomery, "The Appraisal of Good Will," p. 17.

18. Roy B. Kester, *Accounting Theory and Practice*, II (New York: Ronald Press Company, 1919), p. 334.

19. Ibid.

20. Ibid.; and H.G. Stockwell, *How To Read A Financial Statement* (New York: Ronald Press Company, 1925), p. 95.

21. Paton, *Accounting Theory*, pp. 327-330.

22. Ibid.

23. Finney, *Principles of Accounting*, II, Ch. 41, p. 11.

24. See pp. 41-42.

25. "How Much is Goodwill Worth?" *Printers' Ink*, November 21, 1918, p. 53.

26. W.R. Basset, "What Is 'Good Will' Worth?" *System: The Magazine of Business*, April 1918, p. 558.

27. W.H. Bell and J.A. Powelson, *Auditing* (New York: Prentice-Hall, Inc., 1929), p. 242.

28. "Goodwill and Advertising," *The Accountant*, February 28, 1914, p. 289.

29. Ibid.

30. Samuel F. Racine, *Accounting Principles* (Seattle: Western Institute of Accountancy, Commerce and Finance, 1917), p. 172.

31. See pp. 55-56.

32. "Goodwill and Advertising," p. 290.

33. Paton, *Accounting Theory*, p. 320.

34. Freeman, "Valuation of Goodwill," p. 263.

35. Ibid., p. 261.

36. Esquerre', "Goodwill," p. 25.

37. Couchman, *The Balance-Sheet*, p. 138.

38. "Goodwill: Its Nature, Value and Treatment in the Accounts," *The Accountant*, December 6, 1913, p. 817.

39. See p. 33.

40. Henry Rand Hatfield, *Accounting* (New York: D. Appleton and Company, 1927), p. 124.

41. P.D. Leake, "Goodwill: Its Nature and How to Value It," *The Accountant*, January 17, 1914, pp. 83-84.

42. P.D. Leake, *Commercial Goodwill: Its History, Value and Treatment in Accounts*, 3rd ed. (London: Sir Isaac Pitman & Sons, Ltd., 1938), pp. 76-78. Although the passage is from the 3rd edition, the material on this point in the 1st (1921), 2nd (1930), and 4th (1948) editions are the same.

43. "Goodwill," *The Accountant*, March 15, 1919, pp. 199-200.

44. W.R. Hamilton, "Goodwill," *The Accountant*, February 14, 1914, pp. 216-218.

45. Seymour Walton, "Writing off Goodwill," *The Journal of Accountancy*, July 1917, p. 64.

46. Ibid.

47. Roy B. Kester, *Accounting Theory and Practice*, II, 2nd ed., rev. (New York: Ronald Press Company, 1925), pp. 358-359.

48. Hatfield, *Accounting*, p. 115.

49. See pp. 47-48.

50. Kester, *Accounting Theory and Practice*, pp. 358-359.

51. See pp. 47-48.

52. Paton and Stevenson, *Principles of Accounting*, p. 537.

53. "Goodwill and Advertising," pp. 289-290.

54. Paton, *Accounting Theory*, pp. 318-319.

55. See pp. 34-35.

56. David S. Kerr, "Watered Stock and Goodwill," *The Canadian Chartered Accountant*, October 1916, p. 100.

57. "Goodwill," p. 199.

58. See p. 35.

59. Hatfield, *Accounting*, pp. 125-126.

60. American Institute of Accountants, "Uniform Accounting," *The Journal of Accountancy*, June 1917, pp. 401-433.

61. J.M. Yang, *Goodwill and Other Intangibles: Their Significance and Treatment in Accounts* (New York: Ronald Press Company, 1927), p. 184.

62. James H. Bliss, *Management Through Accounts* (New York: Ronald Press Company, 1924), pp. 352-353.

63. American Institute of Accountants, "Verification of Financial Statements," *The Journal of Accountancy*, May 1929, pp. 321-354.

64. George Hillis Newlove, *Consolidated Statements Including Mergers and Consolidations* (Boston: D.C. Heath and Company, 1948), p. 2.

65. H.A. Finney, *Consolidated Statements for Holding Company and Subsidiaries* (New York: Prentice-Hall, Inc., 1922), p. 11.

66. Newlove, *Consolidated Statements Including Mergers and Consolidations*, pp. 49-52.

67. Robert H. Montgomery, *Auditing: Theory and Practice*, I, 2 vols., 3rd ed., rev. and enl. (New York: Ronald Press Company, 1922), p. 346. The first, second, third, and fourth editions of Montgomery's *Auditing: Theory and Practice* are quoted throughout the remainder of this chapter. After the first reference to any particular edition, subsequent references will be cited as: Montgomery, *Auditing*, edition, year, and page number.

68. Paul-Joseph Esquerre', *Accounting* (New York: Ronald Press Company, 1927), p. 130.

69. Montgomery, *Auditing*, 3rd ed., 1922, p. 346.

70. Finney, *Consolidated Statements for Holding Company and Subsidiaries*, p. 34.

71. Ibid., p. 74.

72. Hatfield, *Accounting*, pp. 449-450.

73. Ibid., pp. 450-451.

74. Finney, *Consolidated Statements for Holding Company and Subsidiaries*, pp. 74-75; and Montgomery, *Auditing*, 3rd ed., 1922, p. 400.

75. Robert H. Montgomery, *Auditing: Theory and Practice*, 1st ed. (New York: Ronald Press Company, 1913), p. v.

76. Lawrence R. Dicksee, *Auditing: A Practice Manual for Auditors*, 3rd ed., rev. and enl. (London: Gee & Co., 1898), pp. 8-9. (Hereinafter referred to as *Auditing*.)

77. Ibid., pp. 195-196; see p. 62.

78. Ibid.

79. Lawrence R. Dicksee, *Auditing: A Practical Manual for Auditors*, ed. by Robert H. Montgomery, 2nd ed., Authorized American Edition, revised and enlarged (New York: Ronald Press Co., 1909). The material in this text relating to goodwill (appearing on pp. 190-191) is almost verbatim to that appearing in Dicksee's British edition referred to in the three preceding footnotes.

80. Montgomery, *Auditing*, 1st ed., 1913, pp. v-vi. The same material may be found in the second edition—Robert H. Montgomery, *Auditing: Theory and Practice*, 2nd ed., rev. and enl. (New York: Ronald Press Company, 1917), pp. v-vi.

81. Ibid., pp. 9-11.

82. Ibid., p. 338.

83. Ibid., p. 131.

84. Robert H. Montgomery, *Auditing: Theory and Practice*, 4th ed., rev. and enl. (New York: Ronald Press Company, 1927), pp. 230-232.

85. Ibid., p. 231.

86. DeWitt Carl Eggleston, *Auditing Procedure* (New York: John Wiley & Sons, Inc., 1926), pp. 192-193.

87. Bell and Powelson, *Auditing*, pp. 242-243.

88. Ibid.

89. Robert H. Montgomery, *Income Tax Procedure 1922* (New York: Ronald Press Company, 1922), pp. 627-628.

90. *Revenue Act of 1921, Statutes at Large*, XLII, sec. 206 (a) and (b), 232-233 (1921). (Hereinafter referred to as *Revenue Act of 1921*.)

91. U.S. Treasury Department, Bureau of Internal Revenue, *Regulations 62*, Art. 41, (Washington, D.C.: U.S. Government Printing Office, 1922), p. 37.

92. *Revenue Act of 1921*, sec. 202, pp. 229-231.

93. U.S. Treasury Department, Bureau of Internal Revenue, *Cumulative Bulletin No. 2, January-June, 1920*, Income Tax Rulings, A.R.M. 34 (Washington, D.C.: U.S. Government Printing Office, 1920), p. 31. (Hereinafter referred to as *Cumulative Bulletin No. 2*.)

94. Montgomery, *Income Tax Procedure 1922*, p. 603.

95. J. Royce Miles, *The Treatment of Goodwill in Federal Income Taxation*, Nebraska Studies in Business No. 37 (Lincoln: Extension Division, University of Nebraska, 1935), pp. 13-14. (Hereinafter referred to as *Goodwill in Taxation*.)

96. *Revenue Act of 1921, Statutes at Large*, XL, sec. 234 (a-7), 1078 (1919).

97. Bureau of Internal Revenue, *Regulations 62*, Art. 163, p. 75.

98. Bureau of Internal Revenue, *Cumulative Bulletin No. 2*, Income Tax Rulings, O.D. 472, p. 141.

99. Bureau of Internal Revenue, *Regulations 62*, Art. 143, p. 68.

100. Red Wing Malting Co. v. Willcuts, 8 F. 2d 180 (D. 1925).

101. Red Wing Malting Co. v. Willcuts, 15 F. 2d 626 (8th Cir. 1926).

102. A more detailed account of the case may be found in Miles, *Goodwill in Taxation*, pp. 43-45; and [George Oliver May], "Obsolescence of Goodwill," *The Journal of Accountancy*, March 1930, pp. 161-166.

103. Miles, *Goodwill in Taxation*, p. 45.

104. Harberle Crystal Spring Brewing Co. v. Clarke, 20 F. 2d 540 (D. 1927); Haberle Crystal Spring Brewing Co. v. Clarke, 30 F. 2d 219 (2d Cir. 1929).

105. Clarke v. Haberle Crystal Spring Brewing Company, 280 U.S. 384 (1930).

106. Miles, *Goodwill in Taxation*, p. 45.

107. Henry C. Cox, *Advanced and Analytical Accounting*, Vol. IV of *Business Accounting*, ed. by Harold Dudley Greeley, 5 vols. (New York: Ronald Press Company, 1921), pp. 256-257.

108. Eggleston, *Auditing Procedure*, pp. 192-193.

Chapter V

History 1930-1944

The Business Environment

The Great Depression, beginning late in 1929 and extending well into the 1930s, had a profound effect on accounting. The somewhat optimistic mood prevailing in the twenties vanished, and extremely conservative attitudes developed in business generally and in accounting specifically. This outlook was reflected in strong criticism of unsound or reprehensible business and accounting practices, leading to modifications in accounting for goodwill.

Continuing development of the corporation contributed to changes in accounting practice. Increased salability of ownership had long been recognized as an important characteristic of the corporate form of business. Now, as shares bought and sold were valued in the market at a figure not always corresponding to the valuation of assets shown in the balance sheet, it increasingly became apparent that there was no necessary relationship between book value of the individual assets of the corporation and fair market value of the corporation as a whole. That a stock's market value rested in the earning capacity of a given business finally was given explicit and widespread recognition in the 1930s. As a result, the treatment of goodwill now was considered important because it affected measurements of earning capacity of a business as well as (to a lesser extent) measurements of assets and net worth.

The Accounting Environment

"Experience, n. The wisdom that enables us to recognize as an undesirable old acquaintance the folly that we have already embraced."[1]

As a result of changes in the business environment, the cost basis of fixed asset valuation became one of the best established rules in accounting. According to May, the rule was the result of a revulsion of feeling and went through the stages from postulate to principle in less than a decade.

> The old rule, which permitted and in some cases encouraged the recording of unrealized appreciation on the books of corporations, fell into disrepute because of the abuses that were committed in its name, and because of a change in the general concept of the major objective of accounting from the determination of net worth to the measurement of income and earning capacity.[2]

Emphasis shifted from the balance sheet to the income statement—a fact duly noted and considered in official publications of the accounting profession.[3] Of particular importance was mention of this fact in *General Introduction and Rules Formerly Adopted*, Accounting Research Bulletin No. 1, the first of 51 authoritative bulletins issued by the American Institute of Accountants from 1939 to 1959. (Since June 1, 1957 the organization has been known as the American Institute of Certified Public Accountants.) That bulletin provided a point of reference and departure for all subsequent bulletins, mentioning that the change in emphasis to the income statement was accompanied by conservatism in the statement of income and a tendency to narrowly restrict direct charges to earned surplus. *Accounting for Intangible Assets*, Accounting Research Bulletin No. 24, dealt specifically with the treatment of goodwill.[4] The substantial portions of this chapter dealing with Bulletin No. 24 should be interpreted in light of the foregoing broad remarks in Bulletin No. 1.

By the 1930s, the U.S. accounting profession had developed sufficiently to begin issuing official pronouncements, which increasingly were accepted as authoritative in the formulation of accounting principles. Some of these publications by the American Accounting Association (hereinafter referred to as the Association) and the American Institute of Accountants (hereinafter referred to as the Institute) contained statements either broadly or specifically related to accounting for goodwill. Analysis of these publications constitutes the basis for much of this chapter.

Characteristics of the Literature

In the 1930s, the physical volume of literature devoted to goodwill declined noticeably, probably due more to effects of the depression on publishers and writers generally than to any lack of interest in the subject. The quality of the output rose, however, when viewed in terms of theoretical points discussed, arguments and counter-arguments presented, and decreased repetitiveness as compared with that of the previous twenty years. Much of the discussion was of a critical nature, reflecting the conservative attitude then present.

Literature on goodwill almost ceased to exist for the duration of World War II. Though publications of the Institute and the Association continued to be issued during the war and the important Bulletin No. 24 was issued in December 1944, very few books and articles written in the previous two or three years contained anything directly related to goodwill. The war seems to have brought more pressing problems to the attention of accountants.

Issues and Problems Concerning Goodwill

Initial Valuation

In addition to a discussion of goodwill acquired on the purchase of a going concern, the merits of capitalizing extraordinary advertising expenditures, early losses, and arbitrary write-ups as goodwill were considered in the previous chapter. Although strong criticism had been directed at the treatment of each of the last three items, at least some writers supported one or another of the practices or felt they did no harm.

After the depression, greater emphasis on valuing assets at historical cost directly influenced the acceptance of each of the four items as goodwill. During this period, the position favoring the recognition of goodwill only upon the purchase of a going concern was strengthened; the capitalization of other items as goodwill fell into various degrees of disfavor.

Format of the Initial Valuation Discussion: In the subsequent discussion, a topic is devoted to each practice concerning the effects of general adherence to historical cost valuation (hereinafter referred to as the cost principle). The section on purchase of a going concern is directed in detail to the subject of initial valuation as mentioned in publications of professional accounting organizations in the United States. The sections on advertising, losses, and write-ups include not only initial valuation but subsequent treatment and financial presentation aspects of each of these items, as well. This departure from the usual format of this study was made for two reasons: (1) very little literature appeared on each of these subjects and (2) to illustrate the full extent of criticism leveled at each one.

Purchase of a Going Concern: The trend of thought during this period was toward (1) recognizing only purchased goodwill and (2) recognizing it only at its historical cost. Very little original thought in this regard was added to the accounting literature directly pertaining to goodwill, nor were existing arguments refined to any significant extent. However, attempts by the American Accounting Association and the American Institute of Accountants to develop accounting principles or standards, wherein adherence to historical cost usually was recommended, worked to strengthen the position of recognizing only purchased goodwill. Further, capitalization of advertising expenditures, losses, and write-ups received severe criticism during this period, adding insights to arguments in favor of recording only the historical cost of purchased goodwill.

Publications of the American Accounting Association. In statements issued in 1936 and 1941, the American Accounting Association recommended strict adherence to the cost principle. Accounting was not concerned with valuation, but with "the allocation of historical costs and revenues to current and succeeding fiscal periods."[5] The procedure of revaluing assets up or down had proven unsatisfactory, and it was noted that "a history of cost and cost amortization is a consistent record of actual occurrences measured according to an intelligible formula, and constitutes an essential starting point in financial interpretation."[6]

The pronouncements of the Association did not deal with the treatment of any specific asset. The objective was to set forth fundamental propositions concerning the function of accounting, and one of these propositions dealt with cost. The treatment of goodwill in the same manner as any other asset therefore had to be implied.

The capitalization of arbitrary amounts or early losses as goodwill definitely was precluded by the emphasis on cost and its amortization. Extraordinary advertising expenditures, however, posed a problem. Definite costs had been incurred and recorded, and the benefit to be derived was applicable to future periods. Referring only to these pronouncements, then, the inference could be made that the purchase either of a firm or of extraordinary advertising presented situations where goodwill could be recorded.

In a monograph expanding the ideas presented in the 1936 statement, W.A. Paton and A.C. Littleton clarified their own views concerning advertising expenditures. They felt that the doctrine of capitalizing these expenditures was not intrinsically unsound, but, nevertheless, scarcely deserved support. The influence of these costs on the future was indeterminate, and more dependable reports could not be produced.[7]

Although the monograph represented only the personal views of the authors, both served on the Executive Board of the Association, which had written the 1936 statement. With possibly some reservation, their views reasonably could be imputed to both the 1936 and the 1941 statements.

By inference from the pronouncements, the only items acceptable as goodwill would be goodwill acquired in the purchase of a going concern or through advertising. By imputation from Paton and Littleton's monograph back to the pronouncements, costs of advertising could be eliminated, so that the only situation left to consider was the purchase of an existing firm.

Publications of the American Institute of Accountants. General acceptance of the cost principle for noncurrent assets came about gradually, as reflected in the official pronouncements of the Institute between 1929 and 1944. *Verification of Financial Statements*, issued in 1929 and discussed briefly in the preceding chapter, never specifically mentioned goodwill; therefore its treatment would have to be inferred from the discussion of other noncurrent asset groups.[8] In the discussion of "Fixed Property," reference was made to the cost of property, to the cost of additions, and other like costs.[9] Though occasionally such statements were made, no specific mention was made in this section or elsewhere in the text endorsing or preferring adherence to a cost basis. Such a preference could, at best, be implied. Furthermore, whether or not appraisals were condoned, provision for them was made. "If the property valuation is stated on the basis of an appraisal at a given date that fact should be mentioned in the balance-sheet."[10]

Goodwill could be recognized in at least three instances without violating the intent of the foregoing suggestions: (1) purchase of an existing business, (2) creation through advertising, and (3) reflection in the accounts after an appraisal. A fourth possibility, recognition by capitalization of losses, was not eliminated entirely—though it certainly was not condoned. Whether or not all four items could be treated as goodwill, the pamphlet allowed considerable latitude in those implications that could be drawn from it.

In a letter dated September 22, 1932 to the New York Stock Exchange, the Institute's Special Committee on Co-operation with Stock Exchanges wrote on two topics of interest to the present discussion: (1) expenditures and appraisals and (2) certain broad accounting principles. Concerning the first topic, the committee felt that the central problem of financial accounting was the treatment in accounts of expenditures made in one period with the object of producing profits in the future.[11] In an earlier age, the progress of a firm could be measured by comparison of annual valuations, but the increasing complexity of modern business had made the task of appraisal too vast.

> The variations in appraisal from year to year due to changes in price levels or changes in the mental attitude of the appraisers would in many cases be so great as to reduce all other elements in the computations of the results of operations to relative insignificance.[12]

These remarks appear to imply a definite inclination toward the use of historical cost in accounts, but the accounting principles recommended (and later adopted by the Institute) did not refer to any basis for initial valuation.[13] The list of principles was not meant to be comprehensive, but George O. May, chairman of the committee, stated some years later that, "It is significant that no prohibition against recording unrealized appreciation was included in this list."[14] Evidently, enough of a change in attitude deemphasizing valuation attempts had not yet occurred for the committee to recommend general acceptance of a cost basis.

In *Examination of Financial Statements*, issued in 1936, mention was first made of the basis of intangible assets. "Plant assets, permanent investments and intangibles are usually stated at cost or on some other historical basis without regard to present realizable or replacement value."[15]

This statement still did not preclude writing up goodwill. Using George O. May's phrase concerning the list of principles discussed previously, there was no prohibition against recording unrealized appreciation. Now, however, the usual basis was considered to be cost, implying that any other basis was not usual or ordinary. Arbitrary write-ups no longer would be accepted so readily; they would be subject to question.

Although expressing only the views of its three authors, *A Statement of Accounting Principles*, written in 1938 by Sanders, Hatfield, and Moore, appears to continue the same trend in the application of the cost principle to intangibles as the official pronouncements of the Institute. In accounting practice, according to the study, several general conventions had evolved, one of which was the historical character of the balance sheet. As a result, intangible assets such as goodwill developed within a business were omitted from the balance sheet. Another convention stated that the original basis of fixed asset valuation was cost.[16]

In a section of the study dealing specifically with goodwill, the authors stated:

> It is generally accepted that a value should be placed on goodwill in the books only when goodwill has been purchased. The corollary is that goodwill should not be entered in the books of the business which builds it up.[17]

For a study supposedly basing its statement of accounting principles on experience, this quote taken by itself appears to be a departure from the practice of the time.[18] So the authors, although noting that historical cost was the general rule, stated that two modifications to it had appeared: "(a) the cost of extensive advertising . . .; (b) the operating deficits of the early years of a business."[19]

The difference between a "usual basis" and a "general rule" appears to be slight, but nevertheless a more receptive attitude to the cost principle may be implied. If a practice is considered usual, then following another practice in a given situation implies that something unusual or not customary has been done. Following another practice does not imply that an exception has been taken or that a modification has been made. Exceptions or modifications occur when a "general rule" has been established, and departures therefrom can only be described as exceptional. To depart from a rule certainly is to do something unusual or not customary, but it is to do more than that as well. Either the established rule has been broken, or it has been modified. Applying this analysis to the specific situation, departures from historical cost were not only considered unusual, they now could occur only where some modification from the cost principle had been made.

Arbitrary write-ups of goodwill certainly were placed in an unfavorable position because (1) historical cost was felt to be the general rule and (2) recording appraisal values had not been included as one of the modifications. Furthermore, capitalization of extraordinary advertising expenditures or early losses was acceptable only as a modification of the cost principle. Exclusive recognition of goodwill acquired upon purchase of a going concern was evolving gradually.

Acceptance of the cost principle for goodwill by the Association was finally recommended in Accounting Research Bulletin No. 24 issued in December 1944.

> The initial carrying value of all types of intangibles should be cost, in accordance with the generally accepted accounting principle that assets should be stated at cost when they are acquired.[20]

Of the four items that had at one time or another been treated as goodwill, two could be eliminated immediately. Arbitrary write-ups could be excluded because of adherence to the cost principle. The capitalization of early losses could be excluded because cost was "defined generally as the price paid or consideration given to acquire the asset in question."[21] Those deficits represented the excess of expired costs over revenues realized in a given period, and as expired costs they could never again be used to acquire any asset, much less goodwill.

Goodwill acquired on the purchase of a going concern, the third item, was recognized as the only element completely fitting the committee's definition. The bulletin was concerned in detail with its treatment.

That left one item—extraordinary advertising expenditures. On this point was the following caveat: "The bulletin does not deal with the problems of accounting for intangibles developed in the regular course of business by research, experimentation, advertising, or otherwise."[22] Had that sentence not appeared, a case might have been made for capitalizing some advertising expenditures as goodwill in accordance with provisions of the bulletin. Problems would have been encountered in measuring the subsequent allocation of these expenditures to current and future accounting periods, but these costs would have been deemed legitimate costs of goodwill. With the foregoing statement, the committee recognized that intangibles could be created by advertising but chose to ignore the associated accounting problems in the present bulletin. Possibly the committee felt that by avoiding the issue, difficulties in justifying accounting for advertising as goodwill would lead to the demise of the practice. To some extent this appears to have occurred.

Extraordinary Advertising Expenditures: Although advertising expenditures were discussed to some extent previously, the emphasis was primarily on goodwill acquired upon the purchase of a going concern. Aside from the problems mentioned in connection with the previous subject, goodwill created by advertising was subject to accounting problems related strictly to its own characteristics.

The capitalization of advertising as goodwill was assailed from all directions. In fact, the completely negative tone in accounting literature at this time toward the treatment is quite striking. That advertising might create goodwill was usually conceded, but that was all. Concerning the treatment of its initial cost, George Walker exclaimed that:

> At best, the estimate of the effect of advertising upon the creation
> of goodwill could only be wild speculation. The amount of such an
> estimate would depend very greatly upon the mental attitude of the
> proprietor or appraiser at the time of the investment.[23]

Assuming some figure had been decided on as representing advertising expenditures applicable to future periods, its ultimate disposition was a difficult matter, at best.[24] How could permanent retention be recommended when it was so difficult to determine which expenditures would be permanently beneficial?[25] But how could allocation to future periods be accomplished when, as Paton and Littleton had said, the effect of the costs on the future was indeterminate? And what if, like much advertising, the expenditures were made continuously?

> Many such costs, moreover, are in part regularly recurring, and the adoption of a general policy of capitalization would require the development of a concurrent scheme of amortization—not an easy task.[26]

The criticism and unfavorable attitude toward capitalizing advertising expenditures as goodwill shown in the Institute and Association publications left only one acceptable alternative. Advertising felt to benefit future periods should be capitalized not as goodwill but as prepaid advertising. Then it should be written off as rapidly as possible. Though large amounts incurred before a firm began to produce revenues might be capitalized and retained in the accounts indefinitely, the expenditures would have to be capitalized under some descriptive caption other than goodwill, such as "Organization Costs."

Capitalized Early Losses: The capitalization of early losses never received much support in accounting literature. What little was written on the subject following the depression had the same critical tone and content of the earlier writings. The only publication not mentioning it unfavorably discussed it in a neutral manner. The 1938 study by Sanders, Hatfield, and Moore listed capitalization of early operating deficits as a modification to the general rule of historical cost valuation.[27] The authors had prepared an inventory of accounting principles developed through experience, however, and did not attempt to pass judgment on them.

Unlike extraordinary advertising expenditures, no strong theoretical support existed for the capitalization of deficits. With increased recognition of the cost principle, the practice disappeared.

Arbitrary Write-ups of Goodwill: The practice of recording appraisal values had been a major target (and subsequent casualty) of stricter adherence to the cost principle, and if any doubts still existed through the early forties, they were effectively dispelled with the official and explicit recognition of historical cost as the basis for intangibles in Accounting Research Bulletin No. 24.

Prior to the issuance of the bulletin, and in addition to objections discussed in the previous chapter, several other criticisms were mentioned. Assume that goodwill was written on the books subsequent to an appraisal, that Reappraisal Surplus was credited, and that both accounts were retained indefinitely. Even though Reappraisal Surplus represented one of the least objectionable accounts to have been credited, the ultimate effect of any credit to owners' equity was to increase net worth twice. Net worth would increase once because of the write-up and again as excess profits were earned.[28] Therefore, the same thing would be represented twice, both in owners' equity and in the asset section of the balance sheet.

In a comprehensive article on nonpurchased goodwill, George Walker attacked write-ups on practical grounds, as follows:

> The sales possibilities of the firm are not increased. Neither is the credit position of the firm strengthened, since financiers frequently deduct all intangible values from the net worth section of the balance sheet when a loan is being contemplated.[29]

Along with extraordinary advertising expenditures and early losses, arbitrary write-ups gradually ceased to be an important issue.

Subsequent Treatment

In the more optimistic mood of the twenties, a number of ways for placing goodwill on the books had flourished: purchase of a going concern, capitalization of certain advertising expenditures or early losses, and arbitrary write-up of the account. Most of these practices disappeared with closer adherence to the cost principle advocated in the thirties and forties, leaving only the first treatment mentioned completely acceptable.

Though only one method remained for recording goodwill, several techniques arose for reducing it. The pessimistic outlook fostered by the depression, the desire to be conservative in accounting generally, and awareness of abuses perpetrated in the goodwill account brought increased pressure to expel goodwill from the balance sheet. The practice of writing off goodwill, discussed previously mainly in connection with proprietorships and partnerships, was resurrected for use by corporations.[30] In short, the emphasis had shifted from how to get goodwill on the books to how to get it off.

Three main alternatives existed for the subsequent treatment of goodwill: (1) permanent retention as an asset, (2) gradual reduction, and (3) complete write-off. In addition to the continuous running battle between those advocating permanent retention and those favoring gradual reduction, some new factors appeared that make discussion of each of these positions worthwhile. Those advocating permanent retention were faced with the prospect of maintaining their intransigence in the wake of the greatest business depression in modern times. How they addressed themselves to this problem is discussed in the next topic.

Where the book value of goodwill was to be lowered, the means of reduction became an important point. A choice was required not only between gradual reduction and complete write-off; the charge might be made to current income, earned surplus, or capital surplus. Proper disposition of the charge is discussed in relation to gradual reduction and complete write-off—the second and third topics, respectively.

Publications of professional accounting associations in the United States reflected general indecisiveness in the accounting profession on the question of goodwill's subsequent treatment. Authors of these usually refused to take a stand on the desirability of alternatives. The last of these publications, Accounting Research Bulletin No. 24, represents a culmination of several conflicting factors and a compromise between members of the committee advocating conflicting, but equally acceptable, treatments. These publications, with particular emphasis on Accounting Research Bulletin No. 24, are discussed in the fourth topic.

Permanent Retention as an Asset: "During the eleven-year period 1929-1939, ninety-eight industrial concerns in the United States decreased the values of intangible assets on their books approximately $786,000,000."[31]

The study from which that quote was taken was an analysis of material drawn down from *Moody's Manual of Investments–Industrial Securities* for 346 representative corporations in the United States. The author concluded that a definite trend existed of writing down intangibles and of valuing them, particularly goodwill, at a nominal figure.[32] Evidently, goodwill did not appear quite as permanent to some as it had at one time.

At any rate, the sustained period of adversity must have caused some uneasiness among those who had advocated permanent retention of goodwill in the accounts. In one text, the position was taken that goodwill should be recognized at its cost and should not be depreciated. If it subsequently lost all or a part of its value, a lower rate of profit would be realized on investment.

> The market value of the goodwill has decreased, but there is no depreciation. The goodwill has not worn out, become inadequate, or become obsolete; it has simply failed to earn its anticipated amount of profit.[33]

This argument represents the orthodox viewpoint on permanent retention. One can read into it the older idea that goodwill does not depreciate but aimlessly fluctuates. Whether there are upward pressures as in the twenties or downward pressures as in the thirties, goodwill should remain at cost.

Montgomery, another staunch advocate of permanent retention, expressed the same views in the fifth edition of his *Auditing* in 1934 as in the first edition of 1913.[34] In 1934 he again stated that goodwill may appear at cost and that no objection could be offered to its retention. Although it might be opportune to write off goodwill if earnings were unusually large, "the very existence of earnings sufficient to write it off justifies its retention."[35] While not excluding the practice of writing off goodwill, he did not prefer it and went no further into how the write-off should be accomplished.

Montgomery's text was being used by the accounting profession, teachers, and businessmen, and he mentioned in the preface of his sixth edition in 1940 that a number of changes in practice had occurred since 1934.[36] By inference, one of the changes he quite possibly was referring to was the trend toward reduction of the valuation of intangibles in the accounts. In any event, the practice of reducing intangibles had attained more acceptance, and Montgomery dealt more specifically with it in the sixth edition. "If any adjustments in the book amount of goodwill are made, the offsetting debit or credit should be to earned surplus or capital surplus, whichever is appropriate."[37] As before, he still preferred permanent retention of goodwill; if (from what appears to have been his point of view) an inferior treatment was followed, he at least wanted it handled properly.

The practice of retaining the cost of goodwill was subjected to some criticism, also. One writer, G.A.D. Preinreich, used one of Montgomery's own arguments against him. Montgomery recommended charging off deferred charges if their ultimate benefits were doubtful.

> More than one enterprise has been wrecked by the failure to look preliminary or establishment expenses squarely in the face. The temptation to state the current operations in such a way as to show a profit was too strong; so those concerns have gone along from year to year, the burden increasing instead of diminishing, until the inevitable day of reckoning, when it was realized that liabilities cannot be liquidated with capitalized expenses.[38]

Preinreich thought Montgomery's attitude was proper, but noted:

> The arguments are fully applicable to that goodwill which the same auditors often accept as permanent. An admittedly genuine investment in goodwill and the various forms of deferred charges differ only in degree, not in kind, and therefore the only moot question is the rate or manner of extinguishment, not its necessity.[39]

Despite the adverse business conditions and criticism, the basic position remained intact. The return of more prosperous times as World War II approached could be used to illustrate that goodwill did fluctuate and therefore should remain at cost. It subsequently was incorporated as a major feature of Accounting Research Bulletin No. 24.

Gradual Reduction: Gradual reduction of the goodwill account could be accomplished by charges to current income, earned surplus, or capital surplus. Arguments for amortization to capital surplus usually were not advanced at this time; capital surplus was discussed more frequently in connection with large write-offs of goodwill. The major point of contention was between the other two alternatives: a charged to earned surplus and a charge to income.

Charge to earned surplus. This practice was not in conflict with the assumption that goodwill was permanent; it was a corollary of it. Like Montgomery, some of those advocating the retention of the cost of goodwill based on the asset's assumed permanence recognized that many firms were finding it desirable to reduce the figure at which goodwill was carried on their books. The problem presented was how to accomplish the reduction while maintaining intact the assumption of goodwill's permanence.

The most preferred treatment was unavailable: permanent retention in the accounts. This maintained the assumption but did not accomplish the reduction.

Another treatment was undesirable: charges to income. This accomplished the reduction but violated the assumption. How could one treat an item not subject to depreciation as an expense?

Charges to earned surplus offered a compromise. The practice accomplished the reduction without reporting the charge as an expense. The argument is similar to that advocated several decades back of accumulating a reserve fund out of profits.[40] In that case, however, there was no charge against accumulated profits; there was an allocation of them. Those supporting the assumption of goodwill's permanence had found an alternative—one useful in place of permanent retention—which could contend with the presumed heresy of charges to income.

The method was subject to the same criticism that permanent retention was, that is, that goodwill was not a permanent asset. This was a matter of assumption rather than of method, however, and had been contested for years with little effect one way or the other.

Dropping the assumption of the permanence of goodwill did not entirely preclude charges to earned surplus. Paton noted that, "the periodic charge should be treated as a revenue deduction except in situations in which interpretation as a loss is clearly called for."[41] Though restricted to a special situation, the treatment also could be useful to those favoring amortization to income.

Charge to income. Little was added during this period to support the practice. The old contentions were faithfully restated, but very little, if anything, original was added.

An interesting argument did develop, however, in the form of a criticism of the practice and a rejoinder to it. Assume a firm and its goodwill are purchased, and the new owners, in accordance with acceptable accounting practice, amortize the cost of goodwill to income. Wishing to maintain their acquired goodwill, they advertise and charge the expenditure to current income. If income is charged once for decline of goodwill and charged again for an expenditure made to replenish and retain that goodwill, is not income being charged for the same thing twice?[42]

Paton noted that this argument was used to support permanent retention of goodwill where maintaining a level of income required advertising expenditures at least equal to amortization charges.

> However, the fact that it is not considered feasible to accumulate as a deferred charge costs presumably assignable to future revenues is hardly adequate justification for failure to write off a cost that is presumably expiring.[43]

Paton felt that each item should be considered separately and not be allowed to cancel or offset the other.

This practice was the opposite of permanently retaining goodwill—both in its basic assumption and in the method of its accomplishment. Though the idea of permanent retention was made a dominant feature of Accounting Research Bulletin No. 24, amortization to income was too strongly accepted to be ignored. Amortization also was incorporated as a major feature of the bulletin, though in a roundabout way.[44]

The literature devoted to the question of goodwill's permanence or nonpermanence had become voluminous by this time. One individual summed up the futility of it all when he wrote:

> The interesting cleavage of opinion . . . is probably quite as much a matter of temperament as of principle, and whilst one recognises the strength of the arguments both for and against the writing down of goodwill, one is inclined to question whether, after all, it makes any great deal of difference whether it is written off or retained on the books.[45]

Write-off: The term "write-off" could be and has been used to refer to any type of reduction, whether as a lump sum or as a periodic charge. In this study, the term is used in a much more restricted sense to mean the complete elimination in one entry of a relatively large account from the books. Though two main alternatives for subsequent treatment of goodwill had been in existence for a number of years, the choice of one or the other could be made along clear lines and applied within established practices. The advantages and disadvantages of each had been stated and refined, and both were fully acceptable.

In contrast, vagueness surrounded the practice of writing goodwill off just as it had surrounded the opposite practice of writing it up. When was the write-off to be done? Where was the charge to go? Was disposition of the charge to depend on origin of the goodwill account, amount of the write-off, or both?

The proper timing of the transaction was never considered completely. Those who discussed the practice might assume that the firm already had decided to write off its goodwill and then told how to accomplish it. Presumably a firm would be experiencing low earnings or would desire to follow a more conservative policy in valuing its assets, but little if anything more specific than that was mentioned. Determination of the timing of write-offs, like determination of the amount of write-ups, was largely arbitrary.

Disposition of the charge could be made to a number of accounts: some expense account, earned surplus, capital surplus, or revaluation surplus. The relatively large size of the write-off usually precluded use of an expense account, because current income could be materially affected and distorted. Origin of the goodwill could be used for selecting among the remaining three alternatives.

Earned surplus. If goodwill was acquired on the purchase of a going concern and the new owners decided to write it off, earned surplus was considered the logical account for the charge. The payment for goodwill was made for anticipated future excess income. The account that was expected to receive the credit for this income should also receive the charge which made the income possible.[46]

Those who assumed goodwill to be a permanent asset and who had a conservative bent could make use of the alternative by extending their arguments. As mentioned previously, goodwill could be either retained permanently or written down gradually by periodic charges to earned surplus.

Why not take the corollary of periodic charges one step further and make just one charge for the entire amount?

One special case of the practice should be mentioned—purchase of a going concern and immediate write-off of acquired goodwill. This treatment was discussed in Chapter 3 in connection with partnerships and proprietorships.[47] It had been revived in the United States and used extensively in corporations because no legal barriers against it existed as they did in Great Britain, and the American Institute of Accountants had not yet issued authoritative pronouncements against it. Although the practice was increasingly denounced after World War II, it became a crucial consideration in the seventies.[48]

Revaluation surplus. Probably the least objectionable way in which goodwill could be written up was through an account titled Appraisal Surplus or Revaluation Surplus. Subsequent increased emphasis on cost as a basis for noncurrent assets had led to a general desire to do away with goodwill created in this manner. A good way to remove the account would be to eliminate the appraisal or revaluation surplus created simultaneously with it.

Capital surplus. Several occasions arose in which capital surplus could be used to effect a write-off of goodwill.[49] Sometimes goodwill had been written up and capital surplus had been credited. Though it was not considered correct to begin the write-up with the capital surplus account, the logic of writing off goodwill to its source implied that the surplus account nevertheless should absorb any appreciations credited to it and subsequently written off.

The write-off of purchased goodwill usually was made to earned surplus, but a question arose when that account could not absorb all or part of the charge. Capital surplus, though not the source of the goodwill, could have been used to absorb the charge in excess of amounts carried to available earned surplus. One writer felt this procedure was justified only if full disclosure was made and any future surplus was shown as dating from the time of absorption.[50]

One situation existed that was unique to capital surplus. Capital stock would be issued for assets including goodwill. Subsequently, it would be determined that goodwill had been overstated at acquisition and should be written down. Because the initial valuation resulted from the issuance of stock, then capital accounts, specifically capital surplus, could be charged with the amount of the write-down.

All of these situations assumed that capital surplus was sufficient to absorb the reductions. Either sufficient capital surplus did exist at the time of write-off, or it had to be created for the purpose by reducing legal capital.

Attitudes toward write-offs. The question of goodwill write-offs was part of the larger problem of writing down assets in general. The larger problem had arisen because of sustained low earnings during the depression, but it had never been discussed adequately.[51] In turn, the literature was virtually barren concerning the specific question of the propriety of goodwill write-offs. Symptomatic of this lack of discussion was the question of proper timing referred to earlier. The question of when the charges were to be made could hardly be answered until the reason they were made was considered.

Paton criticized the practice of writing off goodwill as "unduly conservative." While recognizing that the goodwill account had a bad reputation from prior dubious practices, recording and retaining purchased goodwill as an asset was unquestionable, and there was "no reason for its exclusion from the respectable family of assets."[52]

Publications of Professional Accounting Associations:

American Accounting Association. The 1936 and 1941 statements by the American Accounting Association were virtually identical on the subject of cost amortization. Both were so broad that either permanent retention or gradual reduction could be inferred. In 1936, for example, the Executive Committee felt that recognition should be given to all expirations of cost; determination of costs applicable to future periods would have to be based on business judgments, seasoned experience, and expert opinion.[53] But whether goodwill expired had long been a question that seasoned experience and expert opinion had not been able to resolve satisfactorily. In 1941, the Committee mentioned that "a primary basis of classifying fixed assets is that which separates depreciable from nondepreciable property"[54] but left open the question of which assets were depreciable.

Once an assumption was made either way concerning goodwill's permanence, however, no question remained of the asset's subsequent treatment. If goodwill was assumed to be a permanent asset, its cost would be retained permanently on the books. If it was assumed to be nonpermanent, it would be amortized through periodic charges in the income statement. Charges bypassing the income statement through earned surplus were specifically excluded through adherence to an all-inclusive approach in reporting income.[55]

Implications for write-offs of goodwill appear to have been restrictive. Costs applicable to assets that are no longer useful or salable should be eliminated from the accounts, but the statements contained nothing concerning the arbitrary write-off of assets. Presumably write-offs of goodwill should be based on some criteria other than desire.

Assuming a good reason existed for writing off goodwill, the all-inclusive approach dictated that the write-off be treated as a loss or extraordinary charge in the income statement. The write-off ultimately would be reflected in earned surplus, but the initial entry to record the charge would have to be current income.

Capital surplus could be affected indirectly by the write-off. Paid-in surplus, as the account was referred to in the Association's statements, could be used to offset deficits in earned surplus through a recapitalization approved by stockholders, provided that earned surplus was dated from the time of recapitalization.[56] The possibility existed that the deficit in earned surplus was created by recognition of losses in the value of goodwill. Through subsequent recapitalization, capital surplus would be used to absorb indirectly the write-off of the asset.

Subsequent disposition of write-ups was not discussed in the statements. Because strict adherence to the cost principle was recommended, write-ups were not considered correct in the first place, and presumably their subsequent treatment was ignored for that reason.

The treatment of goodwill acquired for capital stock and subsequently found to have been over-valued at acquisition had to be implied. Regardless of whether assets are over-valued or under-valued when purchased, cost is assumed to constitute an essential starting point for financial interpretation.[57] If subsequent examination revealed a discrepancy between book value and the portion of that figure reasonably applicable to future periods, the asset should be reduced with a corresponding reduction of current income. Capital surplus would not be affected by the write-off.

In summary, the Association's statements appear to have dealt only with goodwill acquired at cost. Goodwill then could be either permanently retained at cost or amortized by charges to income. Write-offs could occur only if cost did not reflect the asset's future usefulness and then only by a charge to income. Though subsequently affected, earned surplus could not be used to record the initial write-off, and capital surplus would only be affected in case of recapitalization.

Paton and Littleton's position in their monograph was basically the same as that of the Association, though they were more explicit. They felt goodwill should be amortized to income because the asset represented "an advance recognition of a debit for a portion of income that is expected to materialize later." Writing in 1940 when the depression was still a fresh experience, they based their conclusion on "the fact that there is ample evidence in available business histories to show that extraordinary earning power cannot be expected to persist indefinitely."[58] Their treatment of write-offs can be inferred from their discussion of surplus and appears to be the same as that of the Association.[59]

American Institute of Accountants. The first statement by the Institute of any relevance to the subsequent treatment of goodwill was made in 1932 and concerned the propriety of charges to capital surplus. According to the Special Committee on Co-operation with Stock Exchanges, capital surplus should not be used for charges that should be made against income of either current or future years, though in a reorganization such charges would be permitted. The same result could be accomplished without reorganization if "facts were as fully revealed to and the action as formally approved by the shareholders as in reorganization."[60]

If goodwill was assumed to be a nonpermanent asset, some conclusions might be cautiously drawn. The implications mainly concern write-offs and are of interest for what is excluded rather than for what is permitted. If goodwill was acquired on the purchase of a going concern, the arbitrary write-off of the asset to capital surplus would be improper. Because the firm would have amortized goodwill in accordance with the asset's assumed nonpermanence, current and future income would be relieved of applicable charges. By extension, the same charge made to earned surplus was improper if a deficit was thus created in earned surplus and subsequently closed to capital surplus without disclosure to and approval by stockholders. Under these conditions, charging capital surplus for goodwill write-offs was frowned upon.

Goodwill's permanence or nonpermanence continued to be an unresolved question, however, and the foregoing conclusions could not be made if goodwill was assumed to be a permanent asset. In this situation it would never be written off to current income, so that the write-off of goodwill to either earned surplus or capital surplus would not be relieving income of charges that it otherwise would receive. Such charges thus appear to have been acceptable or at least not criticized.

The treatment of most if not all other asset write-downs or write-offs could be determined by the Institute's statement. But goodwill's appropriate treatment could not be determined until the Institute made an assumption concerning the asset's permanence or specified a treatment to be followed.

Examination of Financial Statements, issued in 1936, contained exactly the same statement as the 1932 publication, with no further elaboration. Though mention was made of amortization of intangibles, the bulletin did not consider the merits of the practice.[61] More specific conclusions concerning write-offs and amortization could not be drawn until later.

The study made in 1938 by Sanders, Hatfield, and Moore presents an excellent view of practices followed at that time.[62] Exaggerations previously made in the goodwill account and distrust of goodwill appearing in the balance sheet had led to reductions of its book value even though substantial goodwill was known to exist. The authors noted that the three main alternatives—permanent retention, gradual reduction, and complete write-off—were acceptable in accounting practice. Amortization was not imperative, but it was not objectionable. Though usually charged to income, it could be charged to capital surplus or earned surplus. If goodwill was written down substantially or written off completely, the charge should be made either to capital surplus or to earned surplus, but not to income.

Sanders, Hatfield, and Moore stated that a pervasive feeling existed that the presence of a goodwill account did not add strength to the balance sheet. And though all three alternatives were acceptable, much writing off had occurred—usually in a few large amounts instead of by systematic amortization.

The rule discussed previously and proposed by the Special Committee on Co-operation with Stock Exchanges was adopted by the Institute in 1934. In September 1939, Accounting Research Bulletin No. 3 was issued to amplify it. After quoting the rule, the bulletin stated:

> If a corporation elects to ... avail itself of the permission to relieve its future income account or *earned-surplus account* of charges which should otherwise be made thereagainst, it should make a clear report to the stockholders of the restatements proposed to be made, and obtain their formal consent.[63] (Italics mine.)

Mention of earned surplus was new; the original rule mentioned only the income account. The amplification may be interpreted to mean that, in a readjustment or quasi-reorganization, the income account and earned surplus may be relieved of certain charges. Conversely, in the absence of a readjustment, the income account and earned surplus may not be so relieved.

In the absence of other statements, those implications would have been significant. Write-offs of purchased goodwill usually were made to earned surplus. Capital surplus should not be used to absorb the write-off instead of earned surplus, nor should it be used to absorb any deficits created in earned surplus by write-off unless the corporation made a readjustment in accordance with the rule and its amplification. Whether goodwill was viewed as permanent or nonpermanent, write-offs to capital surplus directly or indirectly would have been held in disfavor, and one of numerous alternatives would have been eliminated if the bulletin had contained no more. The last paragraph, however, qualified and delimited application of the bulletin's implications.

> It is recognized that charges against capital surplus may take place in other types of readjustments to which the foregoing provisions would have no application. Such cases would include readjustments for the purpose of correcting erroneous credits made to capital surplus in the past, or to eliminate amounts which, by universal agreement, do not give rise to charges in respect to exhaustion or amortization.[64]

"Erroneous credits" might be simply errors of classification, but they also might include an over-valuation of goodwill purchased by stock issuance, which the owners subsequently discovered and wished to write-off. Amounts that did not give rise to charges in the nature of exhaustion or amortization might well include purchased goodwill—many believed the asset was not subject to exhaustion and should not be amortized. As a result, the Institute provided no definitive guidelines concerning subsequent treatment of goodwill.

Accounting Research Bulletin No. 24, *Accounting for Intangible Assets*, thus represented the first time the Institute indicated its preferences concerning goodwill's handling in accounts.[65] Those provisions relating specifically to the subsequent treatment of goodwill are summarized, as follows:

1. Classification of intangibles
   a. Type (a) intangibles—those having a term of existence limited by law, regulation, or agreement, or by their nature—including goodwill as to which there is evidence of limited duration
   b. Type (b) intangibles—those having no limited term of existence and as to which there is, at the time of acquisition, no indication of limited life such as goodwill generally
2. Initial valuation—cost
3. Subsequent treatment
   a. Type (a) intangibles—amortize by systematic charges in the income statement over the period benefited
   b. Type (b) intangibles
      (1) Term of existence remains unlimited
         (a) retain indefinitely at cost
         (b) amortize by systematic charges in the income statement
         (c) write-off to earned surplus or capital surplus
      (2) Term of existence becomes limited
         (a) amortize by systematic charges in the income statement
         (b) partial write-down to earned surplus followed by amortization of remainder in the income statement

(3) Investment becomes partially worthless—situation not covered, but refers to Rule No. 2 of 1934

(4) Investment becomes worthless
    (a) write-off to income statement
    (b) write-off to earned surplus

At the time the bulletin was issued, no clear preference existed in practice for either permanent retention or gradual reduction of goodwill, and a compromise appears to have been worked out. Goodwill generally was regarded as having no limited term of existence, and permanent retention at cost, a treatment consistent with that belief, was the first alternative mentioned as acceptable for handling type (b) intangibles.

To say the least, not everyone agreed with the idea that goodwill was a permanent asset, and accommodation was made to the opposing view. Some goodwill was recognized as having a limited existence and was considered a type (a) intangible subject to amortization in the income statement. Though the provision for type (a) intangibles permitted gradual reduction of the asset, this provision alone would appear to have caused the bulletin to favor permanent retention because goodwill generally was considered a type (b) intangible. If the bulletin was to give equal standing to gradual reduction, some provision would have had to be made for amortization of type (b) intangibles.

> Where a corporation decides that a type (b) intangible may not continue to have value during the entire life of the enterprise, it may amortize the cost of such intangible despite the fact that there are no present indications of such limited life which would require reclassification as type (a), and despite the fact that expenditures are being made to maintain its value.[66]

This statement appears to have given respectability to the treatment of gradual reduction while taking little if any support away from the practice of permanent retention. Those who advocated permanent retention could note that the bulletin assumed goodwill to be a permanent asset, and the first treatment recommended for such an asset was continuous maintenance at cost. A special paragraph had to be added to provide for amortization, and then the amortization had to be formally approved by stockholders, had to be fully disclosed in the financial statements, and was entirely discretionary.

On the other hand, those who advocated gradual reduction might answer that goodwill's continuous existence was not a point of contention; goodwill might be continuously maintained by expenditures made for that purpose or present no indications of limited life. The goodwill originally purchased, however, was constantly diminishing and being replaced; the same amount of goodwill might be maintained, but the goodwill itself was always changing. Goodwill should be amortized accordingly in the income statement.

The two main antagonistic views concerning the handling of goodwill thus were incorporated in the bulletin with no clear indication of which was preferable. This position appears to have corresponded closely to accepted practices.

Another alternative may be viewed as a corollary of the treatment accorded type (a) intangibles. If evidence existed that goodwill previously classified as a type (b) intangible had become limited in duration, it should be reclassified as a type (a) intangible and amortized over its remaining life. As a modification of this treatment, a partial write-down to earned surplus would be allowed if expensing the full amount of the charges would cause distortion in the income statement, and the balance following the write-down would be amortized.

A special case of a type (b) intangible becoming limited in duration might occur. The duration of time might be very short—so short, in fact, that the goodwill might lapse in the current period. In that situation the asset should be written down very quickly or, in effect, written off. The write-off would be to the income statement or to earned surplus, whichever was deemed appropriate.

All of the foregoing practices met with approval by the Committee on Accounting Procedure; none of them involved charges to capital surplus. If a write-down or write-off to earned surplus was made, some reason beyond mere conservatism had to be given. Either the income statement would be distorted by such a large figure or the investment must be considered worthless.

In contrast to the previous write-offs are what might be termed discretionary write-offs made usually on the basis of conservatism only.

> "The committee recognizes that in the past it has been accepted practice to eliminate type (b) intangibles by writing them off against any existing surplus, capital or earned, even though the value of the asset is unimpaired. Since the practice has been long established and widely approved, the committee does not feel warranted in recommending, at this time, adoption of a rule prohibiting such disposition. The committee believes, however, that such dispositions should be discouraged, especially if proposed to be effected by charges to capital surplus.[67]

With this statement, the committee made a compromise between what should have been practiced in the views of its members and what was currently practiced. Discretionary write-offs, though allowed, were discouraged. May pointed out that the committee went further than usual in its attitude toward such write-offs.[68] At this time bulletins of the committee were not rules; their authority rested on their general acceptability, and each bulletin carried a statement to that effect. Though the practice of writing off goodwill had achieved some measure of acceptance, by its negative attitude the committee was leaning slightly toward determination of acceptability rather than reliance on it for its pronouncements.

Charges to capital surplus for amortization, write-down, or write-offs of goodwill either were not mentioned, and therefore not recommended, or were discouraged. Though allowing write-offs to capital surplus in one instance, the committee evidently still felt the account should never be used to absorb reductions of goodwill. This conclusion may also be reached by examining Rule No. 2 of 1934 in retrospect. With the issuance of Bulletin No. 24, the committee finally and continuously evidenced a desire to reduce goodwill (when applicable) through charges to income or earned surplus. As the rule stated that "capital surplus . . . should not be used to relieve the income account of the current or future years of charges which would otherwise fall to be made there against," capital surplus should not be used for reductions of goodwill.[69]

The committee did not concern itself with one final situation—the possibility of type (b) goodwill becoming partially worthless. Goodwill permanently retained on the books might lose a large portion of its value but not all of it. Furthermore, the remainder might appear to have an unlimited term of existence. Presumably, a partial write-down would be in order, but the committee made no comment on how this should be accomplished.

> The problems arising as a result of such partial loss of value (as contrasted with total loss of value discussed above), which are also applicable to tangible assets (such as, loss of commercial value of tangible capital assets not covered by depreciation accounting), are not dealt with herein but are in their broader aspects presently under consideration by the committee.[70]

The committee did draw attention to Rule No. 2 of 1934, so presumably partial write-downs to capital surplus would not be in order or at least not well received.

Summarizing the Institute's position concerning the subsequent treatment of goodwill, either permanent retention or gradual reduction was acceptable and recommended for goodwill having no limited term of existence. Write-offs were acceptable, but were recommended only where the asset had become worthless. Reductions could be made to either income or earned surplus. Capital surplus could be used only for discretionary write-offs, but opposition to this practice existed at two points. Discretionary write-offs were frowned upon and so were any charges to capital surplus. If goodwill's term of existence was limited, the asset should be amortized. If "permanent" goodwill subsequently appeared limited in duration, it could be amortized over its remaining life or partially written down to earned surplus and the remainder amortized.

Subsequent Treatment—Conclusions: Either by implication or by expression, both the Institute and the Association offered fewer alternatives than actually existed in practice at the time. Write-offs to capital surplus either were not allowed or were discouraged by the organizations, and write-offs in general needed justification beyond mere conservatism. Both organizations reflected actual practice by indicating no preference between permanent retention and gradual reduction, though amortization was recommended in the Association's monograph by Paton and Littleton.

The Institute and the Association differed on one point—disposition of substantial charges resulting from write-down or write-off of goodwill. The difference was due not to conflicting views concerning the nature of goodwill, but to the broader problem of the function of the income statement. The all-inclusive approach of the Association precluded placement of charges anywhere other than in the income statement. The Institute allowed write-downs or write-offs to earned surplus if the income statement would be distorted by placing those charges in current or future income. The basic position of both organizations was the same on subsequent handling of goodwill, however, and both were, in effect, advocating improvement in current practice through restriction of allowed alternatives.

Financial Presentation and Disclosure

Coupled with the valuation and treatment aspects of intangible assets in Bulletin No. 24 was the significance of its recommended procedures upon financial presentation. In its discussion section the bulletin contained the following statement: "These questions involve basic accounting principles of balance-sheet presentation and income determination."[71] Conservative attitudes in the valuation and subsequent treatment of goodwill similarly had a direct influence on the asset's financial presentation and disclosure. The next topic is concerned with effects in the balance sheet and income statement of eliminating purchased goodwill in various ways. Certain definite trends appeared in the balance sheet treatment of intangibles that affected financial statement presentation of goodwill; these trends are discussed in the second topic. The last topic is concerned with the continuing interest in trends in the treatment of the difference between cost and book value of assets in consolidated statements.

Effects of Goodwill Eliminations on Financial Statements: Of major significance to interpretation of financial statements was the account to which the elimination was charged—capital surplus, earned surplus, or current income—each with its advantages and disadvantages from several points of view.

If capital surplus was charged either for discretionary write-off of goodwill or because the asset lost value, the present and future operating results of a company would appear improved. If the charges otherwise would have been to current income, the income statement and such ratios or fractions as earnings per share, earnings compared to total assets, and earnings compared to owners' equity would look better. The last two ratios would be improved in one other aspect as well; write-off would lower the denominator of the fraction used to calculate each one.

Asset write-offs to capital surplus obscured the distinction between contributed capital and earned surplus and led to misleading implications concerning a firm's record of operations. According to Marple, capital stock and capital surplus represented the total value of assets contributed to a corporation and left in it by stockholders. These accounts should be increased only if additional capital was contributed or accumulated earnings were capitalized and should be decreased only if capital was returned to stockholders. Earned surplus represented increases in corporate net worth exclusive of stockholders' contributions—the net worth contributed by the business instead of by stockholders.[72] Asset write-offs resulted from activities of the business and did not involve a return of capital to stockholders. If goodwill was written off to capital surplus, contributed capital no longer represented transactions solely with stockholders, and earned surplus did not include all transactions resulting from business activities.[73]

When capital surplus was used for asset charge-offs, earned surplus was shown at a larger figure than otherwise. As Paton said (though in connection with write-downs of plant assets):

> Popular procedure makes it quite possible for the management to eliminate all trace of the unpleasant events from the picture and in many cases in fact the entire adjustment leaves the concern, for good measure, with a nice fat [earned] "surplus" account; and this undoubtedly suggests to the average person examining the revised statement (and is intended to so suggest) that far from having been down in the dumps the concern has just concluded an era of profitable operation.[74]

Apparently due to such reasoning, charge-offs to capital surplus were either implicitly disapproved or explicitly discouraged by pronouncements of both the Association and the Institute.

Write-offs to earned surplus were an answer to the foregoing objections. As before, current income was not affected, and various ratios remained improved. "In this way the entire history of the enterprise is preserved intact and the fact that the concern has absorbed some serious jolts is not obscured."[75]

Though charges to earned surplus were preferable to those to capital surplus, discretionary write-offs were objectionable for being based solely on conservatism. A purchased asset presumably contributing to a firm's income was not shown on the books or statements. Returns on total assets and on owners' equity were more favorably presented than the actual situation warranted, because an asset contributing to those returns was not included in the denominator.

Write-offs to earned surplus due to goodwill's worthlessness removed from the balance sheet an asset that no longer existed. The balance sheet subsequently presented only assets contributing to income, and the income statement was not changed. The desirability of not changing current income was, however, a point of contention. The objective of the Association's all-inclusive approach was presentation of all gains and losses in a firm's assembled income statements for a number of years, with each statement reporting all revenues recognized and costs written off during the period.[76] Charges made directly to earned surplus caused important events to be omitted from the statements, and information on these transactions had to be found elsewhere. By 1944 the Institute had not taken a stand on the broad question of transactions to include in the income statement, but in the specific case of intangibles the Committee on Accounting Procedure allowed write-downs or write-offs to earned surplus if the same charge to current income would distort the income statement.[77]

Amortization to earned surplus offered the same advantages and was subject to the same controversy as write-offs but was open to more criticism. Goodwill was purchased because of its income-producing abilities; if amortized, it should be charged to the revenues its purchase made possible. Earned surplus subsequently would receive the amortization charge when current income was closed to it. If an objective was to bypass the income statement, then goodwill could just as easily be written off in one entry instead of several. Thus amortization to earned surplus appears to have served little purpose—the desired effects of gradual reduction were accomplished by one already established practice, and the means whereby charges to current income were prevented was accomplished by another. Thus the practice seems to have been deemed redundant.

One possible use existed for the practice, however. A lump-sum write-off might affect the account drastically, while amortization to income would allow earned surplus to gradually absorb the charge but would also lower current income. Amortization to earned surplus would result in the best of both—bypassing current income while not affecting earned surplus so harshly. This argument, however, contains the elements of its own demise. Earned surplus could better withstand charges over an extended period only because of the replenishing effects of future income on earned surplus in each of those years in which a charge for goodwill amortization was made. Presumably goodwill was contributing to income in each of those future periods, so the charge for its reduction should be matched in the income statement with the revenues so generated. The process of amortization virtually implied a matching of expired cost to an applicable accounting period, and that sort of matching usually was accomplished in the income statement.

Most of the advantages and disadvantages concerning write-offs or amortization to current income were discussed previously in connection with capital surplus and earned surplus. Briefly, however, writing off goodwill to current income was consistent with the all-inclusive concept, but it risked distortion and possible misinterpretation of reported operating results for a given period. The Association chose the all-inclusive alternative while the Institute, though not excluding that approach, allowed for earned surplus charge-offs in the case of distortion. Amortization to current income was also consistent with all-inclusive income reporting and was an attempt to allocate a cost item to the resulting revenues; but it lowered reported net income, causing various ratios to appear less favorable, and was applied over a somewhat arbitrary length of time.

Disposition in the Balance Sheet:

Separate disclosure. A definite trend toward the separate disclosure of intangible assets was evident in the thirties. In an analysis of 587 balance sheets of companies listed on the New York Stock Exchange for fiscal years ending 1931-1932, E.I. Fjeld noted that 80.4 percent of the statements listing intangibles showed them separately; they were classified with fixed assets in only 14.6 percent of the cases. The same statistics by implication applied specifically to goodwill, and Fjeld further stated that goodwill usually was combined with other intangibles rather than being stated separately.[78] The Institute's *Examination of Financial Statements*, issued in 1936, reflected this trend and evidently approved it, stating that "intangible assets such as patents, trademarks, franchises and goodwill should, if practicable, be shown separately in the balance sheet."[79] In a recommended model balance sheet, an "Intangible Assets" section (with the instruction "describe") followed "Property, Plant and Equipment" and preceded "Deferred Charges" and "Other Assets."[80]

There were several reasons for presenting goodwill separately, in addition to those of facilitating calculation of ratios involving tangible fixed assets and permitting the elimination of intangible assets when no significance was attached to them. The presentation of accumulated depreciation would be a problem if intangible and tangible fixed assets were grouped together. Also, a fundamental difference was presumed to exist between the two categories, because tangible fixed assets were used more directly in production and operation of a business.[81]

At various times, goodwill had been approvingly either lumped together with tangible fixed assets, stated with other intangibles as a separate subsection of fixed assets, or stated with other intangibles as a separate section. By the thirties, the first alternative was disapproved, the second was acceptable, and the third was usually recommended and practiced.

Nominal valuation. The presentation of goodwill at a nominal value had been practiced before, but it became common in this period.[82] Of the 587 balance sheets Fjeld examined, nominal valuations of intangibles (including goodwill, in many cases) appeared in 169 instances. Of the 86 balance sheets showing goodwill as a separate item, 31 of them listed goodwill at $1.00.[83] The practice could have been the result of either a write-up, a write-down, or of amortization of the cost of purchased goodwill until only a nominal valuation remained. A firm possessing no purchased goodwill, but having built up its own, might want to call attention to the asset's existence without inflating assets and net worth. Or, having purchased goodwill, a firm might write it down to $1.00 because of the asset's instability and measurement problems, thus for all practical purposes following the existing popular practice of writing it off.[84]

An indication of how the practice became of sufficient importance for writers to recognize and deal with the subject of nominal valuation may be obtained by comparing successive editions of Montgomery's *Auditing*. In the fourth edition (1927), no mention was made of the subject except in an example illustrating a related (but different) point.[85] By the time of the fifth edition seven years later (1934), the practice was so evident that Montgomery devoted a small section to its reasons and merit. Nominal valuations, he stated, usually were defended on the grounds that no one was misled, and the balance sheet reader was placed on notice that the cost of the concern's intangibles bore no relationship to their present value. Such a practice might be conservative and more justified in the case of intangibles than of other assets.

> But to assume that no one can be misled by it is to assume an ability to understand balance sheets on the part of more persons than the facts warrant. Minority shareholders may easily be deceived with regard to the real value of their stock, when assets are stated at nominal values.[86]

Apparently Montgomery was disapproving of nominal valuations for all intangibles, including goodwill. In the sixth edition (1940), he still felt other intangibles should be amortized, because their write-off would improperly relieve future income of amortization charges, but he reconsidered nominal valuation in the case of goodwill due to his continuously reiterated assumption of the asset's permanence.

> There is less objection to stating goodwill alone at a nominal amount (since it is not subject to amortization through the income account) than there is to arbitrarily writing down such intangibles as patents, when in fact substantial values still remain.[87]

The practice of nominal valuation of goodwill might be viewed as part of the general trend toward conservatism then present. The write-down to $1.00 was only a slight modification of complete write-off of the account, offering the advantages of write-offs while testifying to the presumed existence of the asset. In the case of tangible fixed assets and intangibles whose usefulness was limited in duration, the practice relieved current and future income of charges that otherwise would have been necessary and was criticized for so doing. Goodwill's duration had constantly been a point of contention, however, and the same criticism directed toward goodwill did not carry nearly the same significance.

Goodwill in Consolidated Statements: Before the depression, almost all accounting writers (with some few notable exceptions) had advocated treating the entire excess of cost over book value of a subsidiary's stock as goodwill. After 1930, and with increasing frequency through 1944, more authorities called for analysis of the excess and its allocation to specific assets.[88] Reflecting this trend, Bulletin No. 24 contained a third classification of intangibles in addition to types (a) and (b)—the excess of a parent company's investment in the stock of a subsidiary over its equity in the subsidiary's net assets.

> If practicable, such an excess should be divided as between tangible and intangible assets, and the amount allocated to intangibles should be further allocated as between each type (a) intangible and the aggregate, at least, of all type (b) intangibles. The amounts so allocated should thereafter be dealt with in accordance with the rules hereinbefore set forth.[89]

Newlove felt the trend came about because:

> The published solutions to an Ohio C.P.A. problem involving coal lands (1929) and to American Institute problems involving oil wells (1933) and coal lands (1937) emphasized that the debit differential might well undergo amortization. Since these problems were given at a time when the income statement was being given more importance than it had been previously, they influenced accounting thinking to a marked degree.[90]

Not much change appears to have occurred concerning treatment of the excess of book value over cost. A tendency to analyze the differential had always been present and continued even stronger in the thirties and forties. Through 1944, however, no official pronouncements had been issued by the Institute concerning the matter; Bulletin No. 24 dealt only with excess of cost over book value and not vice versa.

Auditing Considerations

Increasing emphasis on cost valuation of assets for purposes of initial statement, accompanied by criticism of write-ups, directly affected the auditor's consideration of goodwill. Much of Montgomery's concern with the auditor's responsibility for goodwill in the fourth edition of his *Auditing*, in 1927, centered on problems associated with current attempts to reflect the asset's "true value" in the balance sheet.[91] Such attempts noticeably subsided after the twenties and so did the auditor's concern with them. Absent from the sixth edition (1940) was any mention of the auditor's participation in the balance sheet valuation of goodwill. Montgomery said only "that the auditor's responsibility in respect to the item of goodwill is to endeavor to establish that the description of the amount at which it is reflected in the balance sheet presents the facts fairly."[92] The logical culmination of these developments was indicated in another contemporary auditing text. "The method used in arriving at a valuation for goodwill is only of academic interest to the auditor. The asset should not be brought on the books unless bought and paid for."[93]

Emphasis then present on reducing the asset did not lead to as many problems of interpretation as questions of its increase. When both increases and decreases were common practice, Montgomery felt the balance sheet should show how goodwill's valuation arose. "Whether written up from no cost or written down from a large cost, the information is almost essential to balance-sheet analysis."[94] Later, as write-ups became uncommon, Montgomery relaxed this stance, stating, "Goodwill . . . may in the absence of information to the contrary, be assumed by the reader to be stated at cost or less."[95]

Tax Considerations

Very little change occurred at this time in income tax law and regulations concerning goodwill. Valuation at cost and no deduction for depreciation or obsolescence were the two dominant characteristics associated with the asset.

One slight alteration was made in the basis for determining loss on sale of goodwill acquired before March 1, 1913. After 1934, March 1, 1913 value would be considered only for purposes of determining gain; loss could be recognized only in those cases where goodwill was specifically paid for.[96] Though affecting all subsequent sales of goodwill acquired before 1913, the change did not substantially modify general features of the tax law or present any significant implications for broader accounting aspects of the asset.

An interesting development occurred as a result of the effects of World War II on the production and provision of goods and services. Firms unable to produce their normal products nevertheless found it necessary to continue advertising expenditures related to those goods. An affected firm thus found itself making expenditures unquestionably expected to benefit other than the current period, and questions of the outlay's capitalization or deductibility arose. Questioned by businessmen, the government announced that such expenditures would continue to be deductible if reasonable, thus recognizing the need of firms to continue such efforts despite the war.[97]

One possible explanation for attention to peripheral matters only during this period was the absence of business activity involving considerations of goodwill. The onslaught of the depression ended an era of business combinations in which questions of goodwill were present. With slight modification, tax procedures for goodwill thus remained the same, involving only occasional elaboration on special problems arising from such situations as the war.

Summary

The onslaught of the depression, implications of the increasing importance of the corporation, conservative attitudes prevailing in business, and growth of the accounting profession worked as interrelated and, to some extent, interdependent factors in modifying accounting for goodwill. Cost was accepted as the proper basis for purposes of initial statement for assets generally and goodwill specifically. As a result, extraordinary advertising, capitalized early losses, and arbitrary write-ups were subjected to increasingly severe criticism when treated as goodwill. Eventually only goodwill acquired on the purchase of a going concern was recognized.

Concern shifted from ways of getting goodwill on the books to ways of getting it off, and subsequent treatment of the asset was given much more attention than in previous years. Those who favored permanent retention were forced to maintain their position during the greatest economic crisis of modern times, but the return of more prosperous times as World War II approached could be used to support their contention that goodwill did not depreciate but only fluctuated. Through implication or explicit statement, the Institute and the Association allowed permanent retention.

Those wishing to remove the asset from the books could do so gradually or in large write-offs by charges to several accounts. Gradual reduction usually was accomplished by periodic charges to current income or earned surplus, and by 1944 charging goodwill amortization to current income—as opposed to earned surplus—was definitely preferred by both accounting organizations. Amortization to current income appears to have attained equal standing with permanent retention in both organizations' major publications, reflecting current accepted practice. Write-offs were eventually frowned upon or disapproved if based solely on conservatism; disapproval was certain if the charge was made to capital surplus. The Association preferred that write-offs be made only to current income, while the Institute allowed write-offs to earned surplus if the same charge to current income would distort the income statement. Regardless of approach, each position was based on concern for proper presentation of income, illustrating the importance then attached to the income statement.

A trend toward separate disclosure of intangible assets in the balance sheet was evident in the thirties, with goodwill usually lumped together with other intangibles. Nominal valuation of goodwill became common at this time—usually as a modification of the practice of completely writing off the asset. In consolidated balance sheets, a trend toward analyzing the excess of cost over book value arose, which was approved and accepted in Bulletin No. 24 of the Institute. Relatively little change of importance concerning auditing or tax considerations of goodwill occurred during this period.

---

1. Ambrose Bierce, *The Enlarged Devil's Dictionary*, compiled and edited by Earnest J. Hopkins (Garden City, New York: Doubleday & Company, Inc., 1967), p. 89.

2. George O. May, *Financial Accounting: A Distillation of Experience* (New York: MacMillan Company, 1961), p. 39. (Hereinafter referred to as *Financial Accounting.*)

3. American Institute of Accountants, Special Committee on Co-operation with Stock Exchanges, *Audits of Corporate Accounts* (New York: American Institute of Accountants, 1934), p. 8; American Institute of Accountants, *Examination of Financial Statements by Independent Public Accountants* (New York: American Institute of Accountants, 1936), pp. 3-4; and American Institute of Accountants, Committee on Accounting Procedure, *General Introduction and Rules Formerly Adopted*, Accounting Research Bulletin No. 1 (New York: American Institute of Accountants, 1939), p. 2.

4. American Institute of Accountants, Committee on Accounting Procedure, *Accounting for Intangible Assets*, Accounting Research Bulletin No. 24 (New York: American Institute of Accountants, 1944), pp. 195-201.

5. American Accounting Association, Executive Committee, "A Tentative Statement of Accounting Principles Affecting Corporate Reports," *The Accounting Review*, June 1936, p. 188.

6. Ibid., p. 189. The same ideas are contained in American Accounting Association, Executive Committee, "Accounting Principles Underlying Corporate Financial Statements," *The Accounting Review*, June 1941, p. 135.

7. W.A. Paton and A.C. Littleton, *An Introduction to Corporate Accounting Standards*, American Accounting Association Monograph No. 3 (Ann Arbor, Michigan: American Accounting Association, 1940), p. 92.

8. See p. 57.

9. American Institute of Accountants, "Verification of Financial Statements," *The Journal of Accountancy*, May 1929, pp. 336-338.

10. Ibid., p. 338.

11. American Institute of Accountants, Special Committee on Co-operation with Stock Exchanges, *Audits of Corporate Accounts*, p. 5.

12. Ibid.

13. Ibid., pp. 10-11.

14. May, *Financial Accounting*, pp. 91-92.

15. American Institute of Accountants, *Examination of Financial Statements by Independent Public Accountants*, p. 2.

16. Thomas Henry Sanders, Henry Rand Hatfield, and Underhill Moore, *A Statement of Accounting Principles* (New York: American Institute of Accountants, 1938), pp. 56-57.

17. Ibid., p. 67.

18. Ibid., pp. 4-5.

19. Ibid., pp. 67-68.

20. American Institute of Accountants, Committee on Accounting Procedure, *Accounting for Intangible Assets*, pp. 195-196.

21. Ibid., p. 197.

22. Ibid., p. 195.

23. George T. Walker, "Nonpurchased Goodwill," *The Accounting Review*, September 1938, pp. 253-259.

24. For reasons subjects other than initial valuation are discussed at this point, see p. 77.

25. T. Reginald Cloake, "A Discussion of Goodwill," *The New York Certified Public Accountant*, April 1939, p. 311.

26. W.A. Paton, *Advanced Accounting* (New York: MacMillan Company, 1941), p. 405.

27. See pp. 79-80.

28. Earl A. Saliers and Arthur W. Holmes, *Basic Accounting Principles* (Chicago: Business Publications, Inc., 1937), p. 519.

29. Walker, "Nonpurchased Goodwill," p. 259.

30. See pp. 31-32.

31. Harold G. Avery, "Accounting for Intangible Assets," *The Accounting Review*, October 1942, p. 354.

32. Ibid., pp. 356 and 363.

33. Saliers and Holmes, *Basic Accounting Principles*, p. 521.

34. Robert H. Montgomery, *Auditing: Theory and Practice*, 1st ed. (New York: Ronald Press Company, 1913), p. 131; and Robert H. Montgomery, *Auditing: Theory and Practice*, 5th ed. (New York: Ronald Press Company, 1934), p. 312. The first through the sixth editions of Montgomery's *Auditing: Theory and Practice* are quoted throughout this chapter. After the first reference to any particular edition, subsequent references will be cited as: Montgomery, *Auditing*, edition, year, and page number.

35. Ibid. The quote is from the fifth edition, only a slight modification of wording from the first.

36. Robert H. Montgomery, *Auditing: Theory and Practice*, 6th ed. (New York: Ronald Press Company, 1940), p. iii.

37. Ibid., p. 273.

38. Montgomery, *Auditing*, 5th ed., 1934, pp. 300-301.

39. Gabriel A.D. Preinreich, "Goodwill in Accountancy," *The Journal of Accountancy*, July 1937, p. 43.

40. See p. 33.

41. Paton, *Advanced Accounting*, p. 410.

42. Freeman H. Davis, "Goodwill and the Balance Sheet," *The New York Certified Public Accountant*, October 1940, p. 37.

43. Paton, *Advanced Accounting*, p. 409.

44. See p. 93.

45. A.A. Fitzgerald, "Valuation of Goodwill," *The Chartered Accountant in Australia*, September 1932, p. 379.

46. Walker, "Nonpurchased Goodwill," p. 182.

47. See pp. 31-32.

48. See Chapter 7.

49. Raymond P. Marple, *Capital Surplus and Corporate Net Worth* (New York: Ronald Press Company, 1936), pp. 152-154.

50. Ibid.

51. May, *Financial Accounting*, p. 100.

52. Paton, *Advanced Accounting*, p. 409.

53. American Accounting Association, Executive Committee, "A Tentative Statement of Accounting Principles Affecting Corporate Reports," p. 188.

54. American Accounting Association, Executive Committee, "Accounting Principles Underlying Financial Statements," p. 134.

55. American Accounting Association, Executive Committee, "A Tentative Statement of Accounting Principles Affecting Corporate Reports," pp. 189-190.

56. Ibid., p. 191.

57. Ibid., p. 189.

58. Paton and Littleton, *An Introduction to Corporate Accounting Standards*, pp. 92-93.

59. Ibid., pp. 97-117.

60. American Institute of Accountants, Special Committee on Co-operation with Stock Exchanges, *Audits of Corporate Accounts*, p. 11.

61. American Institute of Accountants, *Examination of Financial Statements by Independent Public Accountants*, pp. 22, 30.

62. Sanders, Hatfield, and Moore, *A Statement of Accounting Principles*, pp. 14, 68-69.

63. American Institute of Accountants, Committee on Accounting Procedure, *Quasi-Reorganization or Corporate Readjustment—Amplification of Institute Rule No. 2 of 1934*, Accounting Research Bulletin No. 3 (New York: American Institute of Accountants, 1939), p. 25.

64. Ibid., p. 27.

65. American Institute of Accountants, Committee on Accounting Procedure, *Accounting for Intangible Assets*, pp. 195-201.

66. Ibid., p. 196.

67. Ibid., p. 197.

68. George O. May, "Income Taxes and Intangibles: Two Significant Research Bulletins," *The Journal of Accountancy*, February 1945, p. 129.

69. American Institute of Accountants, Special Committee on Co-operation with Stock Exchanges, *Audits of Corporate Accounts*, p. 11; and American Institute of Accountants, Committee on Accounting Procedure, *General Introduction and Rules Formerly Adopted*, p. 6.

70. American Institute of Accountants, Committee on Accounting Procedure, *Accounting for Intangible Assets*, p. 199.

71. Ibid., p. 197.

72. Marple, *Capital Surplus and Corporate Net Worth*, pp. 167, 171.

73. Ibid., pp. 171-172.

74. W.A. Paton, "Accounting Problems of the Depression," *The Accounting Review*, December 1932, p. 267.

75. Ibid.

76. See p. 89.

77. See pp. 94-95.

78. E.I. Fjeld, "Classification and Terminology of Individual Balance-Sheet Items," *The Accounting Review*, December 1936, pp. 330-345.

79. American Institute of Accountants, *Examination of Financial Statements by Independent Public Accountants*, p. 22.

80. Ibid., p. 38.

81. George T. Walker, "Goodwill on Financial Statements," *The Accounting Review*, June 1938, pp. 178-179.

82. W.A. Paton, ed., *Accountants' Handbook*, 3rd ed. (New York: Ronald Press Company, 1943), p. 844.

83. Fjeld, "Classification and Terminology of Individual Balance-Sheet Items," pp. 332-333.

84. H.S. Noble, W.E. Karrenbrock, and H. Simons, *Advanced Accounting* (Cincinnati: South-Western Publishing Company, 1941), p. 198.

85. Robert H. Montgomery, *Auditing: Theory and Practice*, 4th ed., rev. and enlarged (New York: Ronald Press Company, 1927), p. 232.

86. Montgomery, *Auditing*, 5th ed., 1934, p. 323.

87. Montgomery, *Auditing*, 6th ed., 1940, p. 282.

88. George Hillis Newlove, *Consolidated Statements Including Mergers and Consolidations* (Boston: D.C. Heath and Company, 1948), p. 51. (Hereinafter referred to as *Consolidated Statements*.)

89. American Institute of Accountants, Committee on Accounting Procedure, *Accounting for Intangible Assets*, p. 200.

90. Newlove, *Consolidated Statements*, p. 51.

91. See pp. 59-60. The discussion is repeated almost word for word in the fifth edition seven years later—Montgomery, *Auditing*, 5th ed., 1934, pp. 321-322.

92. Montgomery, *Auditing*, 6th ed., 1940, pp. 281-282.

93. Christian Oehler, *Audits and Examinations* (New York: Fordham University Press, 1940), p. 264.

94. Montgomery, *Auditing*, 4th ed., 1927, p. 227; and Montgomery, *Auditing*, 5th ed., 1934, p. 313.

95. Montgomery, *Auditing*, 6th ed., 1940, p. 273.

96. J. Royce Miles, *The Treatment of Goodwill in Federal Income Taxation*, Nebraska Studies in Business No. 37 (Lincoln: Extension Division, University of Nebraska, 1935), pp. 13-14; *Revenue Act of 1934, Statutes at Large*, XLVIII, sec. 113 (a) (14), 708-709 (1934); and U.S. Treasury Department, Bureau of Internal Revenue, *Regulations 86*, Art. 113 (a) (14)-1 (Washington, D.C.: U.S. Government Printing Office, 1935), pp. 194-196.

97. Robert H. Montgomery, *Montgomery's Federal Taxes on Corporations*, 1943-44, Vol. I: *Gross Income and Deductions* (New York: Ronald Press Company, 1943), p. 701; and U.S. Treasury Department, Bureau of Internal Revenue, *Cumulative Bulletin 1942-2, July-December*, 1942, Office Decisions, I.T. 3581 (Washington, D.C.: U.S. Government Printing Office, 1943), pp. 88-89.

Chapter VI

History 1945-1957

The Business Environment

After World War II ended, prosperity began, and it lasted continuously throughout this period. The slumps that did occur in the economy were relatively minor when compared to the depression of the thirties. As in the twenties, prosperity was accompanied by a significant rise in price levels—an event again causing uneasiness about the stability of the dollar.

Of special importance to accounting for goodwill was the occurrence of a large number of business combinations during the post-war years. Expectations of growth, shortages of managerial ability, technological innovations requiring larger scale operations, and the growing significance of the federal income tax made combinations highly desirable. Unlike earlier periods of merger activity, many combinations involved two corporations of approximately the same size, with neither being dominant in its industry.[1] Accounting for these combinations merited and received a great amount of attention by the profession, and important problems involving the treatment of goodwill arose.

The Accounting Environment

During this time the Institute issued twenty-four bulletins dealing with many facets of accounting. The same number of bulletins were published before and during World War II, but many of those were concerned with special problems created as a result of the war. With the end of the war, attention was directed to matters more closely associated with normal business activities. Whatever may be said concerning the effectiveness of these later pronouncements in attaining their stated objectives, they were of major importance in determining the direction taken in accounting practice.

In the twenties, instability of the monetary unit led to attempted adjustments of accounts to reflect changes in the monetary value placed on various assets, including goodwill. When upward pressures on price levels occurred again in the forties and fifties, uneasiness about the significance of cost valuation for assets arose, but nothing like the earlier practice of writing up assets took place. Recollection of the unsatisfactory results achieved by such practices and the acceptance (not present earlier) of cost for purposes of initial valuation led to the continued use of cost as the basis for the initial recording of goodwill.

The profession already had Bulletin No. 24 (discussed at length throughout the previous chapter) to rely upon in dealing with the trend toward business combinations. Six years later, in 1950, the Institute issued *Business Combinations*, Accounting Research Bulletin No. 40, which introduced the pooling of interests concept.[2] In 1953, *Restatement and Revision of Accounting Research Bulletins*, Accounting Research Bulletin No. 43, incorporated all previous bulletins into one publication.[3] This bulletin modified the provisions relating to Bulletin No. 24 significantly. Finally, in 1957, the section of Bulletin No. 43 that incorporated almost verbatim the 1950 *Business Combinations* statement was superseded by another *Business Combinations*, Accounting Research Bulletin No. 48.[4] Other bulletins dealt indirectly with accounting for goodwill, but the ones that greatly affected its accounting treatment (and discussed throughout this chapter) are Bulletins Nos. 24, 40, 43, and 48.

Characteristics of the Literature

When World War II ended, there were more articles and texts written that included a discussion of goodwill. Bulletin No. 24, employed to establish the point of separation between this chapter and the previous chapter, had a telling effect on the content of the literature. Writers relied greatly on the bulletin for authoritative support, tending to follow or support its provisions as a guide to practice rather than attempting to influence current methods through their own arguments. This tendency is particularly and understandably noticeable in the case of textbooks written for use in accounting courses.

The controversy concerning permanent retention versus gradual reduction of goodwill (which had never completely subsided) again arose after 1950. A change of emphasis from the subsequent treatment position taken in Bulletin No. 24 was clearly evident in Bulletin No. 43, and the pooling of interests accounting treatment introduced in 1950 became a topic of mounting interest as time passed. Because the pooling concept is closely interrelated with accounting for goodwill, and is of increasing importance to it, a separate section entitled "Goodwill and pooling of interests accounting" has been incorporated at the end of this chapter.

Issues and Problems Concerning Goodwill

Initial Valuation

The subject of initial valuation at one time had been one of the most important issues concerning the accounting aspects of goodwill. Determination of a figure for the asset and its initial treatment in accounts had been the subject of much discussion and controversy. Even before this time period, however, valuation procedures had reached such a level of sophistication that greater attempts toward exactness in measuring goodwill were deemed to be rather futile due to the subjectivity and vagueness surrounding it. After discussing in detail various methods of valuing goodwill, one writer stated:

> Use your scientific formulae, yes, but remember, too, that the final result will also be influenced no little by bargaining power, and guess work, for goodwill will ever be like love and the mushroom:—"Something you don't know what you've got until it's too late."[5]

Initial treatment of goodwill, like its initial valuation, ceased to be an area of concern with the prevailing strong conservative trends and the resulting strict adherence to the cost basis for purposes of initial valuation. Advertising expenditures, capitalized early losses, and arbitrary write-ups of goodwill had passed from subjects of current interest to those of historical concern in the twenty years following the onset of the depression. The Institute's position taken in 1944 in Accounting Research Bulletin No. 24[6] (that intangibles should initially be stated at cost) was repeated almost exactly nine years later in *Restatement and Revision of Accounting Research Bulletins,* Accounting Research Bulletin No. 43.[7] Cost valuation for goodwill was hardly mentioned or was even taken for granted in some accounting texts and articles, and aspects of more pressing importance, such as the asset's subsequent treatment, were emphasized. Thus William Werntz was well justified in 1957 in stating

> There is however, one applicable principle on which substantially all accountants, bankers, investors and regulatory agencies agree—that, unless goodwill is purchased, that is validated in amount by an arm's length transaction between a buyer and seller, it should not be entered in the accounts.[8]

The effects of strict adherence to historical cost were considered by Moonitz and Staehling and, though these points were mentioned or implied by earlier authors, they became particularly important with the virtual enthronement of cost valuation. This practice gave the conditions under which accounting, in its present state of development, would sanction recognition of goodwill in published financial statements.

Obviously, goodwill may exist, and yet not be written down anywhere; conversely, an account labeled "goodwill," representing an amount actually paid out some years ago, may appear on someone's ledger in the absence of any evidence that goodwill is present.[9]

The last conclusion belongs more in the discussion of subsequent treatment than in that of initial valuation, but it results from initial recognition of goodwill at its historical cost.

Even as the cost basis for assets was being placed in a dominant position, forces were at work that caused uneasiness about unquestioning allegiance to the rule. In 1948 the American Accounting Association again reiterated adherence to cost valuation in the revision of its 1941 statement.[10] Due to substantial fluctuation in price levels, the Association reexamined its position in 1951, noting that challenges had arisen as to the adequacy of conventional measurements of income. The Association's Committee on Concepts and Standards Underlying Corporate Financial Statements recommended that primary financial statements should continue to be stated at historical dollar costs. In addition, supplementary statements should be included to reflect the effects of fluctuations of the dollar upon net income and financial position by use of a general price index to restate historical costs in current dollars.[11]

Implications for initial treatment of goodwill were the same as those for other assets. Whether in primary or supplementary statements, the basis for goodwill would continue to be cost. In the supplementary balance sheet, however, the cost figure for goodwill would be restated in current dollars. Though somewhat subjective, the aim of the adjustment was not to restate any asset, much less goodwill, in terms of its replacement cost or its "value" as some write-ups of the twenties had been accused of attempting to do. The starting point was historical cost, which then was adjusted for fluctuations in general price levels. In comparison with some practices before the depression, the proposed method was objective in application and mild in effect.

The Association carried its ideas on price level adjustments in supplementary statements further in the last revision of these statements in 1957. General price indexes might be used for adjustment of specific assets. Individual price changes also might be measured by using the asset's replacement cost, with the same goal as previously of evaluating the significance of price fluctuations on financial statements.[12]

The use of specific indexes or replacement cost in the case of goodwill would be very difficult at best. Specific price indexes could not exist for such a subjective asset, and approximations of replacement cost could be based on nothing more than appraisal or conjecture. Whatever the possible applicability to various assets, these suggested practices could be expected to fare no better than did write-up attempts of the twenties when applied to goodwill specifically.

Despite reservations concerning the usefulness of historical cost due to price level changes, cost valuation of assets for purposes of initial statement remained strongly entrenched throughout the immediate post-war period.

Subsequent Treatment

In 1909 Henry Rand Hatfield listed an illustrious group of contemporary accounting authorities who supported amortization and then listed an equally illustrious group who advocated permanent retention.[13] In 1946 an Australian writer used the same approach—listing several current authorities on both sides of the issue.[14] In the almost forty years separating the two writers, little had changed except the names of those involved in the controversy.

Although goodwill's initial valuation may have faded into the background, its subsequent treatment remained a topic of lively debate. After the general lull in the literature on the subject of intangibles in the late forties, several important articles concerning amortization were written. These occurred up to and around the issuance of Accounting Research Bulletin No. 43. Prior to publication of the bulletin, trends toward amortization and against write-offs became apparent. These are discussed in the next section. The second section is concerned with Chapter 5 of Bulletin No. 43, in which important changes of emphasis and substance were made as compared to Bulletin No. 24. The last section covers developments within the four years following the bulletin's issuance.

Trends Toward Amortization and Against Write-offs: Accounting Research Bulletin No. 24, issued in December 1944, appeared to represent a compromise on the amortization question.[15] Amortization, though permitted, was neither encouraged nor discouraged and was given about equal stature with permanent retention. That position apparently was not very stable, however, for emphasis gradually began shifting toward amortization of intangibles.

Position of the Securities and Exchange Commission. The position of the Securities and Exchange Commission in 1945 reflected this trend.

> The Commission has adopted no general rule as to the amortization of goodwill. However, in those cases in which a registrant has retained "goodwill" indefinitely in its accounts, the staff has inquired into the propriety of this accounting treatment. As a result of an analysis of the nature of the account, a number of registrants have undertaken programs of amortization that will result in charging the goodwill to income or, in some cases, earned surplus, over a reasonable number of years.[16]

The Commission's stand on write-offs of goodwill to capital surplus was in close connection with this position and with important consequences in later years. The SEC's Accounting Series Release No. 50, issued just one month after Accounting Research Bulletin No. 24, wherein such write-offs were discouraged, stated:

> The proposed charge to capital surplus is contrary to sound accounting principles. It is clear that if the goodwill here involved is, or were to become, worthless, it would be necessary to write it off.

Preferably such write-off should have been accomplished through timely charges to income, but in no event would it be permissible, under sound accounting principles, to charge the loss to capital surplus.[17]

Of significance is the fact that both the SEC and the Institute, with only slight differences in emphasis, were in broad agreement concerning the subsequent treatment of goodwill. The Institute permitted both permanent retention and amortization as equal alternatives; the Commission appeared to prefer amortization, though it adopted no general rule on this point. The Institute discouraged write-offs to capital surplus, but the SEC went further and disallowed them altogether. In moving from an examination of the Institute's position to that of the Commission, the slight changes indicate the direction in which the profession was moving.

Arguments concerning amortization. One indication of opinion in the early fifties concerning amortization of goodwill was the lack of new articles and texts advocating permanent retention of the asset. Authorities such as Montgomery and May could be cited as supporting nonamortization, but such references generally were five to ten years out of date. Even Montgomery's auditing text, in which through six previous editions a strong preference for permanent retention was indicated, contained increased support in the seventh edition (1949) for amortization of the asset.

Some accountants believe, therefore, that no objection should be offered to its continued reflection at cost, but there are also those who believe otherwise. Reasonable discretionary amortization, even where there is no evidence of loss of value, is certainly permissible.[18]

An argument for permanent retention was advanced by Walter Staub in 1945, which George Walker noted was similar in outline and reasoning to Accounting Research Bulletin No. 24.[19] The argument is as interesting for the criticism it drew as for its own merits. Staub stated,

It follows that there is no basic reason for, or scientific method of, writing-off or amortizing the cost of Type B intangibles, the value of which is continuing. To require the compulsory amortization of intangibles, the value of which is being currently maintained or even enhanced, seems a departure from the "going concern" concept of financial statements and an attempt to provide for losses which may be sustained upon termination or liquidation of an enterprise at some time in the future. If, however, a corporation decided to amortize the cost of a Type B intangible, as to which there is no present indication of limited existence or loss of value, by systematic charges in the income statement, long established custom indicates such procedure to be permissible despite the fact that expenditures are being made to maintain its value.[20]

Walker quoted this argument and then recommended substituting "building" for "intangibles" and "depreciation" for "amortization" in it. Walker felt the paraphrase indicated a lack of consistency in reasoning and was reminiscent of depreciation practices of bygone days when little, much, or no depreciation was charged, depending on the amount of income one wished to report. He concluded by stating: "It is as incorrect to relate amortization to the value of intangibles as it is to relate depreciation to the value of fixed assets."[21]

Staub's statement also was criticized for maintaining that writing off or amortizing goodwill was a departure from the going concern concept. K.G. Emery felt that the concept should be interpreted to mean that individual assets, which were existing and recognizable, could be carried at a residual cost higher than their market values upon dissolution; it should not be used to justify indefinite retention of every investment cost incurred since inception of the enterprise.[22]

An argument that had been advanced for some time held that goodwill should be retained permanently when advertising expenditures were maintaining the asset's reported "value" by creating new goodwill as fast as the old goodwill expired. The reasoning was countered in one text that read:

> The alleged identity holds, however, only if the amount of advertising outlay charged to [sic] asset account is precisely equal to the amount of goodwill which should be amortized. If this relationship should persist for many years, it would be a strange and wondrous coincidence indeed.[23]

The argument also was dismissed by reference to the principle of matching costs with applicable revenues. A function of accounting was not to account for changes in value; depreciation on buildings, for example, was not computed with any concept of market value in mind. Accounting was concerned with the allocation of costs, and the allocation of goodwill to revenues generated from the asset should be no different from the apportionment of the cost of any other asset to appropriate accounting periods. Although the amount of the charge might present a difficult problem of estimation, similar problems were encountered with other long-lived assets.[24]

An argument that utilized the matching concept was advanced for amortization. This argument was mentioned incidentally in 1951 by Emery, who stated:

> It must be realized that all factors giving rise to goodwill value are finite or temporal. ... It is as though the earning capacity of the going business had acquired momentum in the hands of the seller and, hence, continued to function effectively for the benefit of the purchaser until it ran down, at which time the final dollar of goodwill cost should be written off the books.[25]

The "momentum theory" was given fuller expression a few years later by Robert Nelson, who compared it to the ideas of writers, such as Paton and Leake, who advocated an annuity theory. The annuity theory held that the buyer was investing in a series of excess earnings, and it rationalized in a neat logical manner the calculation of purchase price. In Nelson's words, "The Momentum Theory is the hypothesis that a businessman purchases a promotional push instead of an annuity and that the 'push' dissipates like momentum."[26] The investment therefore should be amortized over the expected life of the momentum, with the buyer's estimate of life being the controlling factor. Straight-line amortization probably should be used due to meagerness of knowledge concerning dissipation of the momentum.[27]

Although the momentum and annuity theories were somewhat closely related, the momentum theory recognized the futility of exacting calculations (as indicated in Leake's work) that the other might entail.[28] The annuity theory might be interpreted to imply that the purchaser had a right to receive excess profits merely by investment in a firm expected to make them; the momentum theory more clearly implied that the purchaser had a right merely to attempt to make excess profits as a result of his investment. His investment provided access to an opportunity but was no guarantee of reward.

Such comments as these favoring amortization would have drawn substantial criticism if they had been made twenty or more years before. But advocates of permanent retention were relatively silent in the early and middle fifties, and no one appears to have attempted to counter the momentum theory during that time. The shift of emphasis in literature was accompanied by another shift in a very important publication—Accounting Research Bulletin No. 43. Although the chapter concerning intangibles allowed both permanent retention and amortization as had its predecessor, Bulletin No. 24, it now appeared to favor amortization.

Write-offs, earned surplus, and capital surplus. Somewhat overshadowed by major developments concerning goodwill was the fact that one relatively minor problem was solved in *Income and Earned Surplus*, Accounting Research Bulletin No. 32, issued in December 1947. Partial write-downs of intangibles expressly had not been considered in Bulletin No. 24, because the Committee on Accounting Procedure was considering the broader aspects of partial losses in value applicable to all assets.[29] Bulletin No. 32 stated that generally all items of profit and loss recognized in a period should be used to determine net income for that period. Exceptions to this rule would be items material in relation to income and not identifiable with, or resulting from, usual or typical operations of the period. One of several examples of an extraordinary item excludable from net income was "The write-off of a material amount of intangibles, such as the complete elimination of goodwill."[30]

As far as the subsequent treatment of goodwill was involved, a distinction between partial and complete elimination of the asset no longer was necessary. Disposition of the charge turned on its significance relative to current reported net income rather than on its absolute amount. Furthermore, Bulletin No. 32 did not contradict what had already been established as recommended treatment for complete write-off of intangibles in Bulletin No. 24; it merely extended the same general procedure to partial write-offs.

Although pertinent sections of Bulletin No. 32 might be viewed as dealing with how a write-off should be accomplished, questions concerning why goodwill should be written off in the first place arose elsewhere. The American Accounting Association evidently felt the practice of discretionary write-offs had attained enough use, while being sufficiently objectionable, that it justified comment in its 1948 revision. In addition to the usual plea for cost valuation and against arbitrary write-ups, it added: "Adherence to the cost basis of accounting requires that there should be no suppression or unwarranted assignment to expense of the costs of existing assets."[31]

The Institute also began to consider the appropriateness of revising its stance on write-offs taken in 1944. Although discretionary write-offs to capital surplus had been discouraged in Bulletin No. 24, the Institute's Research Department wrote in 1952 that: "The committee is now considering whether it should go beyond a recommendation to discourage this practice."[32] The department stated that few instances of writing off intangibles to capital surplus had been noted, and it concluded that "their absence seems to indicate general recognition of the undesirability of this procedure."[33]

Aside from charges to capital surplus, discretionary write-offs in general were being questioned by the committee. To make a purchase and then immediately write the asset off was not in accordance with the principles and procedures by which any other type of asset was accounted for, so the committee was favorably considering the position that no write-downs (except amortization) should be made until a loss had occurred. While these comments represented the current trend of committee thinking, it hoped to get as many views as possible before any firm decisions were made in this regard.[34]

Accounting Research Bulletin No. 43, Chapter 5:

Write-offs, earned surplus, and capital surplus. The committee evidently felt its views were justified, for about a year after calling for comments on its views it wholeheartedly adopted them in Bulletin No. 43. Write-off of intangibles to reflect a recognizable loss should be made to current income or, alternatively, to earned surplus if misleading inferences would be drawn from income charges. Concerning capital surplus and discretionary write-offs, it was stated that: "Lump-sum write-offs of intangibles should not be made to earned surplus immediately after acquisition, nor should intangibles be charged against capital surplus."[35]

Summarizing the Institute's position by recommended treatment and comparing it with its position nine years previously, it now permitted write-downs or write-offs only in the event of a loss. Before, discretionary write-offs also were permitted, though they were discouraged.

Examining the Institute's position by the account to be charged, it no longer considered capital surplus to constitute an acceptable account for any write-offs. Earned surplus, once recommended as the best account for both discretionary charge-offs and charges to reflect losses, could receive only charges to reflect losses, and then only when current net income reported would be distorted by including the item within the income statement. The income statement now was considered the appropriate place to reflect write-offs; they should be made to earned surplus only if such charges would cause misleading inferences in the income statement.

The effects of such procedures on accounting for goodwill were significant. Arbitrary write-offs, once a method for relieving financial statements of an undesirable item and presenting a company's financial situation more favorably, no longer were allowed. In those statements in which goodwill was presented, more credibility could now be attached to the item, assuming the more stringent provisions of Bulletin No. 43, Chapter 5 were followed.

Emphasis on amortization. The fact that no substantial changes concerning amortization of intangibles occurred in Bulletin No. 43 is important. Both permanent retention and gradual reduction of goodwill were permitted, as before, but both a reading of Chapter 5 by itself and a comparison between it and Bulletin No. 24 indicate that permanent retention at cost was deemphasized.

The first mention of any subsequent treatment recommended for type (b) intangibles in Bulletin No. 24 had stated that the cost of those assets might be carried continuously unless and until it became reasonably evident that their term of existence had become limited or that they had become worthless.[36] Bulletin No. 43 contained no such reference in the comparable section (paragraph 6), describing only those procedures for type (b) intangibles whose life had become limited or that had become worthless.[37] The next section discussed discretionary amortization of type (b) intangibles in much the same terms as Bulletin No. 24. The only explicit mention in Bulletin No. 43 of permanent retention at cost was made in one of the last sections of the chapter—a section not directly concerned with the amortization issue. In "Limitation on Write-off of Intangibles," paragraph 9, the bulletin stated: "If not amortized systematically, intangibles should be carried at cost until an event has taken place which indicates a loss or a limitation on the useful life of the intangibles."[38]

Admittedly the statement is much the same as that found in Bulletin No. 24, but it was not prominently placed in juxtaposition to the amortization arguments as it previously had been, and it contained a preface indicating it applied where systematic amortization was not being taken. Initial consideration and discussion of amortization, coupled with the preceding quotation, indicate that amortization was preferable, though permanent retention could be substituted if desired.

Subsequent Developments: According to one source, the section that limited write-offs of intangibles did not immediately attract attention when published:

> It was not until a combination of rising stock market prices, coupled with a trend to expand through acquisitions, that company heads began to realize that they could no longer write off part of the purchase price except through amortization and the consequent penalty of reduced earnings.[39]

About two years after issuance of the bulletin, officials of companies that recently had acquired or were acquiring other companies began writing letters to the Committee on Accounting Procedure asking it to change its position on limiting write-offs so that immediate write-offs would be acceptable. In March 1956 the committee considered the suggestions, but concluded by an "overwhelming majority" that its position was sound and did not necessitate revision.[40]

Although apparently consistent with conservative accounting principles applicable to other assets, the effects of limiting write-offs could be very unfavorable on a firm's financial statements. As mentioned before, wherever goodwill appeared, more confidence could be placed in the figure at which it was shown, but the undesirable consequences associated with its appearance developed pressures to avoid presentation of the asset at all. An outlet was provided through employment of pooling of interests accounting, discussed later in this chapter.

Financial Presentation and Disclosure

As in the previous period, emphasis was placed on keeping goodwill out of the accounts and financial statements. With capital surplus and earned surplus no longer available to absorb discretionary write-offs of goodwill, however, procedures were utilized to avoid recording it at all. The reasons such procedures were felt to be necessary are discussed in the next section, "Effects on Financial Statements of Various Treatments."

A regular series of reliable statistical information on many accounting matters, entitled *Accounting Trends and Techniques*, became available for the first time shortly after the end of World War II. Published annually by the Institute, these volumes furnish valuable information on the disposition of goodwill in financial statements, the subject of the second section.

Goodwill in consolidated statements was accorded the same treatment in Bulletin No. 43, Chapter 5, as it was in Bulletin No. 24. Normally the subject of a separate section, discussion on this subject is deferred until Chapter VII, in which *Consolidated Financial Statements*, Accounting Research Bulletin No. 51, issued in 1959, is covered.

Effects on Financial Statements of Various Treatments: Assuming a firm was considering acquisition of another company possessing substantial goodwill, the acquiring firm had on first appearance two alternatives for treatment of the prospective intangible asset: amortization and permanent retention. Amortization, the preferable treatment under Bulletin No. 43, had several important disadvantages for analyses involving the balance sheet, income statement, and various ratios. First of all, the treatment reduced reported net income—which in turn reduced earnings per share, income as a percentage of net worth, and income as a percentage of total assets. But because net worth and total assets were made even larger by the inclusion of goodwill, the latter two ratios were reduced even more. If goodwill was retained at cost indefinitely, reported net income and earnings per share were not affected, and return on net worth and total assets were reduced only once. Apparently, the favored accounting treatment from the standpoint of accounting principles gave less desirable results from the standpoint of the company faced with prospects of implementing the recommended procedures.

Under Bulletin No. 24, the firm, if it so desired, could arbitrarily write off its goodwill to earned or capital surplus immediately after purchase of another company. Although such practice was frowned upon, effects on all the financial measurements mentioned previously were most favorable, since net income and earnings per share were not lowered and net worth and total assets were not burdened with a substantial intangible asset. The least desirable accounting treatment from one point of view gave the best results from that of another point of view.

Bulletin No. 43, Chapter 5, expressly disallowed discretionary write-offs of intangibles, and companies wishing to acquire others had to look elsewhere to avoid the consequences of recording purchased goodwill. Pooling of interests accounting afforded such an opportunity. While the accounting procedure involved was quite distinct from that accorded combinations treated as purchases, the criteria for distinguishing between a pooling and a purchase were subjective. After 1953 application of these criteria in practice gradually deteriorated to the extent that by the late fifties almost any combination could be treated either way.[41]

When the pooling treatment was employed, stock given by one company was recorded at the book value of the assets rather than at the fair value of either the consideration given or received, because no purchase was deemed to have taken place. Assuming the combination was really a purchase and the pooling criteria was being stretched or misconstrued to accommodate the wishes of the acquiring company, goodwill that had been purchased was not being shown; *it had in effect been written off immediately to capital surplus since the stock given for it was never recorded at its fair value.*[42] If the effects desired could not be obtained in one manner, they could be, and were, obtained in another.

Disposition of Goodwill in Financial Statements:

Separate disclosure. The trends indicated from available data in the previous period continued into the fifties.[43] Exhibit 1 indicates that goodwill was classified separately or with other intangibles as a separate balance sheet group by approximately 85 to 90 percent of the companies disclosing the existence of intangibles in any given year. The remaining firms usually classified goodwill under "Other Assets"; only a negligible portion of companies presented it in some other way. Compared with Fjeld's study of balance sheets in the early thirties, the manner in which goodwill was presented had changed very little.[44]

Valuation of goodwill. Exhibit 2 indicates that nominal valuation of the asset was preferred throughout the period. Use of that treatment reached a peak in 1953-1954, however, and thereafter it steadily declined throughout the remainder of the period under study.[45] At approximately the time that the practice of nominal valuation began to decline in use, the practices of amortizing goodwill and of presenting it at an unamortized figure began to increase.

Part of the explanation for such a great emphasis on nominal valuation might be due to the large number of firms that had written down their goodwill to $1

Exhibit 1: Classification of Goodwill in the Balance Sheet

Years	Separately Set Forth	Under Fixed Assets	Under Other Assets	Under Deferred Charges
1951-1952[a]	161	1	7	0
1952-1953[b]	150	3	18	2
1953-1954	152	2	16	1
1954-1955	147	1	13	0
1955[c]	137	2	21	0
1956	145	2	23	2
1957	138	3	18	4

[a]Data for 1951-1952 covers 525 companies. Data for 1952-1953 onward covers 600 companies.

[b]From 1952-1953 onward, "Goodwill" and "Goodwill re: Subsidiary" as shown in the original source have been combined.

[c]Collection of data changes to a calendar year basis beginning in 1955. Data for 1954-1955 and 1955 therefore overlap.

Source: American Institute of Accountants, Research Department, *Accounting Trends and Techniques*, Vols. VI-XII (New York: American Institute of Accountants, 1952-1958).

around the time of the depression and had continued to present it at an insignificant figure over the years. Another reason could have been the opportunity under Bulletin No. 24 of arbitrarily writing down the asset. The decline of the practice probably was influenced by the position taken in Bulletin No. 43 of disallowing discretionary write-offs, permitting permanent retention, and preferring gradual reduction. Where it was necessary to present goodwill, the asset would be shown at cost or cost less amortization; nominal valuation could occur only when amortization reduced goodwill to that amount—a relatively slow process compared to a lump-sum write-off. (Two other minor possibilities for nominal valuations of goodwill would be (1) determination and recognition of the asset's loss, and (2) arbitrarily placing it on the books at $1.) Therefore, goodwill generally would be shown at a substantial figure, or it would not be shown at all due to the use of pooling of interests accounting. Nominal valuation gradually would decline in importance as companies contemplating business combinations were required to select among alternatives that, under the new procedures of Bulletin No. 43, were not conducive to its use.

Auditing Considerations

Accounting Research Bulletin No. 24 simplified auditing considerations of goodwill to some extent. Initial valuation at cost of assets generally was well

Exhibit 2: Valuation of Goodwill

Years	Amortized (1)	Not Amortized (2)	Total Columns 1 and 2 (3)	Nominal Valuation (4)
1947-1948[a]	d	d	32	122
1948-1949	d	d	30	125
1949-1950[b]	d	d	35	121
1950-1951[b]	d	d	28	127
1951-1952[c]	12	18	30	138
1952-1953[b]	26	20	46	127
1953-1954	16	25	51	131
1954-1955	13	24	37	124
1955[e]	24	26	50	111
1956	38	27	65	107
1957	39	30	69	95

[a]Data for 1947-1948 to 1950-1951 covers 525 companies.

[b]For 1949-1950, 1950-1951, and from 1952-1953 onward, "Goodwill" and "Goodwill re: Subsidiary" as shown in the original source have been combined.

[c]Data for 1952-1953 onward covers 600 companies.

[d]Information not available.

[e]Collection of data changes to a calendar year basis beginning in 1955. Data for 1954-1955 and 1955 therefore overlap.

Source: American Institute of Accountants, Research Department, *Accounting Trends and Techniques*, Vols. II-XII (New York: American Institute of Accountants, 1948-1958).

established after the thirties, but Bulletin No. 24 (and subsequently Bulletin No. 43) expressly codified cost valuation for intangibles and goodwill specifically. Thus the auditor now had an official pronouncement to rely on for determining whether valuation and subsequent treatment of goodwill were consistent with generally accepted accounting principles.

Tax Considerations

Several points of distinction between goodwill and covenants not to compete or franchises were discussed and elaborated on in the tax literature. Also mentioned occasionally were problems associated with changing from a corporate to a noncorporate form of business and whether or not goodwill should be recognized in such situations. While constituting an interesting subject from the standpoint of tax law, and undoubtedly a matter of concern to parties involved in litigation, such issues did not bear directly on financial accounting aspects of goodwill. The essential and important areas of tax law related to the asset's accounting treatment remained the provisions and cases found in the first twenty years of existence of the federal income tax.

An area of tax law indirectly related to goodwill became important during this time—tax-free corporate reorganizations were allowed if certain standards were met. One of these provisions concerning exchanges of stock for stock became especially significant when attention began focusing on pooling of interests accounting for business combinations. Wyatt summed up the advnatages of this provision to the individual disposing of his firm in the following words:

> Considered in conjunction with rising price levels, a booming American economy, and a generally strong and rising stock market, the influence of the tax law becomes apparent. Potential vendors are far more inclined to sell their businesses for shares of stock than for cash, since the latter would result in an immediate tax liability.[46]

Furthermore, the vendor could lessen his tax liability, as well as postpone its recognition, through gradual sale of the stock received for his investment.[47]

The buyer, meanwhile, had one main disadvantage to contemplate when such reorganization provisions were followed. His tax basis in the properties received would be the same as that in the vendor's hands and generally would be lower than if the transaction were treated as a purchase for tax purposes. A lower basis meant lower depreciation charges in the years to follow, higher taxable income, and thus higher taxes. Advantages to the buyer, on the other hand, included conservation of cash (since stock was used in the combination), the reporting of higher income and consequent presentation of more favorable financial ratios, and use of the same asset basis for both tax and accounting purposes.[48] The advantages to both parties evidently outweighed the disadvantages involved, for pooling of interests accounting and the tax reorganization provisions were used together frequently.

The emphasis given in accounting to amortization of goodwill, with a concomitant disallowance of discretionary write-off of the asset, made pooling accounting and the parallel reorganization procedures for tax purposes important. The amortization emphasis had other ramifications for the tax law as well. For many years, proponents of permanent retention of goodwill had cited as one reason for their stance the refusal by the Internal Revenue Service to allow its amortization as a deduction for tax purposes. To an extent, therefore, tax procedures influenced accounting practice. With increasing acceptance of amortizing goodwill for accounting purposes, the tax procedures denying deduction were attacked. In 1955 Gordon Hill argued for acceptance of amortization of goodwill for tax purposes, apparently using the accountant's traditional concepts of going concern and matching expenses and revenues. According to Hill,

> In our present economic system the end of any major business enterprise is not anticipated. Therefore, the practice of disallowing intangible items as tax deductions until such time as loss or gain thereon shall have been determined by their disposition or by proof of determinable loss, is a poor one.[49]

The deduction for a cost incurred was forever denied, and, like any other cost, it should be absorbed in operations. The government's position probably was due to the taxpayer's inability to prove a specific period to which the intangible should be allocated.[50]

> The cost can, of course, be charged off against proceeds of a sale, or upon abandonment or other complete loss of useful value, but these avenues rarely become available. While it seems appropriate that the taxpayer have the burden of supporting a reasonable position, it is not reasonable to defer a write-off until a company ceases operations and there is no income against which it can be charged.[51]

While accepted accounting practice for once was being used to put pressure on tax provisions concerning treatment of goodwill, the deduction for tax purposes still was denied over twenty years after Hill's article.

Goodwill and Pooling of Interests Accounting

Pooling of interests accounting is a subject closely interrelated to accounting aspects of goodwill, and many implications concerning goodwill's treatment follow from its use. Accounting for poolings, however, is worthy of being the subject of separate study emphasizing its own features. Although some of these features are mentioned in the following discussion, primary concern is directed to goodwill, its relation to the pooling issue, and how use of the pooling treatment affected accounting for the asset.

Basic Concept of Pooling of Interests: An idealistic example of a pooling of interests might involve two lawyers considering formation of a partnership. Having specialized in separate areas of law, each practitioner might feel he could gain from being associated with another in a complementary field of endeavor. Neither will possess more or less ownership interest in the proposed combination than previously; neither wishes to dominate the arrangement. Each desires to continue much as before—contributing about the same effort and resources to his livelihood with almost the same freedom of choice. Each prospective partner, however, now will act to benefit the partnership, for their once diverse economic aims and interests are now common or pooled. The economic change in question is not one of acquisition but of association.

The example can be expanded to two large corporations having substantial and equal investments in assets and desiring to combine their operations. In this situation, the owners and managers of each corporation probably would be different, but continuity of ownership and of management of each firm still would be necessary. Though the modification is important, the basic idea is the same—neither corporation has purchased the other. Two formerly independent entities now are acting as one.

Accounting Research Bulletin No. 40: The accounting treatment incident to a pooling of interests was being discussed as early as the 1920s, and the term "pooling of interests" used to describe this type of business combination (and later the accounting treatment itself) was evolving in the mid-1940s.[52] In September 1950, the Committee on Accounting Procedure issued *Business Combinations*, Accounting Research Bulletin No. 40.[53] The bulletin attempted to differentiate between two types of combinations: a pooling of interests and a purchase. All attendant circumstances (rather than any legal designations) governed classification as one or the other, with major consideration given to whether or not "all or substantially all of the equity interests in predecessor corporations continue, as such, in a surviving corporation."[54] If so, the transaction could be classified as a pooling. Important also would be the relative sizes of the constitutent companies, continuity of management, and whether or not activities of the companies were similar or complementary. In attaching weight to these characteristics, the bulletin stated, "No one of these factors would necessarily be determinative, but their presence or absence would be cumulative in effect."[55]

Classification as a purchase meant that one of the companies would be considered an acquiring corporation and the other an acquired one. The acquiring firm would record the other's assets at cost—customarily defined as the fair market value of consideration given or received, whichever was more readily determinable. Classification as a pooling of interests, however, meant that corresponding asset and equity account carrying values should merely be combined, with no new basis of accountability being called for.

Of major significance to the accounting treatment for poolings was the concept that, given all circumstances mentioned previously, nothing had been acquired. Or, stating the same thought in the form of a question, who had acquired whom? Going further, who could have acquired whom? Costs arose only upon acquisition, and no acquisition had taken place. In this case, cost of any asset was its purchase price to one of the predecessor corporations, modified by previous assignment of applicable portions to income.

Like any other asset, goodwill had not been purchased; the superior earning power of one firm had been pooled with that of another. Though recognized to exist by both parties, the goodwill built up by each prior to the combination was not recorded by either, because neither had purchased it. Applying a rule established by hard experience, nonpurchased goodwill should not be placed on the books of a business; recording the asset could be viewed as an arbitrary write-up—a practice definitely not approved. Pooling of interests accounting could be looked upon as a modification of the cost principle, but it also could be viewed as a strict application of it to a unique situation at a time when the cost principle was held in high esteem.

The effects of the pooling treatment on accounting for goodwill were not important initially. After issuance of Bulletin No. 24 six years before (in 1944), write-offs to capital surplus became rare, but write-offs to earned surplus still were made (though discouraged when based on nothing more than conservatism). By treating a business combination as a purchase, recording assets other than goodwill at approximately their old book values, charging goodwill for the excess of total cost over other assets, and then writing off goodwill to earned surplus, virtually the same effect as the pooling treatment could be obtained. For the time being, need for the effects obtained by pooling accounting was dormant, but nevertheless latent. The method became very important a short time later.

Accounting Research Bulletin No. 43: Three years after Bulletin No. 40 was issued, *Restatement and Revision of Accounting Research Bulletins* (1953) was published. No substantial changes concerning business combinations (incorporated as Chapter 7, Section C in the new bulletin) were made. The important changes occurred in Chapter 5, "Intangible Assets." Attempts by the Committee to improve accounting for intangibles had a significant effect on goodwill's treatment, but not in the manner that the Committee apparently intended. Write-offs of goodwill to capital surplus were disallowed, but the stance had little impact, because the practice had been unpopular after being discredited in Bulletin No. 24. Disallowing write-offs to earned surplus immediately after acquisition, discouraging charges to earned surplus in general, and favoring amortization of goodwill to income were the crucial recommendations having major ramifications. No longer could the same effects on financial presentation be obtained by either purchase or pooling of interests accounting. A sharp distinction had been drawn with dismaying clarity; for the first time, pooling of interests accounting became important.[56]

> Our study indicated the likelihood that this new position on accounting for intangibles had a significant influence upon the accounting for business combinations. Since the pooling accounting treatment would not create any excess of cost over book value of assets, pressures developed to employ this treatment. In a period of rising prices such as the 1950s the pressures to avoid the future charges to income that the purchase treatment involved were almost irresistible.[57]

Previously, a combination would be considered and the appropriate accounting treatment would be applied according to the combination's characteristics. Now the combination's characteristics would be determined to some extent by the accounting treatment desired.

The Securities and Exchange Commission also gave impetus to use of the pooling treatment by recommending generally the same accounting treatment for intangibles and business combinations as did the Institute. The SEC encouraged amortization of goodwill while approving of pooling of interests.

> The pooling of interests concept has often been the lesser of the two evils to the SEC since it results in a presentation of historical

costs without the difficult valuation problems attendant to purchases. . . . The Commission has also on occasion regarded the substantial intangible asset (which need not be amortized) resulting from purchase treatment as a less desirable presentation than historical cost.[58]

Provisions of the federal income tax law concerning tax-free exchanges contained few drawbacks and several major advantages for use of the pooling treatment.[59] Although the tax provisions appear not to have been designed for the purpose of facilitating pooling of interests accounting, their existence at the time the practice became important added to other factors encouraging its use.

Kripke summarized the effects of these developments on accounting for goodwill when he stated:

> But let us see what has been accomplished. *The effect is to nullify the accounting principles requiring substantially all charges to go through the income account.* Here the charge to eliminate the goodwill is, in effect, made in advance. It is made not to income and not to earned surplus, but to capital surplus or the capital account, through the convenient device of never recording the goodwill by never recording the full consideration for which the capital stock was issued. *Thus, pooling has had the unintended seeming effect of nullifying principles of conservative income accounting for which leading members of the accounting profession had waged a victorious battle.*[60] (Italics added.)

In substance, charges to capital surplus that were disallowed by one accounting treatment were allowed in another.

In addition to making combinations fit the desired accounting treatment, attempts were made to stretch the criteria for treating a combination as a pooling of interests. Trends toward diversification undermined the similarity-of-activities criterion, since "complementary business operations had little or no relation to the economic and financial aspects of a pooling."[61] In Accounting Research Bulletin No. 48, issued in January 1957 to supersede Chapter 7, Section C, of Bulletin No. 43, the criterion was no longer mentioned.[62] While prior to 1957 the size guideline generally was followed, Bulletin No. 48 greatly de-emphasized it, and it virtually ceased to exist. Continuity of equity interests proved a difficult concept to define, and Arthur Wyatt found sufficient examples after 1957 to believe the factor was not deemed essential. The general deterioration of these criteria and their application in practice progressed to the point that almost any business combination could be treated as either a purchase or a pooling at the discretion of the parties involved.[63]

A Summary of the Significance of the Pooling of Interests Concept to Accounting for Goodwill: Before 1953, criteria for distinguishing between purchase and pooling accounting generally were followed, but about the same accounting treatment could be obtained by either method. After issuance of Accounting Research Bulletin No. 43, wherein differences in accounting were clarified, the distinguishing criteria were criticized, extended in application to the point of being misconstrued, and gradually deteriorated as meaningful guidelines. After Bulletin No. 48 was issued, however, either method could be used, because the criteria were considered to be either inappropriate or inadequate.[64]

Summary

The continuous period of prosperity after World War II was accompanied by a general rise in price levels, which again caused questions to arise concerning the significance of historical cost as a basis for initial valuation of assets. Cost valuation was well established by this time, however, and its use for purposes of initially stating goodwill, in effect, was taken for granted.

In 1950 the Institute issued Bulletin No. 40, which introduced the pooling of interests concept of accounting for business combinations and mentioned criteria for distinguishing between that method and a purchase. The Bulletin was not immediately significant because the same effect in financial statements and ratios could be obtained by either treatment; immediate write-offs of goodwill to earned or capital surplus upon purchase of a firm, though discouraged, were allowed in Bulletin No. 24. If the other assets purchased were recorded at the acquired firm's book values, no difference existed between the combination's being recorded as a purchase or as a pooling.

The trend of authoritative thought and practice toward emphasizing amortization and disallowing arbitrary write-offs of goodwill was reflected in Bulletin No. 43, which significantly modified procedures found in Bulletin No. 24. Changes in wording and presentation of the sections regarding subsequent treatment indicated that amortization of goodwill appeared to be preferable to permanent retention of its cost in the accounts. Write-offs to capital surplus and discretionary write-offs to any account were disallowed; however, with such write-offs expressly disapproved, and with Bulletin No. 40 restated almost word for word in Bulletin No. 43, a clear distinction now was evident between purchase and pooling accounting. Due to the unfavorable effects of the purchase treatment on reported income and various ratios, in comparison to those of pooling accounting, pressures arose to employ the pooling treatment where possible. The subjective criteria for distinguishing between the two treatments—and their application in practice—deteriorated steadily. After issuance of Bulletin No. 48, which revised the criteria, any business combination involving stock given for property or more stock could be accounted for as either a purchase or a pooling.

---

1. Arthur R. Wyatt, *A Critical Study of Accounting for Business Combinations*, Accounting Research Study No. 5 (New York: American Institute of Certified Public Accountants, 1963), pp. 4-5. (Hereinafter referred to as *Accounting for Business Combinations*.)

2. American Institute of Accountants, Committee on Accounting Procedure, *Business Combinations*, Accounting Research Bulletin No. 40 (New York: American Institute of Accountants, 1950), pp. 299-301.

3. American Institute of Accountants, Committee on Accounting Procedures, *Restatement and Revision of Accounting Research Bulletins*, Accounting Research Bulletin No. 43 (New York: American Institute of Accountants, 1953).

4. American Institute of Accountants, Committee on Accounting Procedures, *Business Combinations*, Accounting Research Bulletin No. 48 (New York: American Institute of Accountants, 1957).

5. B.J. Sanderson, "Goodwill and Its Valuation," *The Chartered Accountant in Australia*, July 1950, p. 37.

6. See p. 80.

7. American Institute of Accountants, Committee on Accounting Procedures, *Restatement and Revision of Accounting Research Bulletins*, Accounting Research Bulletin No. 43, p. 38.

8. William W. Werntz, "Intangibles in Business Combinations," *The Journal of Accountancy*, May 1957, p. 46.

9. Maurice Moonitz and C.C. Staehling, *Accounting—An Analysis of Its Problems* (Brooklyn: Foundation Press, Inc., 1952), pp. 451-452. (Hereinafter referred to as *Accounting*.)

10. American Accounting Association, Executive Committee, "Accounting Concepts and Standards Underlying Corporate Financial Statements: 1948 Revision," *The Accounting Review*, October 1948, p. 339.

11. American Accounting Association, Committee on Concepts and Standards Underlying Corporate Financial Statements, "Price Level Changes and Financial Statements: Supplementary Statement No. 2," *The Accounting Review*, October 1951, pp. 468-474.

12. American Accounting Association, Executive Committee, "Accounting and Reporting Standards for Corporate Financial Statements: 1957 Revision," *The Accounting Review*, October 1957, p. 544.

13. Henry Rand Hatfield, *Modern Accounting* (New York: D. Appleton and Company, 1913), p. 116.

14. Norman S. Young, "Valuation of Goodwill and Its Treatment in Accounts," *The Australian Accountant*, November 1946, pp. 532-533.

15. See p. 80.

16. William W. Werntz and Edmund B. Rickard, "Requirements of the Securities and Exchange Commission," in *Contemporary Accounting*, ed. Thomas W. Leland (New York: American Institute of Accountants, 1945), ch. 38, pp. 5-6. Werntz was chief accountant of the Securities and Exchange Commission from 1938 to 1947.

17. U.S. Securities and Exchange Commission, *The Propriety of Writing Down Goodwill by Means of Charges to Capital Surplus*, Accounting Series Release No. 50 (Washington: U.S. Government Printing Office, 1956), p. 123.

18. Robert H. Montgomery, Norman J. Lenhart, and Alvin R. Jennings, *Montgomery's Auditing*, 7th ed. (New York: Ronald Press Company, 1949), p. 294.

19. George T. Walker, "Why Purchased Goodwill Should be Amortized on a Systematic Basis," *The Journal of Accountancy*, February 1953, pp. 210-211. (Hereinafter referred to as "Purchased Goodwill.")

20. Walter A. Staub, "Intangible Assets," in *Contemporary Accounting*, ed. Thomas W. Leland (New York: American Institute of Accountants, 1945), ch. 8, p. 5.

21. Walker, "Purchased Goodwill," p. 211.

22. Kenneth C. Emery, "Should Goodwill Be Written Off?" *The Accounting Review*, October 1951, p. 565. In the 90 years in which goodwill has been discussed, Emery's article represents one of the best summaries of arguments for and against amortization of goodwill.

23. Moonitz and Staehling, *Accounting*, p. 462.

24. Walker, "Purchased Goodwill," pp. 213-215.

25. Emery, "Should Goodwill Be Written Off?" p. 566.

26. Robert H. Nelson, "The Momentum Theory of Goodwill," *The Accounting Review*, October 1953, p. 492.

27. Ibid., pp. 492, 498.

28. P.D. Leake, *Commercial Goodwill; Its History, Value, and Treatment*, 3rd ed. (London: Sir Isaac Pitman & Sons, Ltd., 1938).

29. See p. 95.

30. American Institute of Accountants, Committee on Accounting Procedure, *Income and Earned Surplus*, Accounting Research Bulletin No. 32 (New York: American Institute of Accountants, 1947), p. 263.

31. American Accounting Association, Executive Committee, "Accounting Concepts and Standards Underlying Corporate Financial Statements: 1948 Revision," p. 340.

32. American Institute of Accountants, Research Department, "Should Goodwill Be Written Off?" *The Journal of Accountancy*, April 1952, p. 464.

33. Ibid., p. 465.

34. Ibid.

35. American Institute of Accountants, Committee on Accounting Procedure, *Restatement and Revision of Accounting Research Bulletins*, pp. 39-40.

36. American Institute of Accountants, Committee on Accounting Procedure, *Income and Earned Surplus,* p. 196; see pp. 92-93.

37. American Institute of Accountants, Committee on Accounting Procedures, *Restatement and Revision of Accounting Bulletins*, pp. 38-39.

38. Ibid., p. 40.

39. John Peoples, "Accounting for Intangibles in the United States," *The Canadian Chartered Accountant*, July 1957, p. 17.

40. Carman G. Blough, "Writing Off Goodwill," *The Journal of Accountancy*, June 1956, p. 60.

41. See p. 129.

42. Ibid.

43. See pp. 98-99.

44. Ibid.

45. See Exhibit 4, ch. 7. The trend continued steadily through 1973 when only four companies were reported to be utilizing nominal valuation. After 1973, information on nominal valuation of goodwill was not given.

46. Wyatt, *Accounting for Business Combinations*, p. 58.

47. Ibid., p. 40.

48. Ibid., pp. 41, 58.

49. Gordon M. Hill, "Wanted: Solutions to Three Major Technical Problems," *The Journal of Accountancy*, August 1955, p. 45.

50. Ibid., pp. 45, 46.

51. Ibid.

52. For more detailed information on this point, see Accounting Research Study Number 5—especially chapter 3.

53. American Institute of Accountants, Committee on Accounting Procedure, *Business Combinations*, pp. 299-301.

54. Ibid.

55. Ibid.

56. Dean S. Eiteman, *Pooling and Purchase Accounting* (Ann Arbor, Michigan: University of Michigan, 1967), p. 64.

57. Wyatt, *Accounting for Business Combinations*, p. 39.

58. William C. Suttle and William G. Mecklenburg, "Pooling of Interests," *The Texas CPA*, January 1969, p. 37. Though intangibles need not be amortized, amortization was preferred by the SEC. See pp. 115-116.

59. See pp. 124-126.

60. Homer Kripke, "A Good Look at Goodwill in Corporate Acquisitions," *The Banking Law Journal*, December 1961, pp. 1034-1035.

61. Suttle and Mecklenburg, "Pooling of Interests," p. 37.

62. American Institute of Accountants, Committee on Accounting Procedure, *Business Combinations*, Accounting Research Bulletin No. 48.

63. Wyatt, *Accounting for Business Combinations*, pp. 27-28, 36-39.

64. George R. Catlett and Norman O. Olson, *Accounting for Goodwill*, Accounting Research Study No. 10 (New York: American Institute of Certified Public Accountants, 1968), p. 49.

Chapter VII

History 1958-1980

The Business Environment

Trends discernible in the previous period continued with even greater force and impact into the sixties and early seventies. An even larger number of business combinations, coupled initially with prosperity and incessantly with inflation, affected accounting for goodwill in a significant manner. Even though the economy experienced some downturns in the mid-to-late seventies, lower stock prices made many firms attractive targets for acquisition.

Inflated asset and stock prices caused some firms involved in business combinations to account for the transactions in such a manner as to avoid reflecting the inflated prices in accounts and financial reports. The accounting profession was subsequently criticized for permitting such abusive practices to occur, but when it attempted to curtail them, its proposed accounting guidelines were so restrictive they drew national attention because they were viewed by some as threatening to affect the merger movement adversely. Thus the fact that accounting practice was not only a part of or a result of the business environment but could have an impact as well was illustrated forcefully.

The Accounting Environment

The most important and dramatic events of this period were those associated with the creation and then the demise of the Institute's Accounting Principles Board. In 1959 the Board superseded the Committee on Accounting Procedure, and the authority of its opinions, like those of its predecessor, initially rested on general acceptability. But with the issuance of a special bulletin in October 1964, the pronouncements themselves were considered to have substantial authoritative support; that is, the Board's opinions were deemed to constitute generally accepted accounting principles.[1]

With the enhanced authoritativeness and potential economic impact of its opinions, the Board seemed always surrounded by controversy. Many phases of the Accounting Principles Board (APB), such as its methods of operation, membership, and content of pronouncements, escaped criticism. Late in the life of the APB, the Board's Chairman stated that "the Accounting Principles Board has produced four statements, twenty-one opinions, and a thousand critics."[2]

The pronouncements concerning business combinations and intangibles were no exception to the controversy—in fact, the pooling-purchase-goodwill issue may have been the most controversial issue in the APB's history. The documentation of that debate appears throughout this chapter, and in it may be seen some of the larger issues associated with the operation of the APB itself. In the process of tackling the business-combination problem, some critics were disappointed by the Board's first taking a stand and then backing down. This action, which was particularly apparent in the pooling-of-interests debate, was believed by some to indicate that the APB was not sufficiently free from client and other pressures. The business combinations issue had the most protracted history of any ever appearing before the APB; a research study was not issued until August 1970.[3] That a very urgent matter had taken a very long time to resolve pointed to the problems of utilizing a part-time volunteer organization. These and other problems were cited by the Wheat Committee as necessitating "more than minor modifications in the present arrangements," and the pooling-purchase-goodwill issue constituted at least a valid illustration of many of the imperfections of the APB.[4]

Various interpretations may be made of the impact of the business combinations-intangibles issue on the demise of the APB. It may have been anything from the straw that broke the camel's back to an issue illustrating and/or bound up with fundamental deficiencies in the APB. Regardless, in March 1971 only seven months after the business combinations-intangibles issue resulted in opinions, Marshall Armstrong, president of the American Institute of Certified Public Accountants, appointed a committee to determine how accounting principles should be established.[5] One year later, this committee proposed that a Financial Accounting Standards Board (FASB) should take the place of the APB, and in June 1973 that action was accomplished.[6]

Because its members serve full time, are salaried, have no other affiliations, and are drawn from business and academia, as well as public practice, it was hoped that the FASB would be more independent and responsive than its predecessor. Whether or not the FASB is more independent and responsive is a matter of opinion, but its authoritative pronouncements have continued and even accelerated an earlier APB trend toward more technical and detailed procedures.

The tendency to define more specifically what constituted adherence to its pronouncements was an important issue at the time the APB issued its opinions on business combinations and intangibles. The corporate accountant's flexibility in selecting from alternative principles was curtailed, the auditor's ability to exercise professional judgment was threatened, and concern was voiced over what role the APB should occupy in affecting the practice and profession of accounting. As a result, the treatment of goodwill and the criteria for business combinations involved not only theoretical questions but the appropriateness of issuing very precise opinions. The issues became inextricably entangled.

The APB ultimately opted for specific criteria. While the Wheat Committee criticized many aspects of the APB, the committee defended this approach. Concerning APB Opinion No. 15 on earnings per share, the opinion immediately preceding those on business combinations and intangibles, the Wheat Committee stated:

> It is virtually certain that, if the Board contented itself with broad generalizations, it might placate some critics but would provoke others, for it would be accused of uttering platitudes. It is extremely doubtful that broad generalizations would satisfy the needs of public investors as seen by the SEC. The detailed prescriptions of Opinion 15 were, in fact, prompted by the ineffectiveness of the broader standards for reporting earnings per share in Part II of Opinion No. 9.[7]

The business combinations issue had an obvious and perhaps more painful parallel to the earnings-per-share opinions. As described in the last chapter, and as continued in this one, the vague criteria for distinguishing a purchase from a pooling of interests had been brushed aside; abuses florished, and much criticism of the accounting profession was the result.

When the APB was accused of utilizing a cookbook approach, the Wheat Committee stated, "Good cooks do not sneer at cookbooks; and they would not think much of a recipe which called for 'a fair amount of flour' or 'an appropriate number of eggs.' "[8] A trend toward more specific pronouncements was thus carried forward and firmly established in the APB's opinions concerning goodwill.

Characteristics of the Literature

The most significant event of the current period concerning goodwill was the simultaneous issuance of Accounting Principles Board Opinions Nos. 16 and 17 in August 1970.[9] Prior to their release, all aspects of goodwill's treatment were energetically debated in an unprecedented and seemingly incessant outpouring of articles in accounting journals. Since accounting for goodwill affected such an important aspect of modern-day business as the trend toward business combinations, the subject also gained national prominence in such periodicals as *Time, Newsweek, Business Week, Financial World, The New York Times,* and *The Wall Street Journal.*

Unlike a great many articles written in the past that dealt exclusively with goodwill, many articles that appeared before and after APB Opinions Nos. 16

and 17 were concerned with goodwill in its relation to the larger problem of business combinations. In addition, the abuses surrounding pooling of interests accounting achieved a dubious distinction for their notoriety. Thus as in the previous chapter, the interrelationship of goodwill with this subject is incorporated into a separate section entitled "Goodwill and Pooling of Interests Accounting."

After Opinions Nos. 16 and 17, very few articles were written debating the treatment of goodwill. Much of the literature that followed was written in the spirit of an aftermath providing a climactic event—adding embellishment and insight to what had already transpired, but offering very little, if anything, new.

The larger issue of business combinations involving pooling-purchase considerations suffered no such fate, however. Many articles were written and numerous interpretations were issued to clarify the application of the business combination criteria. Some loopholes were found and attempts were made to close them. These issues are worthy of an entirely separate discussion, and thus they are mentioned only to the extent that they bear on the treatment of goodwill.

Issues and Problems Concerning Goodwill

Initial Valuation of Goodwill

To some extent, developments concerning the initial valuation of goodwill followed patterns of the previous period. Amounts includable in the initial figure for the asset were more strictly defined, suggesting continued close adherence to a cost basis. However, strong inflationary pressures in the economy caused some to question the validity of historical cost or asset valuations in general. This questioning, in turn, affected considerations of goodwill's initial valuation.

In 1944 the Institute had accepted historical cost as a basis for initial valuation of intangibles. At about the same time, the costs of developing and maintaining goodwill ceased to be recorded as an asset. Though the practice had met criticism for many years, the Committee on Accounting Procedure decided not to deal with the problems of accounting for intangibles developed in the regular course of business.[10] Therefore, no official pronouncement by the Institute on that subject existed until twenty-six years later, when Opinion No. 17 was issued.

In addition to covering "the accounting for both identifiable and unidentifiable intangible assets that a company acquires," the new opinion also covered "accounting for costs of developing goodwill and other unidentifiable intangible assets with indeterminate lives."[11] After noting that costs of developing intangible assets with indeterminate lives were ordinarily not distinguishable from current operating costs and were thus not assignable to specific assets, the board concluded

> that a company should record as assets the costs of intangible assets acquired from other enterprises or individuals. Costs of developing,

maintaining, or restoring intangible assets which are not specifically identifiable, have indeterminate lives, or are inherent in a continuing business and related to an enterprise as a whole—such as goodwill—should be deducted from income when incurred.[12]

By explicitly restricting the recognition of goodwill to those instances in which a going concern was acquired, the Opinion followed an approach that had been advocated by several writers half a century earlier and that unequivocally had been considered good practice for at least twenty-five years. Some passages of Opinions Nos. 16 and 17 attracted national attention in financial circles, but the restriction just quoted passed virtually unnoticed. While a significant official step may appear to have been taken, the actual effect was to dispose of a relic long disregarded in practice.

Attempts to cope with changes in price levels usually consisted of adjusting asset costs through the use of general or specific price indexes or restating them in terms of replacement or current costs—the terms "replacement" and "current" being subject to various interpretations. Probably the most elementary form of financial statement adjustment was the use of a general price-level index to account for changes in the purchasing power of the dollar. The American Accounting Association had recommended such an approach in 1951 for use in supplementary statements,[13] and the Institute recommended experimentation with a similar approach in 1969.[14] In this situation, the initial cost of goodwill would be restated in terms of the current purchasing power of the dollar; no attempt would be made to value the asset at its current or replacement cost.

Although more exacting and difficult adjustments could be attempted, they usually ran into trouble when applied to goodwill.[15] The Association's 1966 Statement recommended use of current cost information as well as historical cost and elaborated on the application of current cost to specific assets. Discussing intangibles generally, however, the Association noted that traditionally these assets were recorded only at cost or were even understated in some cases: "The difficulties encountered in determining historical cost seem minor when compared with the near-insoluble task of determining the current cost of such assets."[16]

In discussion devoted specifically to goodwill, the Association expressed the opinion that the most reasonable approach to valuing the asset was through valuation of the entire entity—a procedure that involved estimation of future income and that lacked verifiability and objectivity.

> Where goodwill has been recorded as a result of purchase, the unamortized amount may appropriately be adjusted by use of a general price-level index. It does not appear feasible to attempt more than this to obtain a current valuation of goodwill.[17]

The FASB's dealings with changing price levels culminated in the historic *Financial Reporting and Changing Prices* issued in September 1979.[18] The Board required price-level adjusted data and current cost information of a supplementary nature in published annual reports by large companies meeting certain size requirements. In its minimum reporting requirements, the Board stipulated that only "inventory and property, plant, and equipment" needed to be restated for either the price level or current cost adjustments, so that goodwill was excluded. The Board did indicate the experimental and tentative nature of its requirements, however, so that it would be possible to add more comprehensive adjustments at a later date—presumably to include those associated with goodwill.[19] However, it would appear difficult, though not impossible, for goodwill to be stated at other than historical cost adjusted for price-level changes for reasons just mentioned.

The upward movement of prices had another effect on goodwill through high and fluctuating prices in the stock market. If an acquiring company gave a large amount of its high-priced stock for all of the stock of or a controlling interest in another company, the difference between the market value of the acquired company's assets could be large. The treatment of this difference as goodwill and its subsequent amortization to income could drastically affect reported net income and earnings per share. If, through various maneuvers, the transaction could be reported as a pooling of interests rather than as a purchase, these consequences could be avoided.

The pooling of interests treatment was not necessarily an attempt to escape the consequences of truth, for, as Backman noted, the stock market was open to serious question as a satisfactory basis for the valuation of assets. Stock prices could fluctuate widely for reasons which had little or no relationship to a company's books of account or operations. Thus stock prices, affected by such diverse influences as speculative trading, population problems, the death or illness of a president, and interest rates, could result in meaningless book values and distortion in reported earnings.[20]

The problems associated with high initial valuations of goodwill, coupled with compulsory amortization of the asset as required in Opinion No. 17, are closely interrelated with accounting for business combinations in general and are discussed throughout the remainder of this chapter.

Subsequent Treatment in Accounts

In the February 1964 issue of *The Journal of Accountancy*, Leonard Spacek set forth his views on "The Treatment of Goodwill in the Corporate Balance Sheet,'" a substantial article that appeared at a crucial time.[21] Aside from the merits of the position taken, the article, and subsequent examination of its points in later issues of the periodical, emphasized two characteristics of the contemporary discussion pertaining to disposition of goodwill: (1) the asset's subsequent treatment was not a dead issue in any sense, and (2) accounting for intangibles was the source of general and mounting dissatisfaction. Ultimately, the APB attempted to resolve the issue by specifying mandatory amortization of intangibles to income. The reasons for this particular solution are discussed in this section.

The first segment covers the effects of Accounting Principles Board Opinion No. 9, issued in December 1966 and related subsequent pronouncements on the alternatives for handling goodwill.[22] The arguments advanced for each of these alternatives are presented, followed by a discussion of Opinion No. 17.[23] The final segment is concerned with the implications of trends toward amortization for the broader issue of business combinations in general.

Accounting Principles Board Opinion No. 9 and Related Pronouncements: Part I of Opinion No. 9, "Net Income and the Treatment of Extraordinary Items and Prior Period Adjustments," had an important effect on write-off of goodwill. Prior to the Opinion's issuance, goodwill could be partially written off to retained earnings (followed by periodic amortization of the remainder to current income) if its existence was or became limited and if the large amortization charges in the absence of any write-off would result in distortion of the income statement. Furthermore, the asset could be completely written off when it became reasonably evident that it had become worthless.[24] This position, in effect from 1953 to 1966, represented a significant restriction of alternatives in comparison with earlier practices and was in turn superseded by yet stricter alternatives. In 1966 the Board concluded that all items of profit and loss recognized during the period, including those classifiable as extraordinary items (for which criteria were given), should be reflected in net income. Only certain rare material items termed "prior-period adjustments" could be written off to retained earnings:

> Adjustments related to prior periods—and thus excluded in the determination of net income for the current period—are limited to those material adjustments which (a) can be specifically identified with and directly related to the business activities of particular prior periods, and (b) are not attributable to economic events occurring subsequent to the date of the financial statements for the prior period, and (c) depend primarily on determinations by persons other than management and (d) were not susceptible of reasonable estimation prior to such determination.[25]

Such criteria virtually eliminated the write-off of goodwill to retained earnings. Most attempted write-offs of the asset failed to qualify for such a deduction because of attributes (a) and (b) alone, since the determination of its period of expected benefit had always been a subjective estimate at best. One of the main reasons for write-offs to earned surplus had been the avoidance of such charges in the income statement. Though write-offs of goodwill could still be made under the new restrictions, they could only be made through current income. "The write-off of goodwill due to unusual events or developments within the period" was given, in fact, as an example of an extraordinary item, as opposed to a prior-period adjustment. (Extraordinary items were defined as "events and transactions of material effect which would not be expected to recur frequently and which would not be considered as recurring factors in any evaluation of the ordinary operating processes of the business.")[26] While such extraordinary transactions were segregated in the income statement from ordinary items, they were still charged to current income.

Later pronouncements that either updated Opinion No. 9 or were applied in connection with it were even more restrictive. Opinion No. 17 reaffirmed Opinion No. 9 and further discouraged write-offs.[27] In 1973 Opinion No. 30 refined the definition of extraordinary items to be those events and transactions which were both unusual in nature and infrequent in occurrence. Write-offs of intangibles were specifically excluded from extraordinary treatment except as a direct result of a major casualty, an expropriation, or passage of a new prohibitive law.[28] And in 1977 the FASB's Standard No. 16 redefined prior-period adjustments to be only the correction of an error or adjustment concerning certain tax benefits.[29] Only some error concerning goodwill's initial computation or subsequent treatment could thus be taken directly to retained earnings.

Arguments for either permanent retention or gradual reduction of goodwill do not appear to have been affected by the virtual change to the all-inclusive approach to reporting income, nor did their relative standing to each other prior to Opinion No. 17 appear to have been altered. With the changes brought by Opinion No. 9, however, write-offs of retained earnings were no longer generally accepted. Writers thereafter advocated (though unsuccessfully) reinstatement of the practice on other grounds, which are discussed in the following section.

Permanent Retention vs. Write-off vs. Amortization:

Permanent retention. During this period, permanent retention seems largely to have passed from active debate concerning the subsequent treatment of goodwill. Not only were no new arguments advanced for it, virtually no one argued against it—which seems to indicate it was no longer considered a serious contender.[30] The battle seems to have gone elsewhere. Those advocating capitalization of some amount as goodwill usually argued that it should be treated as any other asset and should ultimately be disposed of, while their opponents questioned either its status as an asset or the amount at which it was capitalized. The contestants fought on the basis of an amortizable asset versus its immediate write-off. Neither side seemed to consider permanent retention as either an alternative or a compromise.[31]

Write-off. The practice of writing off goodwill to either earned or capital surplus followed an interesting course of events in the period from 1958 to 1971. Since the thirties, write-offs to other than current income had been subject to increasing restrictions, which culminated in the virtual elimination of such charges in Opinion No. 9. As a result, arguments supporting the practice shifted from circumstances in which goodwill was assumed to have declined substantially in value to the question of capitalizing goodwill as an asset in the first place. Timing of the transaction was similarly affected; write-off was advocated immediately after placing the asset on the books rather than at the time of a presumed decline in value.

Much of the renewed support in accounting literature for the immediate write-off of goodwill came from members of the accounting firm of Arthur Andersen & Co. Two of the more important writings were Spacek's article in 1964, which was referred to earlier, and *Accounting for Goodwill,* by George Catlett and Norman Olson, published as an Accounting Research Study by the Institute in 1968.[32] A fundamental contention for this treatment was that goodwill was not an asset. When a business was purchased, the excess of the total price over the fair value of its producing assets constituted "a cost to the buyer of earnings over and above the cost of the assets required to produce those earnings."[33]

> Goodwill is not a resource or property right that is consumed or utilized in the production of earnings. Rather it is a result of earnings, or of the expectations of them, as appraised by investors.[34]

The appraisal by investors was reflected in the market price of a company's stock, which was influenced by a number of factors.

> The role of accounting is to provide information which the investor can use in arriving at his opinion of the value of a business; accounting does not determine that value.[35]

Accounting should therefore record the fair value of the producing assets of the business purchased and (1) immediately write off the expenditure for goodwill to retained earnings or capital surplus or (2) show goodwill as a reduction of stockholders' equity. Otherwise, goodwill would be determining the value of a business rather than furnishing the investor with information that he could use for that purpose.

This argument was attacked on its major premise that goodwill was not an asset and on the implications of the accounting treatment accorded amounts recorded as goodwill. Paton, in critical comments concerning Catlett and Olson's study, stated:

> Assets are not inherently tangible or physical. An asset is an *economic quantum.* It may be attached to or represented by some physical object, or it may not. One of the common mistakes we all tend to make is that of attributing too much significance to the molecular conception of property. A brick wall is nothing but mud on edge if its capacity to render economic service has disappeared; the molecules are still there and the wall may be as solid as ever but the value is gone. . . . the distinction between tangibles, so-called, and intangibles, so-called, is not a fundamental line of cleavage. In principle, the intangible asset is just as admissible to the respectable, recognizable company of business property as something you can stub your toe on. This point should be stressed, not submerged, in any analysis of the nature of the intangibles.[36]

Setting up goodwill as an asset and subsequently amortizing it resulted in charges in the income statement for cost of earning power that, according to Spacek, were wrong and potentially misleading.[37] Hylton countered this opinion with "What charges are there on an income statement which do *not* represent the cost of earning power?"[38] To defend his argument, Spacek returned to the point that goodwill was not a producing asset:

The cost charged to the income account should represent the cost of producing the earnings and not the cost of earning power. . . .

. . . When this risk element representing future earning power is sold from one stockholder to another, we have the sale and purchase of goodwill—the sale and the purchase of the opportunity to secure the earning power of the particular company for the future. It is the cost of the right to future earnings, but such earnings are not assured.[39]

This particular argument does not appear to have been immediately pursued by critics of the write-off approach, but it can be attacked in much the same manner as Hylton's attack on the initial statement by Spacek. Goodwill certainly represented the sale and purchase of the opportunity to secure the earning power of a company in the future. But did not the payment for any asset represent payment for such an opportunity? Once an asset has been acquired, the purchaser enjoys the right to any future earnings resulting from employment of the asset in a profit-making manner, but in Spacek's own words, "such earnings are not assured." Immediately after a building is purchased it could burn down, thus emphasizing the fact that the purchaser's right to any asset, not only goodwill, is just an opportunity and not an assurance. Thus, the distinction between goodwill and other assets on the basis that its purchase represented an opportunity only was not valid.

The major premise of the direct write-off approach as just interpreted implied the accounting treatment for the intangible, but the accounting treatment had implications of its own. One writer felt that immediately writing off goodwill was "tantamount to saying that someone deliberately threw his money away."[40] In addition to inferring that goodwill was not an asset, the direct write-off method also implied that it did not subsequently become an expense and should not be deducted in the income statement.

Thus, income for which an expenditure was made will appear on the income statement with no indication that an expenditure was made to acquire this income. Should the expected income not be realized, again, income will not be offset by the cost incurred in hope of that future income. . . . The hallowed directive to 'match revenue with related expense' seems to be ignored by the direct charge-off.[41]

If goodwill was considered neither an asset nor an expense, then the write-off presumably represented some sort of capital contraction. After evaluating and discarding the available alternatives of goodwill's treatment as a dividend, a gift, a capital contraction, and a correction of prior years' income, Hylton concluded that implications of the treatment appeared to cast serious doubt on the propriety of any such entry.[42]

The write-off alternative was not merely the subject of academic discussion. Those involved in the argument treated the proposal seriously as a possible alternative for handling goodwill, with generally more against the method than for it. When Catlett and Olson's work was published, most of the members of their Project Advisory Committee (whose comments were published with the study) disagreed with the recommendation of immediate write-off, and the Director of Accounting Research, Reed K. Storey, authorized publication only with reservations.[43]

Of fifty letters received by the Accounting Research Division of the Institute commenting on Accounting Research Study No. 10, about two thirds disagreed with the immediate write-off proposal.[44] A staff proposal of the Securities and Exchange Commission also rejected the idea.[45] The subject was discussed with such intensity that the writers occasionally bordered on insulting each other, and the write-off treatment remained controversial, particularly from 1964 until the subsequent treatment issue was settled in Opinion No. 17 in 1970.[46]

Amortization. The general position expressed by various writers favoring amortization of goodwill, was that the intangible asset was like any other asset and should be treated accordingly—an idea also used, as mentioned previously, to attack the write-off method. Just as other assets were subject to eventual exhaustion, so was goodwill. While the idea was by no means novel, it was advocated with increasing frequency and was subsequently embodied in Accounting Principles Board Opinion No. 17.

The approach was in conflict with the write-off method in regard to whether the asset, presumed to exist by both approaches, was sufficiently different from other assets to merit special treatment (nonamortization versus amortization).

Specific arguments for and against the position predictably echoed arguments of the previous eighty years. These arguments still had partisan appeal and gave no recognition to the fact that they had been ably dispatched—in some cases a generation earlier. Occasionally, however, a slightly different argument was presented or an old approach was altered to fit modern circumstances. These situations deserve consideration.

H.C. Knortz, attacking the compulsory amortization proposed in the exposure draft preceding Opinion No. 17, stated:

> The draft suggests that the turning pages of the calendar are sufficient evidence of a deterioration in residual goodwill values although, in fact, it nowhere asserts that these values are necessarily lost with the passage of time.[47]

This objection can be answered in two ways. George Walker, quoted in the previous chapter, felt that it was as incorrect to relate amortization to the value of intangibles as it was to relate depreciation to the value of fixed assets.[48] In addition to accounting considerations, there were questions concerning the life of the asset. Wolff concluded that

> when dealing with unlimited-term intangibles, the term should be understood to mean that at present the point in time at which their value will expire cannot be foreseen, not that they will have value eternally. When viewed in this manner, the question resolves itself into the problem of choosing an appropriate term for amortization purposes.[49]

Another argument maintained against amortization was the following:

> Thus, the more that is paid for a company, the less would be earned
> under purchase accounting. This is unrealistic and indicates that the
> mandatory amortization of artifically created goodwill does not
> make much economic sense.[50]

On the surface the argument appears to be easily answered, since the more that
is paid for a company, the smaller is the expected return due to a matching of
greater costs with the same revenue. The real problem, however, is not the
mandatory amortization policy, but the figure that is subject to such treatment.

The questionable initial valuation of goodwill (discussed earlier) due to
fluctuating stock market prices led to serious questions concerning its subsequent amortization.[51] In its brief presented to the Accounting Principles
Board concerning business combinations and intangible assets, the firm of
Arthur Andersen & Co. presented probably the strongest arguments against
amortization of goodwill. The firm pointed out that the consideration given for
goodwill was based on stock-market prices representing stock-market speculation
about the future and reflected the stock market's optimism at only one point in
time. The value thus established had no permanence because it was as volatile as
the moods that determine stock-market prices. The question was then asked,
"With such elusive qualities, what does it mean to reflect goodwill as an asset in
a statement of financial position?" Arthur Andersen & Co., however, did not
question the reliability of the stock market as an indicator of goodwill's value;
the market valuation of the intangible was reliable but very unstable:

> Since stock prices are representative of all the continuously varying
> circumstances and moods of the market place, neither the prices nor
> the goodwill determined by those prices can be stable. No asset
> qualifying for a place in the statement of financial position of a
> company can have such characteristics if it is to be useful to any
> investor or reader of the statement.[52]

This argument may be rebutted on two levels: (1) by examining certain characteristics of assets and goodwill and (2) by reference to some specific accounting
considerations. Briefly, goodwill is no different from other assets—noticeable
discrepancies are differences of degree rather than of nature. Accounting conventions geared to handle the asset should be the same as those for other long-lived
assets; specifically, that goodwill should be recorded at cost and amortized over
its expected life.

Examining these considerations in detail, the earlier question may be
countered with a similar one, "Why should the price of any long-lived asset as of
a moment of time affect results of operations for the next generation or more by
subsequent depreciation or amortization against income?" The difference in
price stability between goodwill and other long-lived assets is not due to a
difference in the nature of goodwill and other assets; it is a difference of
relativity or degree. The price fluctuations of land or plant and equipment, for

example, might be less pronounced or obvious than goodwill; nevertheless, such fluctuations are evident. One question that perplexed these writers was the fact that the price paid for goodwill would thwart an otherwise advantageous business combination. Such a combination would be possibly beneficial to many groups—the management of various other firms, the firm's owners, its customers, its employees, the economy. Why should "scratches on paper" stifle all of these worthwhile occurrences? Again, however, the price of land or plant and equipment in a given instance could deter advantageous results from the viewpoint of various segments of society. Thus the difference is one of degree since the difficulties associated with the acquisition of both goodwill in one case and land in the other are due to the workings of the economic system and the accounting conventions that are used to measure the system's results.

In a profit-oriented economy, a traditional indicator of the success of a firm has been through the application of accounting conventions that measure profitability in terms of money. Attempts to require amortization of goodwill represent the logical extension of accounting conventions to goodwill that are applied to other assets. Based on the premise that goodwill is an asset, the treatment represents uncompromising adherence to determination of profitability through matching of expired costs with revenues. If stockholders or managers act on the basis of information furnished in financial statements (presumed to be more exacting in the measurement of profits with the inclusion of goodwill's amortization), productivity or operations of a firm (as noted previously) certainly could be affected. Aside from profitability, the art of accounting has generally not been directed toward such factors, except to determine how changes to them would affect the earnings potential. The acquisition cost of any long-lived asset and its subsequent allocation to future periods of presumed benefit has exactly the same effect as similar allocation of goodwill's initial cost. The strictures of the previously quoted writers may be viewed as misdirected, since what they presumed to be a unique characteristic of goodwill is common to all things called assets. In substance, they brought out a characteristic of the economic system rather than a trait of a particular asset.

Accounting Principles Board Opinion No. 17: On February 23, 1970, the Accounting Principles Board issued an exposure draft on a proposed opinion concerning business combinations and intangible assets. The board solicited and duly received comments from many interested individuals, groups, and firms concerning its recommendations and presented its conclusions in two opinions in August 1970. Opinion No. 16, discussed later in this chapter, dealt with business combinations in general, describing the criteria for distinguishing between combinations classifiable as purchases and those classifiable as poolings of interests. Opinion No. 17 outlined the treatment to be accorded intangible assets, superseding all of Chapter 5 of Accounting Research Bulletin No. 43 except for one paragraph that was superseded by Opinion No. 16.[53] While that portion of the exposure draft incorporated in Opinion No. 16 was significantly changed, the remainder, with only slight rearrangement or elaboration and no changes in substance, was placed in Opinion No. 17.

While Opinion No. 17 was concerned with the treatment of intangible assets in general, controversy—much of which was discussed in the preceding section— arose from the application of its provisions to goodwill specifically. The basic reasoning underlying the stipulated treatment for intangibles was that intangibles (and therefore goodwill) were like other assets and should be treated accordingly.

> Accounting for an intangible asset involves the same kinds of problems as accounting for other long-lived assets, namely, determining an initial carrying amount, accounting for that amount after acquisition under normal business conditions (amortization), and accounting for that amount if the value declines substantially and permanently. . . .
>
> . . . All assets which are represented by deferred costs are essentially alike in historical-cost based accounting. . . .
>
> . . . The basic accounting treatment does not depend on whether the asset is a building, a piece of equipment, an element of inventory, a prepaid insurance premium, or whether it is tangible or intangible. The cost of goodwill and similar intangible assets is therefore essentially the same as the cost of land, buildings, or equipment under historical cost based accounting.[54]

Application of the accounting principle of matching revenues with expenses to certain intangible assets, particularly goodwill, could be difficult due to the asset's indeterminate life.

> Amortizing the cost of goodwill and similar intangible assets on arbitrary bases in the absence of evidence of limited lives or decreased values may recognize expenses and decreases of assets prematurely, but delaying amortization of the cost until a loss is evident may recognize the decreases after the fact.[55]

The Board felt that a solution to the dilemma was to set minimum and maximum amortization periods. Such a solution, incidentally, excluded both immediate write-off and permanent retention.

> Few, if any, intangible assets last forever, although some may seem to last almost indefinitely. Allocating the cost of goodwill or other intangible assets with an indeterminate life over time is necessary because the value almost inevitably becomes zero at some future date. Since the date at which the value becomes zero is indeterminate the end of the useful life must necessarily be set arbitrarily at some point or within some range of time for accounting purposes.

Accordingly, the Board concluded that "the value of intangible assets at any one date eventually disappears and that the recorded costs of intangible assets should be amortized by systematic charges to income over the periods estimated to be benefited."[56]

A number of factors were listed that should be considered in determining the estimated life of an intangible, such as legal provisions, effects of obsolescence, demand, competition, service life of employees, and expected actions of competitors. The asset should then be amortized over its estimated life and—apparently with reference to goodwill—should not be written off in the period of acquisition. If the asset's life was indeterminate and apparently unlimited, its cost should be amortized over a maximum of forty years, therefore excluding the permanent retention alternative acceptable before issuance of this Opinion. Amortization on a straight-line basis was recommended and should be subject to continual review for changes in estimates of the asset's useful life. If the life of the intangible appeared to be changed, then the unamortized cost should be amortized over the increased or reduced number of years. Closing a possible loophole, the Board stated that the revised useful life could not exceed forty years after acquisition. If the asset's life or value changed substantially, an extraordinary charge to income might be in order, but "a single loss year or even a few loss years together do not necessarily justify an extraordinary charge to income for all or a large part of the unamortized cost of intangible assets."[57]

Opinion 17 represented a significant restriction of alternatives in comparison to its predecessor, Accounting Research Bulletin No. 24, issued twenty-six years before, or even to Chapter 5 of Accounting Research Bulletin No. 43, issued in 1953. Amortization to current income was mandatory for goodwill—the only acceptable treatment for the asset in ordinary circumstances. As a result of this and previous opinions, write-down of the asset was permitted, but only to current income as an extraordinary charge and only with sufficient justification. Write-offs to contributed capital in excess of par or stated value (capital surplus), write-offs to retained earnings (earned surplus), discretionary write-offs, immediate write-off upon acquisition, and permanent retention had been eliminated gradually since 1944. Only amortization to current income and write-down of the asset remained as viable practices, and they were not alternatives for each other but were mutually exclusive.

Opinion 17 was adopted with the votes of thirteen of the Board's eighteen members. George Catlett, the Arthur Andersen partner who coauthored Accounting Research Study No. 10 advocating immediate write-off, dissented and echoed the views espousing the write-off treatment. The other four dissenters objected to the exclusion of permanent retention as an alternative and restated the main arguments in favor of that treatment. They concluded with a statement that supported their position but had wider implications concerning the general approach of the Opinion and of the Board in its attempts to solve accounting problems: "In all cases, the amortization of intangible assets should be based on professional judgment, rather than arbitrary rules."[58]

Criticisms based on considerations other than immediate goodwill accounting issues were that the forty-year arbitrary amortization limit for goodwill was adopted merely as a compromise[59] and that, furthermore, the forty-year rule was an attempt to evade a decision "on concepts by minimizing the related effects through extended write-off periods."[60]

The criticisms in the preceding paragraph voiced in the exposure draft stage and the others voiced in the Opinion itself were countered by Philip L.

Defliese—a Board member who voted for the Opinion—in an article published six months after its release. Defliese noted that in decisions concerning business combinations and goodwill the APB was following the basic concepts of historical cost and of matching costs with revenue and that the matching concept had a large bearing on the question of goodwill's subsequent treatment.

> To achieve their objectives, these Opinions had to set up some rigid (and occasionally arbitrary) guidelines. This is always an easy target for those who disagree with an Opinion in principle.[61]

After thus answering the charge of arbitrariness, he then summarized many of the problems associated with goodwill and the Board's reason for mandatory amortization:

> Goodwill has been an accounting enigma for decades. Purchased goodwill, when amortized, creates a form of double charge when expenditures for its regeneration are made simultaneously. Since goodwill cannot be assumed to be perpetual, some method of eliminating the cost of goodwill had to be devised; at the same time, most accountants refuse to defer the regeneration charges to the future because there is no objective way to do it. The use of a long period of amortization—a maximum of 40 years—therefore was the most practical and objective solution.[62]

Implications of Compulsory Amortization on the Issue of Business Combinations: The trend toward amortization and the subsequent adoption of the treatment to the exclusion of other alternatives, particularly permanent retention, would undoubtedly have led to heated debate, but there would have been less argument had it not been for the presence of other factors. These will be discussed shortly. One individual, a charter member of the APB whose firm was still represented on the Board, stated publicly, "As far as I'm concerned, the Accounting Principles Board has gone off its rocker."[63]

One reason for the controversy was the increased authoritativeness of the APB Opinions.[64] Furthermore, required amortization would unfavorably affect earnings per share and other similar indicators of corporate profitability. The main problem, however, was the concurrent development of more stringent provisions governing the treatment of a business as either a pooling of interests or as a purchase—provisions designed to significantly limit use of the pooling treatment. If compulsory amortization alone had been adopted, then firms could have resorted easily to use of the pooling treatment to effect their combinations, since the virtually lifeless provisions of Accounting Research Bulletin No. 48 were no longer seriously followed. If, instead, the pooling criteria had been strengthened and the provisions relating to goodwill had remained unchanged, firms could still have resorted to permanent retention of an asset if the transaction did not qualify for treatment as a pooling. What eventually occurred was, from the viewpoint of those whose financial statements were affected, the worst of both possible worlds. Faced in most cases with strict pooling criteria, firms were often required to record and amortize a large amount of goodwill.

As a result, the battle was fought on two fronts. Compulsory amortization was strongly attacked, and the business combination proposals were vociferously taken to task as well. When the smoke cleared, the amortization proposals remained intact while the combination provisions had been modified. Those provisions were an improvement, however, and would curb many of the earlier abuses associated with pooling of interests.

After the issuance of Opinion No. 17, goodwill's subsequent treatment generally became a dead issue. Only a few scattered articles appeared in the entire decade of the seventies—representing one of the few lulls in the almost one hundred years of controversy surrounding accounting for goodwill. Goodwill's compulsory amortization was virtually taken for granted; the new issue was the implementation of the business combination criteria. In other words, concern shifted from the subsequent treatment of goodwill to the initial avoidance of the asset by finding ways to record a combination as a pooling of interests.

Financial Presentation and Disclosure

The influence of the APB is particularly evident insofar as the disposition of goodwill in financial statements is concerned. The pronouncements of the Board's predecessor, the Committee on Accounting Procedure, were never so authoritative nor so specific. The effects of APB Opinions on financial statements are therefore discussed in the first topic.

Accounting Trends and Techniques, published annually by the American Institute of Certified Public Accountants, continued to furnish information on the disposition of goodwill in financial statements. This data proved comparable to that presented in the previous chapter. Discussion and analysis of the trends contained therein constitute the subject of the second topic.

Always something of an enigma, negative goodwill or the excess of book value over cost was finally dealt with by the Committee on Accounting Procedure and again by the APB. Recommendations by those authorities for its treatment and its relation to the business combination issue in general constitute the subject of the third topic.

Effects of APB Opinions on Financial Statements: In 1964, as noted previously, the Institute's Council adopted a proposal requiring auditors to disclose any departures from principles enunciated in Board Opinions or Accounting Research Bulletins. Before this proposal went into effect on December 31, 1965, the Accounting Principles Board reviewed all Accounting Research Bulletins to "determine whether any of them should be revised or withdrawn."[65] The Board felt that some provisions of the Bulletins no longer applied and, therefore, "it should revise certain of the Bulletins in order to obviate conflicts between present accepted practice and provisions of outstanding Bulletins which would otherwise require unwarranted disclosure."[66]

As one of its changes, the Board deleted paragraph 7 of Chapter 5 of Accounting Research Bulletin No. 43[67] which was concerned with discretionary amortization of unlimited life intangibles and stated that "the procedure should be formally approved and the reason for amortization, the rate used, and the shareholders' or directors' approval thereof should be disclosed in the financial statements."[68]

The Board's deletion was evidently in the nature of housecleaning; a provision which was not being followed in practice was being removed since "the revisions set forth in this Opinion are made in the light of currently accepted practices followed in preparing financial statements and reporting upon them."[69]

APB Opinion No. 9, discussed previously in connection with goodwill's subsequent treatment, had an important bearing on the asset's financial presentation. After the Opinion's issuance, charges to amortize, write down, or write off goodwill could be made only in the income statement. The statement of retained earnings could no longer be utilized for amortization or write-down of the intangible. By essentially embracing the all-inclusive concept, the Board's action thus represented one more step in decreasing the alternatives for handling goodwill. The write-off of goodwill due to unusual events or developments over a period of time was still considered to be an extraordinary item and, as such, was excludable from ordinary items in computing operating income. After income before extraordinary items was determined, however, material write-off of goodwill had to be deducted on the income statement to determine net income for the period.

Even after Opinion No. 9 was issued, though, the income statement could still escape charges for goodwill if a company simply refused to amortize the asset—an acceptable alternative under Chapter 5 of Bulletin No. 43, then still in effect. Opinions Nos. 16 and 17 came as a shock, therefore, since Opinion No. 16 significantly restricted the pooling alternative, making goodwill's recognition more probable, and Opinion No. 17 specified mandatory amortization of the asset in the income statement. Finally, Opinion No. 30's redefinition of extraordinary items specified only three circumstances wherein those few write-offs still permitted could escape ordinary treatment. Thus, the asset's subsequent treatment and financial presentation were virtually placed in a straitjacket.

To summarize briefly, the Board's Special Bulletin in 1964 strengthened the force of its pronouncements; Opinion No. 9 restricted elimination of goodwill to the income statement; Opinion No. 16 restricted the situations in which the recognition of the asset could be avoided; and Opinion No. 17 required amortization. There was practically no escape except to avoid recognition of goodwill.

Disposition of Goodwill in Financial Statements:

Separate disclosure. Accounting Trends and Techniques indicated that separately classifying goodwill or presenting it with other intangibles as a separate balance-sheet group was the preferred treatment, as it had been in the previous period.[70] Exhibit 3 indicates that goodwill was disclosed in this manner approximately 75 percent of the time—a slight decrease from the 85 to 90 percent of the previous period. Meanwhile the classification of goodwill as "other assets" increased approximately 20 to 25 percent. Thus, irrespective of

Exhibit 3: Classification of Goodwill in the Balance Sheet

Years	Separately Set Forth	Under Fixed Assets	Under Other Assets	Under Deferred Charges
1958*	149	2	20	3
1959	151	0	22	3
1960	144	0	33	0
1961	137	1	40	4
1962	139	1	41	3
1963	127	2	38	7
1964	131	1	42	4
1965	132	2	53	5
1966	125	2	51	6
1967†	147	2	48	3

*For all years, "Goodwill," "Goodwill (not otherwise indicated)," and "Goodwill re: Subsidiary" as shown in the original source, have been combined. Data covers 600 companies for all years.
†No comparable information was presented after 1967.
Source: American Institute of Certified Public Accountants, *Accounting Trends & Techniques,* Vols. XIII-XXII (New York: American Institute of Certified Public Accountants, 1959-1968).

almost fifty years of discussion in the literature, the manner of goodwill's presentation had remained about the same.

Valuation of goodwill. Exhibit 4 indicates that the use of nominal valuation, once the preferred treatment for goodwill, continued to steadily decline until by 1979 it was used by less than 1 percent of the companies disclosing goodwill. In the remaining instances, a policy of amortization appears to have been slightly preferred through 1963, but thereafter through the sixties nonamortization was increasingly utilized until by 1969 the policy was favored almost three to one over amortization. Even taking into account the increasing number of instances "not determinable," which tend to obscure analysis of trends, nonamortization was obviously and increasingly favored to all alternatives throughout the mid- and late-sixties.

Although nonamortization continued to increase in popularity until reaching a peak of 207 in 1972, the effects of Opinion No. 17 (issued in late 1970) are apparent. Amortization increased dramatically in 1971 and 1972 and steadily increased each year with two exceptions through 1978. Even with the decreases noted in 1975 and 1976, amortization increased proportionately every year from 1969 forward in comparison with nonamortization and with all alterna-

Exhibit 4: Valuation of Goodwill

Years	Amortized	Not Amortized	Total Columns 1, 2	Nominal Valuation	Not Determinable
1958*	48	35	83	91	--
1959	51	43	94	84	--
1960	55	46	101	82	--
1961	60	52	112	71	--
1962	59	46	106	64	17
1963	51	46	97	57	21
1964	44	51	95	55	32
1965	50	64	114	46	37
1966	43	72	115	35	42
1967	43	72	115	31	58
1968	46	108	154	24	71
1969	47	138	185	20	65
1970	70	166	236	11	49
1971	129	162	291	5	40
1972	217	207	424	6	11
1973	250	197	447	4	11
1974	262	187	449	--	--
1975	261	182	443	--	--
1976	253	174	427	--	--
1977	288	175	463	--	--
1978	296	165	461	--	--
1979	285	156	441	--	--

*For all years, "Goodwill" and "Goodwill re: Subsidiary" as shown in the source have been combined. Through the years, "Goodwill" was variously titled "Goodwill (not otherwise indicated)" and "Goodwill (source not indicated)." Likewise, the caption "Goodwill re: Subsidiary" was changed to "Excess Acquisition Costs (including goodwill)," and then to "Goodwill recognized in a business combination." For 1978 and 1979, the only caption presented was "Goodwill recognized in a business combination." Data covers 600 companies.

Source: American Institute of Certified Public Accountants, *Accounting Trends and Techniques,* Vols. XIII-XXXIV (New York: American Institute of Certified Public Accountants, 1959-1980).

tives. Interestingly, while amortization had been mandatory for nine years by 1979, nonamortization was being utilized about as often as it had been in 1970—the year the opinion excluding nonamortization was issued. Presumably the nonretroactive provisions of the Opinion, allowing goodwill purchased prior to November 1, 1970, to be retained permanently and thus obtain the treatment's generally favorable effect relative to amortization, explains its lingering popularity.

Negative Goodwill—The Excess of Book Value Over Cost: Accounting Research Bulletin No. 51, *Consolidated Financial Statements,* issued in August 1959 represented the first time the Institute attempted to deal with the subject of excess book value over cost. It reiterated its earlier position found in Accounting Research Bulletin No. 43 concerning the excess of cost over book value.[71] This position stated that to the extent the excess was attributable to particular assets, tangible or intangible, it should be allocated to them. Any amounts allocable to intangibles should further be allocated, if possible, between type (a) and type (b) intangibles and treated accordingly.[72] Then, in specifically considering negative goodwill, the Committee stated, "in general, parallel procedures should be followed in the reverse type of case."[73] Therefore, the cost of specific assets should absorb the excess to the extent it was thought attributable to them. If any of the excess remained unabsorbed after this allocation—a circumstance the Committee considered to be unusual—it could be shown in a credit account and would ordinarily be taken into income in future periods on a reasonable and systematic basis.[74]

Put in context with the available literature on the subject, the Committee's recommendations simply codified what had been considered good practice since the twenties.[75] In a similar vein, it moved to discredit the practice of crediting capital surplus with the excess, stating that "such a procedure is not now considered acceptable."[76] Thus, the Committee was codifying accounting principles concerning negative goodwill rather than formulating them.

As did other items in the business combination area, negative goodwill succumbed to the abuses associated with the pooling method. At the time Bulletin 51 was issued in 1959, the pooling criteria were in an advanced stage of deterioration. Shortly thereafter, any business combination could be accounted for with a minimum of difficulty as either a purchase or a pooling. As befits the subject of negative goodwill, its abuse occurred in reverse fashion from that of most of the other abuses. Occasions still arose where some believed that the pooling treatment should legitimately have been applied. In weighing alternative accounting treatments, however, parties to a business combination might determine that if the transaction were treated as a purchase by one of the firms, a negative goodwill element would result that could be amortized and therefore increase income. Since the pooling criteria were practically defunct, the transaction would then be treated as a purchase, and amortization would be allowed. Therefore deterioration of the criteria because businesses were trying to escape the consequences of the purchase method of accounting also worked in reverse for those attempting to escape the effects of the pooling method.[77]

Opinion No. 16 attempted to alleviate the problem in two ways. The first was to delineate clearly with specific criteria the difference between a pooling and a purchase. (This difference is discussed later in this chapter.) The second way was to describe the proper method of accounting for the excess of the book value of acquired net assets over cost. After the market or appraised value had been determined for noncurrent assets, any excess over cost was to be applied proportionately to the values assigned them.[78] If the noncurrent assets are reduced to zero, the remainder should be classified as a deferred credit and amortized systematically to income for a period not to exceed forty years, with the method and period of amortization disclosed.[79] Thus the issue of negative goodwill, at least for the time being, appears to have been resolved. With the provisions of Opinion No. 16, most of the loopholes have been closed and the appearance of negative goodwill on balance sheets of the future will be rare indeed.

Auditing Considerations

Auditing considerations applicable to goodwill as a result of the issuance of Opinions Nos. 16 and 17 were not so important in themselves as they were for indicating the direction of the profession itself. The accounting profession had found itself in an awkward, compromising position when its criteria for distinguishing between a purchase and a pooling of interests were not so specific. The auditor had wide latitude in which to determine, in his or her professional judgment, whether a given transaction qualified for pooling or purchase treatment. The profession, however, found itself subject to mounting criticism when the criteria were abused, ignored, and distorted—in some cases with the help of the auditor himself.

> In brief, talking with members of the APB over the years, man to man, has made me painfully aware of the fact that they know better than I'll ever know just how pooling had been perverted in practice—they see the way their clients were doing it and, in fact, were there and then counselling clients on the ways in which this ill-fated accounting method could be utilized to produce instant and specious earnings.[80]

When the more stringent and specific provisions of Opinions Nos. 16 and 17 were promulgated, the auditor had at his disposal guidelines for determining the asset's initial valuation, subsequent treatment, financial presentation, and necessary disclosure. His guidelines were also his straitjacket, however, for he had little discretion in their application. In an attempt to eliminate abuse, the profession thus appeared to be eliminating at least some of its professional judgment as well.

> We are not yet subject to full-fledged dictation, but we are surely on the way; complete regimentation of the profession lies ahead if the

march in that direction is not checked. And in no other established professional field is a stultifying, rigid book of rules the boss.[81]

Even though the criteria were more objective, nothing kept accountants from merely making more adroit attempts to avoid the specific guidelines. This occurred particularly in the case of Opinion No. 16. Thus, the professional accountant found himself in a position of following rules that might be interpreted as eliminating his professional judgment while only rechanneling the possibility and method of abuse.

Tax Considerations

In 1965, Walter C. Frank wrote some rather picturesque comments concerning goodwill's duration and its tax treatment:

> Science fiction, hard pressed to stay several steps ahead of technical developments, still has two undiscovered marvels to keep its devotees breathless amidst the exciting life and times of the twenty-second century and beyond: the ability to become invisible and the ability to live forever. Invisibility and unlimited life are as old as folklore, tribal traditions, and the Bible. Some recent full page newspaper advertisements not-withstanding, eternal life on this or any other planet and invisibility are still regarded to be in the realm of pure fantasy.
>
> Implicit in these two dream developments is the concept of indestructibility. It is that concept which leads us away from the escape hatch of science fiction to the realities of taxation as we consider an item which is invisible, lives forever (or thereabouts), and is indestructible. Well, at least it wears well, or does it?
>
> Goodwill: intangible, inexhaustible, non-depreciable, non-amortizable. People sell it, pay for and buy it, compute it, haggle about it—but do they really own it? Does it last and last as long as the business with which it is associated?[82]

Frank's article concluded with a call for reexamination of goodwill's tax treatment, representing one of a still small, but growing, group of individuals calling for goodwill's amortization for tax purposes.

Some of the more imposing reasons why such amortization was denied for tax purposes were abuses in what was recorded as goodwill, indefinite duration of the asset regardless of the fact that it was eventually exhausted, and, as a result, the ability to manipulate the amortization charge. Most of the abuses that occurred in initially recording the asset, such as arbitrarily writing the account up or charging the account with operating losses that occurred in the early phases of a firm's existence, had long since met their demise. A more contemporary source of trouble existed with the ability of firms to manipulate the classification of a business combination as either a purchase or a pooling. Furthermore, the problem of goodwill's subsequent treatment still existed.

Several factors gradually arose that had important implications. The first of these was the increasing authoritativeness of the accounting pronouncements of the Accounting Principles Board. In the past, the treatment of an item for taxation purposes had been a strong influence on the way accountants handled an item—a good example being goodwill's nonamortization for tax purposes. Though certain to continue for a long time, this relationship was not immune to change.

Another factor, also connected with the Accounting Principles Board, was the increasingly specific nature of guidelines in the Board's pronouncements. Although at times the Board became precise to the point of being arbitrary, its trend in that direction represented an attempt to curtail abuses in the application of accounting principles, and Opinions Nos. 16 and 17 certainly continued the trend.

When examined with tax considerations in mind, the Board's views on business combinations and intangibles were much more specific than they had been in the past concerning the classification of a business combination as a pooling or a purchase and therefore were more specific regarding goodwill's initial recognition. In accordance with the prevailing view that goodwill was eventually exhaustible, the Board set an arbitrary maximum amortization period for its subsequent treatment. Abuses were still possible but certainly would be more difficult to accomplish. The old tax nonamortization ideas appeared to be definitely weakened. The tax law thus specified a treatment for reasons that had been at least partially negated by an increasingly influential accounting authority. As a result, a rather unique situation arose whereby a well-entrenched tax treatment was viewed as not being in accordance with accepted accounting principles. The following comments preceded an article by Henry Hill espousing a change in tax rules: "The treatment of goodwill under the Internal Revenue Code does not conform to the treatment of goodwill under the recent Opinions No. 16 and 17 of the APB."[83] Edwin L. Cohen, Assistant Secretary of the Treasury for Tax Policy, aware that an accounting principle was available that could possibly be used by taxing authorities, believed that amortization of goodwill would result in balancing capital gains applicable to the seller with ordinary deductions applicable to the buyer. Countering this argument, Henry Hill stated that

> this objection fails to take into account that the capital gains tax would be imposed immediately and the ordinary deduction would be spread over future periods. There is not enough difference between capital gain and ordinary income rates of corporations to offset the discounted effect of anything but a very short amortization period. Thus, on balance, the government would be ahead.[84]

Notwithstanding these arguments and a few other articles scattered through the seventies, nonamortization for tax purposes appeared firmly entrenched as the eighties began. The policy never appears to have been seriously threatened or reconsidered, and the precedents established in the twenties continued unchanged.

Goodwill and Pooling of Interests Accounting

In the following discussion as in the comparable section of Chapter VI, primary concern is directed to goodwill, its relation to the pooling issue, and how use of the pooling treatment affected accounting for the asset.[85] Pooling of interests accounting is considered only insofar as it bears on these points.

Significance and Scope of the Problem: As noted earlier, accounting for business combinations became entangled in a wide range of problems affecting accounting and the profession. As a result of the trend in accounting literature toward amortization of intangibles that eventually culminated in Opinion No. 17's required amortization of goodwill, many firms attempted to avoid the effects of this treatment in their financial statements by resorting to pooling of interests accounting. In a period of rising prices, the pooling treatment avoided the effects of recording higher figures for other assets as well. The pooling treatment soon became a refuge for merger-minded firms as the result of deterioration in the criteria concerning its use. Erosion of the standards, with the possible aid of the accounting firms themselves, led to abuses in use of pooling as well as scathing criticism of the accounting profession. Evidence of this deterioration, examples of abuse and of the resulting criticism of accountants, efforts of the profession to cope with the situation, the approach taken, and the results achieved constitute the subject matter of this section.

Erosion of the Pooling Criteria: The demise of the criteria has already been mentioned, and only the completion of that discussion remains.[86] Briefly, the similarity of interests criterion and the size criterion were eliminated by Accounting Research Bulletin No. 48. Continuity of equity interests and continuity of management proved difficult to define. The latter was once generally interpreted to mean representation on the board of directors by the parties being pooled. "Now it is sufficient if only "key personnel" come along, and satisfactory resolution of this can almost always be found or rationalized."[87]

Disregard for the standards had progressed to such an extent by 1965 that the Accounting Principles Board issued the following statement:

> The Board believes that Accounting Research Bulletin No. 48 should be continued as an expression of the general philosophy for differentiating business combinations that are purchases from those that are poolings of interests but emphasizes that the criteria set forth in paragraphs 5 and 6 are illustrative guides and not necessarily literal requirements.[88]

Ignored in practice and liberally construed by the accounting profession, the standards virtually ceased to exist. The Securities and Exchange Commission provided the only effective limitations on employment of the pooling treatment.

APB 6 is considered by some to be the professional acknowledgement that in actual practice the *coup de grace* had been rendered with respect to pooling standards. The word "professional" has been used because the SEC stands in the background and it has in fact largely set what standards there remain by refusing to go beyond certain limits as set by it. This is a very unhealthy state of affairs.[89]

Criticism of the Accounting Profession: When the criteria were effectively abandoned, the accounting treatment for pooling was used by acquisition-minded firm managers to manipulate published reports of earnings with the possible acquiescence and help of public accountants and governmental or regulatory agencies. Briloff, discussing the pooling problem from the viewpoint of misleading stockholders and diluting their shares, stated:

> The process of shareholder delusion through share dilution continues unabated. It can, in my opinion, be fairly inferred that this delusion-dilution process goes on with the specific approval, and probably also the guidance, of the independent auditors for the acquiring entity, and with the direct knowledge and consent of the Securities and Exchange Commission, as well as the committees on stock listing for the several exchanges, including the New York Stock Exchange.[90]

Several interesting practices arose such as the part-purchase/part-pooling method, and retroactive pooling. Part-purchase/part-pooling was used where a substantial part of the acquired entity's stock had been obtained by cash and the remainder was purchased with the acquiring firm's stock. The purchasing company would then contend that the portion of the absorbed firm's stock obtained with stock was in effect a pooling of interest—albeit only partially. Thus the acquiring firm achieved the advantages of the pooling method in proportion to that part of the transaction involving stock traded for stock. The method was therefore useful "for keeping goodwill to a minimum and building immediate earnings."

> If neither of these elements presents a problem in a given transaction, the acquisition is likely to be treated as a purchase. This "doublethink" is objectionable from a theoretical viewpoint and represents an example of Gresham's Law in operation because the door is hereby opened to opportunistic accounting.
> The partial-pooling, because it has not been logically conceived, will eventually become a "hot potato" and an additional source of embarrassment to the profession if it continues to be used.[91]

Retroactive poolings, occurring mainly from 1957 to 1963, were the result of a unique set of circumstances. At the time of the issuance of Bulletin No. 48 in 1957, the pooling criteria either were dropped or were in various stages of decay.[92] Furthermore, the Bulletin's more liberal provisions would have allowed some transactions that had been treated as purchases before 1957 to be treated as poolings. Some of the firms so affected then changed their financial statements from the year of the acquisition forward in order to portray the business combination as if it had been treated as a pooling of interests in the first place. The pooling treatment therefore became retroactive in the accounts of the firm.

A. N. Mosich harshly criticized the method and the profession. Finding no retroactive poolings after 1963, he stated, "After that, if pooling treatment was the more advantageous for acquiring company, it was probably adopted at the outset."[93]

When the change was put into effect, the company stated in supplemental listing applications to the New York Stock Exchange that its independent accountants had found the change to be in accordance with generally accepted accounting principles. "Of course, in each of these cases, the original use of purchase accounting to record the merger was viewed by the same accountants as being in accordance with generally accepted accounting principles."[94]

The magnitude of the issue can be appreciated upon realizing, as Mosich noted, that most of the retroactive poolings were approved by the largest and most prominent accounting firms in the world. "Only one of the largest eight accounting firms failed to approve any such changes."[95]

What appears to be a classic example of abuse through this treatment occurred when one firm treated as a retroactive pooling its combination with another and three years later sold the firm with which it had retroactively pooled.

> Although the concept of pooling does not necessarily prohibit the sale of a previously pooled unit, the cohesive force of the "corporate marriage" (pooling) may be questioned when one party to the "marriage" can readily sell of [sic] dispose of the other.[96]

Terms other than "marriage" might better describe the relationship. Mosich concluded that

> if guidelines established by the accounting profession continue to be overly permissive in this area, then the accounting profession must share the blame with management for any onerous consequences accruing to users of financial statements as a result of applying such loose guidelines.[97]

Studies during this period sponsored by the American Institute of Certified Public Accountants and the American Accounting Association called for curtailment or abolition of pooling of interests accounting. Six years after Bulletin No. 48 was issued, Wyatt's study of business combinations advocated restricting pooling accounting to certain rare instances and then advocated a pooling treatment unlike that currently used.[98] In 1966 the Association's statement on accounting theory recommended disallowance of the technique, stating that "this is perhaps the classic case of quantifiability and verifiability warring with relevance," with the question of relevance too large to be ignored.[99] The

Institute's study on goodwill by Catlett and Olson in 1968 recommended doing away with the treatment.[100]

Meanwhile, time was passing. Eleven years transpired between the issuance of Bulletin No. 48 and the Institute's Accounting Research Study No. 10. While the largest business combination movement in history was taking place, no official guides for the profession beyond the practically defunct ones of Bulletin No. 48 had appeared for the handling of mergers. Therefore, in testimony before the House Committee on Interstate and Foreign Commerce on February 25, 1969, Hamer Budge, then chairman of the Securities and Exchange Commission, stated in relation to the business combination issue:

> We recognize that this is a highly controversial area of accounting in which many judgment factors are involved, both in the matter of the initial accounting for the acquisition and in the disposition of goodwill when it appears. Consistent with our practice ever since 1933, we have supported efforts of the accounting profession to solve these problems. If this does not lead to prompt action, the urgency of the situation may dictate rule-making by the Commission.[101]

The issues and problems surrounding goodwill in accounting had thus transcended the immediate aspects of the asset's treatment in accounts and now involved an important aspect of the future direction of the accounting profession.

Accounting Principles Board Opinion No. 16: In the following discussion, events occurring in 1969 and in 1970 through the issuance of Opinion No. 16 are listed in chronological order and some aspects of the Opinion are summarized. The impact of the events and the Opinion are then discussed and analyzed.

Summary of events. In June 1969 the APB held a symposium on accounting for business combinations in which representatives of fifteen business and professional organizations were invited to submit memorandums on the issue. The basic decision confronting the APB was "whether (1) all business combinations should be accounted for by a single method or (2) differing circumstances should require or permit two or more accepted methods."[102]

At its November meeting the Board concluded that pooling should be abolished but changed its mind a month later, stating that both the pooling and purchase methods should be retained—but not as alternatives.[103] Issued in late February 1970, the exposure draft's provisions would have significantly limited the pooling treatment, containing among other things a controversial clause restricting the pooling treatment to companies at least one-third as large as the firm with which they were combining.[104] Amid rising debate and threats of lawsuits, the size test was relaxed at the Board's June meeting from a ratio of three to one to a ratio of nine to one and was dropped altogether when APB Opinion No. 16 was issued in August.[105]

Impact of the Opinion. As noted earlier, the trend, due to the abuse of the pooling treatment and the bad publicity given the profession, was to completely do away with the pooling treatment, and such an idea was originally proposed in pre-exposure draft meetings. The pooling treatment was included in the exposure draft but was restricted in its application through very specific guidelines. Such restrictions would have been hard enough on the business community had they been the only thing proposed for handling business combinations, but a concurrent move was made to reduce the number of alternatives for handling the goodwill asset by requiring its amortization.

The debate concerning the proposed treatment focused on two points: (1) the required amortization of goodwill, discussed earlier in this chapter, and (2) the criteria for determining the treatment of a transaction as either a purchase or a pooling. One attempt was aimed at liberalizing the treatment of goodwill once it had been recorded; the other was an attempt to keep it from being recorded in the first place. The required amortization provisions remained the same, but the pooling-purchase provisions, though still substantially restrictive, were liberalized to allow more poolings of interests.

The most general criticism leveled at the business combinations provisions of the Accounting Principles Board was that the Board was trying to restrict business combinations. In the absence of an Opinion or proposed Opinion by the Board, a combination could take place. Otherwise, the proposed accounting treatment would have too much of an unfavorable effect on the merger for it to be carried out.

Particularly under attack was the Board's size test, which held that a purchase was presumed to take place when the ratio of the size of the companies was greater than three to one. Under mounting attack and a threatened law suit by companies that stood to be affected by the provision, the size test was changed from three to one in its original form to nine to one in later meetings and was finally dropped altogether, although complaints were still voiced that the revised provisions similarly restricted business combinations. Those who felt that the APB's goals should not restrict business combinations presumably believed that accounting methods should not be adopted that would affect the occurrence of mergers. Such a point of view was unrealistic, however. If indeed it ever had been, it was no longer possible to idealistically propose accounting rules that would not be embroiled in merger decisions, since accounting methods, and particularly the pooling treatment, were already being used to manipulate data in financial statements. Any new rules would most certainly affect the outcome of business combinations. The old ones had been used for that purpose for years.

The size test was further attacked because it was arbitrary—a serious criticism that could be leveled at almost all of the criteria. Part of the problem of less specific criteria, as evidenced in the demise of the pooling criteria, was that they were very liberally construed and eventually ignored. Seidman, in specifically defending the size test, admitted that it was arbitrary but felt that guidelines must be established in order to implement any basic principle.

> He drew an analogy with the accepted legal and social principle that certain rights, such as the right to vote or enter into contracts, are

denied to minors. Once this principle is accepted, he said, an arbitrary parameter, such as an individual's twenty-first birthday, must be adopted to distinguish childhood from adulthood.[106]

The size test was eventually dropped, but the remaining criteria were retained in their explicit form. Still, there were those who felt that the APB's aim to limit poolings could be bypassed. As one writer noted: "Unfortunately, a detailed 'legislative' approach which eliminated judgment places a premium on deft maneuvering."[107]

Aside from various characteristics of the solution, final judgment has to rest with the content and subsequent effect of the solution itself. Opinion No. 16, curtailing but not abolishing the use of the pooling method, represented a compromise between the Board and its critics. The compromise approach, which appears to be kin to the legislative idea discussed earlier, was itself subject to severe criticism. A *Wall Street Journal* article written shortly after the three-to-one size test had been relaxed to nine to one stated: "The accounting profession's top rule-making body took a step toward tightening the guidelines for corporate mergers. What ended as a step, however, started as a long stride."[108]

An interesting point of conjecture is how the above quote would have been worded after the nine-to-one test itself had been abolished. More damaging than that, however, are the words of the Institute's own executive vice-president, Leonard Savoie, in an address delivered in September 1969 (before even the exposure draft was released), which stated that a forthcoming draft abolishing pooling and requiring mandatory amortization would be issued. He went on to say: "Anything less than this solution will mean simply a 'repositioning' of the abuses which have become so rampant in recent years."[109]

After the exposure draft was released and before Opinion No. 16 was issued, Briloff quoted these remarks and noted with some degree of acerbity and premonition:

> Late February brought the anxiously-awaited exposure draft of the APB proposed Opinion on "Business Combinations and Intangible Assets." I leave it to the reader to judge whether this is a "forthright solution" or a "repositioning of the abuses." More importantly, the reader is urged to apply the Savoie standards to evaluate what may ultimately evolve as the APB's Opinion on this "current crisis."[110]

Relating the preceding discussion specifically to the asset goodwill, the criteria for restricting poolings of interests were conversely the criteria for recognizing goodwill in the accounts. Therefore, the problems just discussed in connection with Opinion No. 16 were not only applicable to poolings of interests but also to initial recognition of goodwill—a point not lost on those still seeking to avoid the asset's recognition. In the four years after Opinion No. 16 was issued, the American Institute of Certified Public Accountants issued thirty-nine interpretations and the SEC issued four Accounting Series Releases in an attempt to facilitate implementation of the criteria and to close existing "loopholes."[111]

Notwithstanding the great amount of time and energy expended on accounting for business combinations, the issue has always seemed to smolder, even during those rare and relatively tranquil moments in its troubled history—now extending to over thirty years. The very nature of pooling versus purchase accounting is an interesting but exasperating practical and theoretical quagmire—made more difficult by the issues and problems surrounding accounting for goodwill. In its first month of existence, the FASB issued an open letter requesting views on previous APB pronouncements. The FASB found that Opinions Nos. 16 and 17 most needed the Board's attention. While the discussion memorandum *Accounting for Business Combinations and Purchased Intangibles* was issued in 1976, no action had been taken for several years, pending completion of various aspects of the Board's conceptual framework project.[112]

Notwithstanding a statement dealing with intangible assets of motor carriers, the Board in 1981 finally dropped consideration of the larger issue of business combinations and purchased intangibles because of the project's "low priority in relation to other existing and potential projects."[113]

Summary

Accounting for goodwill, either directly or in connection with related issues, is not entirely settled. This assessment is not a complaint, however, for it could have been made in any of the previous one hundred years and, regardless of the FASB's ultimate actions, may be applicable for many years to come. The issues and problems surrounding accounting for goodwill continue to be intriguing and puzzling to accounting practitioners, authoritative groups, academicians, and accounting historians. The last chapter has not been written on this asset. It thus appears fitting to close the historical sections of this study covering almost one hundred years and approximately one thousand articles and books by stating that "the jury is still out."

---

1. Council of the American Institute of Certified Public Accountants, *Special Bulletin: Disclosure of Departures from Opinions of Accounting Principles Board,* reprinted in American Institute of Certified Public Accountants, Accounting Principles Board, *Status of Accounting Research Bulletins,* Opinions of the Accounting Principles Board, No. 6 (New York: American Institute of Certified Public Accountants, Inc., 1965), p. 48; Emmett S. Harrington, "Important Issues Being Discussed by the Accounting Principles Board," *Management Accounting,* December 1970, p. 10.

2. Study on Establishment of Accounting Principles, *Establishing Financial Accounting Standards: Report of the Study on Establishment of Accounting Principles* (New York: American Institute of Certified Public Accountants, Inc., 1972), p. 35.

3. Ibid., p. 36.

4. Ibid., p. 8.

5. Ibid., p. 1.

6. Ibid., pp. 7-11.

7. Ibid., p. 37.

8. Ibid., p. 38.

9. American Institute of Certified Public Accountants, Accounting Principles Board, *Business Combinations,* Opinions of the Accounting Principles Board, No. 16 (New York: American Institute of Certified Public Accountants, Inc., 1970), pp. 279-327; American Institute of Certified Public Accountants, Accounting Principles Board, *Intangible Assets,* Opinions of the Accounting Principles Board, No. 17 (New York: American Institute of Certified Public Accountants, Inc., 1970), pp. 331-344.

10. See pp. 80-82.

11. Accounting Principles Board, *Intangible Assets*, p. 333.

12. Ibid., pp. 336, 338-339.

13. See p. 114.

14. American Institute of Certified Public Accountants, Accounting Principles Board, *Financial Statements Restated for General Price-Level Changes*, Statement of the Accounting Principles Board, No. 3 (New York: American Institute of Certified Public Accountants, Inc. 1969).

15. See p. 114.

16. American Accounting Association, Committee to Prepare a Statement of Basic Accounting Theory, *A Statement of Basic Accounting Theory* (Evanston, Illinois: American Accounting Association, 1966), p. 78.

17. Ibid., p. 79.

18. Financial Accounting Standards Board, *Financial Reporting and Changing Prices,* Statement of Financial Accounting Standards No. 33 (Stamford, Connecticut: Financial Accounting Standards Board, 1979).

19. Ibid., pp. 6, 10-12.

20. Jules Backman, "An Economist Looks at Accounting for Business Combinations," *Financial Analysts Journal,* July-August, 1970, pp. 43-45.

21. Leonard Spacek, "The Treatment of Goodwill in the Corporate Balance Sheet," *The Journal of Accountancy,* February 1964, pp. 35-40.

22. American Institute of Certified Public Accountants, Accounting Principles Board, *Reporting the Results of Operations,* Opinions of the Accounting Principles Board, No. 9 (New York: American Institute of Certified Public Accountants, Inc., 1967), pp. 35-40.

23. Ibid., *Intangible Assets.*

24. See pp. 119-120.

25. Accounting Principles Board, *Reporting the Results of Operations,* pp. 112-115.

26. Ibid.

27. See p. 149.

28. American Institute of Certified Public Accountants, Accounting Principles Board, *Reporting the Results of Operations–Reporting the Effects of Disposal of a Business, and Extraordinary, Unusual and Infrequently Occurring Events and Transactions,* Opinions of the Accounting Principles Board, No. 30 (New York: American Institute of Certified Public Accountants, Inc., 1973) pp. 556, 564-566.

29. Financial Accounting Standards Board, *Prior Period Adjustments,* Statement of Financial Accounting Standards No. 16 (Stamford, Connecticut: Financial Accounting Standards Board, 1977), p. 5.

30. In actual practice, however, the treatment was retaining its popularity. See pp. 152-154.

31. One of the few writers during this period who appeared to support the permanent retention of goodwill was Knortz. Herbert C. Knortz, "Economic Realism and Business Combinations," *Financial Executive,* April 1970, pp. 48-60.

32. George R. Catlett and Norman O. Olson, *Accounting for Goodwill,* Accounting Research Study No. 10 (New York: American Institute of Certified Public Accountants, Inc., 1968).

33. Spacek, "The Treatment of Goodwill in the Corporate Balance Sheet," p. 36.

34. Catlett and Olson, *Accounting for Goodwill,* p. 107.

35. Ibid.

36. William A. Paton, "Comments of William A. Paton," in Catlett and Olson, *Accounting for Goodwill,* p. 143.

37. Spacek, "The Treatment of Goodwill in the Corporate Balance Sheet," p. 39.

38. Delmer P. Hylton, "The Treatment of Goodwill" (Letters to the Editor), *The Journal of Accountancy,* April 1964, p. 30.

39. Leonard Spacek, "The Treatment of Goodwill" (Letters to the Editor), *The Journal of Accountancy,* April 1964, p. 31.

40. Wolfgang Wolff, "Accounting for Intangibles," *The Canadian Chartered Accountant,* October 1967, p. 258.

41. Delmer P. Hylton, "Implications of the Direct Write-off of Goodwill," *The New York Certified Public Accountant,* December 1966, p. 918.

42. Ibid., p. 919.

43. Catlett and Olson, *Accounting for Goodwill,* pp. xii, 116-166.

44. Paul A. Pacter, "Accounting for Business Combinations: The Evolution of an APB Opinion," *The Journal of Accountancy,* August 1969, pp. 66-67.

45. "SEC Chairman Budge Testifies on 'Poolings' and Goodwill," *The Journal of Accountancy,* April 1969, p. 16.

46. See, for example, the exchange of letters between Alexander Eulenberg and Leonard Spacek, "More Comments and Replies on Goodwill," *The Journal of Accountancy,* July 1964, pp. 53-55. Also see Piaker's article and subsequent correspondence between Robert L. May and Piaker. Philip M. Piaker, " 'Non-Accounting' for Goodwill—A Critical Analysis of Accounting Research," Study No. 10, *The New York Certified Public Accountant,* November 1969, pp. 837-844; Robert L. May, "Criticizes 'Illogical' Assumption in Professor Piaker's

Article (Letters to the Editor)," Ibid., March 1970, p. 181; Piaker and May, "More on 'Non-Accounting for Goodwill—A Critical Analysis of Accounting Research Study No. 10'," Ibid., August 1970, pp. 613-614.

47. Herbert C. Knortz, "The Realities of Business Combinations," *Financial Analysts Journal,* July-August 1970, p. 31.

48. See p. 117.

49. Wolff, "Accounting for Intangibles," p. 258.

50. Backman, "An Economist Looks at Accounting for Business Combinations," p. 45.

51. See p. 140.

52. Arthur Andersen & Co., "Before the Accounting Principles Board: Proposed Opinion: Business Combinations and Intangible Assets: Brief and Argument of Arthur Andersen & Co.," May 15, 1970. (Hereinafter referred to as "Brief and Argument.")

53. Accounting Principles Board, *Intangible Assets,* p. 333.

54. Ibid., pp. 332, 338.

55. Ibid.

56. Ibid., pp. 338-340.

57. Ibid., pp. 339-341.

58. Ibid., pp. 342-343.

59. Arthur Andersen & Co., "Brief and Argument," p. 4.

60. Knortz, "Economic Realism and Business Combinations," p. 58.

61. Philip L. Defliese, "The APB and Its Recent and Pending Opinions," *The Journal of Accountancy,* February 1971, p. 68.

62. Ibid.

63. Frederic Andrews, "Proposed Measurement of Corporate Goodwill May Curb Acquisitions," *The Wall Street Journaal,* February 27, 1970, p. 1.

64. See p. 136.

65. American Institute of Certified Public Accountants, Accounting Principles Board, *Status of Accounting Research Bulletins,* Opinions of the Accounting Principles Board, No. 6 (New York: American Institute of Certified Public Accountants, Inc., 1965), p. 37.

66. Ibid., p. 38.

67. Ibid., p. 41.

68. American Institute of Accountants, Committee on Accounting Procedure, *Restatement and Revision of Accounting Research Bulletins,* Accounting Research Bulletins, No. 43 (New York: American Institute of Accountants, 1953), p. 39.

69. Accounting Principles Board, *Status of Accounting Research Bulletins,* p. 38.

70. See p. 122.

71. Committee on Accounting Procedure, *Restatement and Revision of Accounting Research Bulletins* p. 40.

72. Ibid.; American Institute of Certified Public Accountants, Committee on Accounting Procedure, *Consolidated Financial Statements,* Accounting Research Bulletins, No. 51 (New York: American Institute of Certified Public Accountants, 1959), p. 43.

73. Committee on Accounting Procedure, *Consolidated Financial Statements,* p. 43.

74. Ibid., p. 44.

75. See pp. 59-61.

76. Ibid., pp. 60-61; Committee on Accounting Procedure, *Consolidated Financial Statements,* p. 44.

77. "SEC Chief Accountant Speaks Before NYSSCPA," *The Journal of Accountancy,* January 1970, p. 16; Leonard Spacek, "The Merger Accounting Dilemma—Proposed Solutions," *Financial Executive,* February 1970, p. 39.

78. Long-term investments in marketable securities were excluded from the allocation.

79. Accounting Principles Board, *Business Combinations,* p. 321.

80. Abraham J. Briloff, "The Accounting Profession at the Hump of the Decades," *Financial Analysts Journal*, May-June 1970, p. 61.

81. William A. Paton, "Earmarks of a Profession—and the APB," *The Journal of Accountancy*, January 1971, p. 43.

82. Walter C. Frank, "Goodwill is Not Immortal: A Proposal to Deduct the Exhaustion of Purchased Goodwill," *The Journal of Taxation*, December 1965, p. 380.

83. Henry P. Hill, "Accounting for Goodwill—Half Way Home," *Financial Executive*, March 1971, p. 42.

84. Ibid., pp. 42, 44.

85. See pp. 126-130.

86. Ibid.

87. Robert Beyer, "Goodwill and Pooling of Interests: A Re-Assessment," *Management Accounting*, February 1969, p. 11.

88. Accounting Principles Board, *Status of Accounting Research Bulletins*, p. 44.

89. Beyer, "Goodwill and Pooling of Interests: A Re-Assessment," p. 11.

90. Abraham J. Briloff, "Dirty Pooling," *The Accounting Review*, July 1967, p. 489.

91. Samuel P. Gunther, "Part Purchase—Part Pooling: The Infusion of Confusion Into Fusion," *The New York Certified Public Accountant*, April 1969, p. 247.

92. A. N. Mosich, "Retroactive Poolings in Corporate Mergers," *The Journal of Business*, July 1968, p. 357.

93. Ibid.

94. Ibid., p. 359.

95. Ibid., p. 360.

96. Ibid.

97. Ibid. p. 362.

98. Arthur R. Wyatt, *A Critical Study of Accounting for Business Combinations,* Accounting Research Study No. 5 (New York: American Institute of Certified Public Accountants, 1963), pp. 105, 107.

99. Committee to Prepare a Statement of Basic Accounting Theory, *A Statement of Basic Accounting Theory,* p. 33.

100. Catlett and Olson, *Accounting for Goodwill,* p. 106.

101. "SEC Chief Accountant Speaks Before NYSSCPA," pp. 16 and 19.

102. Pacter, "Accounting for Business Combinations: the Evolution of an APB Opinion," pp. 64-65.

103. "APB May Abolish Pooling of Interests," *The Journal of Accountancy,* November 1969, p. 19; "APB: Accounting for Business Combinations, Ibid., January 1970, p. 8.

104. American Institute of Certified Public Accountants, Accounting Principles Board, *Exposure Draft: Proposed APB Opinion: Business Combinations and Intangible Assets* (New York: American Institute of Certified Public Accountants, Inc., 1970), p. 11.

105. "Accounting Group Moves to Tighten Rules on Mergers," *The Wall Street Journal,* June 29, 1970, p. 3.

106. "Accounting Principles Board Proposes 'Merger' Opinion," *The Journal of Accountancy,* April 1970, p. 12.

107. Samuel P. Gunther, "Poolings—Purchase—Goodwill," *The New York Certified Public Accountant,* January 1971, p. 35.

108. "Accounting Group Moves to Tighten Rules on Mergers," p. 3.

109. Briloff, "The Accounting Profession at the Hump of the Decades," p. 61.

110. Ibid.

111. The twelve criteria, their implementation, interpretation, and problems associated therewith, are discussed in detail in several articles by Samuel P. Gunther. Three of his articles—very illuminative on the subject—are Gunther, "Poolings—Purchase—Goodwill," pp. 25-37; Samuel P. Gunther, "Financial Reporting for Mergers and Acquisitions: Current Problems with Pooling and Purchasing," *Mergers & Acquisitions: The Journal of Corporate Venture,* Winter 1974, pp. 8-20; Samuel P. Gunther, "Financial Reporting for Mergers and Acquisitions Revisited: Current Problems with Pooling and Purchasing," *Ibid.,* Spring 1977, pp. 4-8.

112. Financial Accounting Standards Board, "Status Report No. 96, January 11, 1980" (Stamford, Connecticut: Financial Accounting Standards Board, 1980), p. 3.

113. Financial Accounting Standards Board, "Status Report No. 114, April 10, 1981" (Stamford, Connecticut: Financial Accounting Standards Board, 1981), p. 3. Financial Accounting Standards Board, *Accounting for Intangibles Assets of Motor Carriers,* Statement of Financial Accounting Standards No. 44 (Stamford, Connecticut: Financial Accounting Standards Board, 1980).

Chapter VIII

An Inquiry into the Nature of Goodwill

Introduction

> It differs from other property, inasmuch as, while other property is palpable, goodwill is impalpable. Other property can be handled, weighed, or measured, its nature ascertained by inspection, its quality tested by sight, smell, feeling, or analysis, or the annual income receivable from it identified. But goodwill—how can its quality be ascertained? The difference between the two kinds of property is like that between matter and life, or between a man's estate and a man's character—one is ponderable, the other imponderable.[1]

More than a century has passed since the first accounting article on goodwill appeared, and in that time goodwill has been defined in literally hundreds of ways. In fact the most striking feature of this literature is not that most of the definitions are similar, but that many of them are different and in some cases, as pointed out in Chapter I, even conflicting. Much of this variation arises from the subjectivity inherent in the asset goodwill. Subjectivity pervades the asset, and although some attempts have been made to ignore it or even to define goodwill precisely in spite of it, the fact remains that subjectivity is a central feature of goodwill as an asset and, consequently, a central feature of the nature of goodwill. This rather nebulous quality thus becomes a matter not to be avoided but addressed, and one important goal of this chapter is to explain subjectivity where possible or at least to help the reader understand why it exists.

Objectives and Limitations

In this study, goodwill has been viewed on three levels: (1) the nature of goodwill, (2) the accountant's perception of goodwill, and (3) the accountant's treatment of the asset in accounting records and financial statements. In the previous five chapters, goodwill was discussed with reference primarily to its accounting aspects and how its treatment has evolved in the ten or so decades since the 1880s. In this chapter, the main emphasis is on the analysis of the nature of goodwill in order to gain an understanding of the economic significance of the asset and the role or function of goodwill within the framework of business enterprise.

As noted in Chapter I, goodwill has been considered throughout the study to be a product of its environment—a reflection of the dominant form of business existing at any point in time. Therefore, before goodwill can be analyzed and understood, the current business environment must be depicted.

The institutional framework and ideas of Thorstein Veblen and John Kenneth Galbraith were utilized as authoritative sources to provide a setting of the current business environment. Their ideas constitute a point of departure for an inquiry into the nature of goodwill.

Organization of the Chapter

In this chapter, goodwill's inception and evolution are traced and analyzed within an institutional framework, culminating in a definition of goodwill that is applicable to the contemporary economic environment. Then, characteristics traditionally associated with the goodwill asset are reconsidered, and the asset is examined in relation to its accounting treatment. Thus, this chapter introduces a contemporary theory of goodwill, offering both a broad view of goodwill and a detailed analysis of specific traits and characteristics. Specifically, the chapter is organized in the following manner:

1. A "working definition" of goodwill is first presented in which both objective and subjective aspects of the asset are introduced.

2. The framework used is that contained in Thorstein Veblen's two articles entitled "On the Nature of Capital."[2] This section summarizes and interprets those portions of his argument relevant to the present discussion and applies them to patents and goodwill.

3. Much has changed in the business world since 1908 when Veblen wrote his articles, and an interpretation of these changes has been documented by John Kenneth Galbraith in his book, *The New Industrial State.*[3] In this section some of Galbraith's ideas are sketched, to provide a basis for new implications concerning the development and maintenance of goodwill, resulting in a contemporary definition of the asset.

4. A number of characteristics of intangibles generally and goodwill specifically have been discussed in accounting literature for over seventy years. Each of these are reexamined in this section with regard to the modern environment.

5. The last section ties together ideas concerning the nature of goodwill and its contemporary accounting concept and treatment.

Goodwill—a Working Definition

Returning to the "working definition" of goodwill offered in Chapter II, goodwill may be thought of as the differential ability of one business, in comparison with another or an assumed average firm, to make a profit. The concrete aspects of this broad and fundamental view are that goodwill is a phenomenon of business enterprise, and its presence is indicated by better than ordinary profits. Furthermore, the profits that manifest. the existence of goodwill must be compared with some standard or norm, either actual or assumed.

The subjective aspects of goodwill arise from the same elements of goodwill that provide its objectivity. In an economic sense, goodwill has virtually no meaning apart from business enterprise—indeed, it is defined in terms of business success. Discussed at length in Chapter II, however, was the evolution and evolutionary nature of business—even now an ongoing process that continuously influences the way in which goodwill arises, the forms in which it appears, and the manner in which it may be sustained.

Historically, the ability to make and sustain profits was directly associated with the rise of business. The goal of livelihood in feudal times was gradually replaced by the goal of profit, and comparisons with other businesses or, ultimately, to some normal business or profit figure resulted in the measurement and conceptualization of goodwill.

> Because, theoretically, if there were not the presupposition of a normal return in business there could be no value attributable to the various intangible factors, and all income would be looked upon as the direct product of the investment in other assets, leaving no credit for any intangible property.[4]

If a "normal return" is a construct of the mind, then goodwill itself is a figment of our imagination and changes with our perception of what constitutes a normal return. At different times and for different industries a normal return may vary, causing the measurement if not the perception of goodwill to change accordingly.

Summary and Interpretation of Ideas from Veblen

Tangible Assets

In a two-part study "On the Nature of Capital," published in 1908, Thorstein Veblen presented among other points an evolutionary analysis of the origin and accumulation of capital involving the relationship of capital to the community, the development of property rights, and the advent of business enterprise. His study provides a more detailed analysis of goodwill and its evolution by examining the necessary elements preceding its development, by contrasting tangible and intangible assets, and by contrasting goodwill and other intangibles.

Early in his work, Veblen pointed out that at any given time there is in the keeping of a community a stock of knowledge that all members of society draw on for their needs. The level of knowledge is gradually augmented by individuals in the group, though the particular contribution of each individual to a particular invention may be relatively insignificant as compared to the previous knowledge embodied in it. This knowledge has always been held loosely by the community at large, and in early cultural states the material contrivances necessary to use the knowledge were held in the same manner. At that point, any individual with the requisite diligence and intelligence could make the implements necessary for his well-being. Eventually, however, the body of knowledge grew to the point that the tangible equipment required to put the knowledge into effect became more complex relative to the capacity of the individual. In other words, the tools became harder to produce and replace.[5]

At this point, certain important conclusions from Veblen's work may be drawn. Notice that in any cultural setting, whether quite primitive or very modern, the tools merely represent or use the level of knowledge present at any given time. Veblen's analysis points out that at some point the tools become quite difficult to manufacture. Although the interrelation of knowledge and equipment remains as before, the equipment is so hard to obtain that it becomes a matter of strategic consequence.

As a result, property rights arose, and men took steps to insure the ownership of their property; those who possessed the contrivances had the advantage over those who did not.[6] Regardless of who possessed the skill to operate the equipment, the individual who *owned* the equipment *controlled* its employment. In other words, he who controls the equipment controls to that extent the manifestations of a community's knowledge.

As technology changes, the ability of a specific object to confer strategic economic advantage also changes. At various stages of civilization the strategic emphasis has been on labor (thus promoting slavery), cattle, land, and—more recently—industrial equipment.[7]

Once individuals acquired control of strategic property and the private enterprise system evolved, properties could be examined from two points of view: (1) that of the community as a whole and (2) that of the individual or enterprise owning them. The community might benefit from employment of the items, but such benefit was not the controlling issue. The main consideration focused on the individual who sought to profit from the advantages derived from property rights. In brief, the things the individual controlled were valuable to the community to the extent they contributed to its welfare, but they were of value to the individual (and were capitalized) to the extent they augmented that person's profits.[8]

When profitability became a primary goal of ownership, and the items owned were valued according to how much profit they rendered, then these items began to be thought of in the modern-day connotation as assets. While other characteristics may well be added to ownership and profitability, such as the ability to sell or transfer the equipment, and although exceptions might be pointed out, these are, at least initially, two important ingredients of an asset and, to a great extent, still convey the term "asset," as it is commonly understood.

Once business enterprise has developed, however, it becomes possible for goodwill to be fostered and ultimately sustained; thus the necessary prerequisites for goodwill's existence are complete. There must exist a level of knowledge sufficiently complex to bring about ownership, and ownership must exist within a framework of business enterprise. Whatever the previous goal of ownership, the new goal becomes profit. Thus by inference, the individual who uses strategically valuable property (strategic since it controls employment of a portion of the community's knowledge) more profitably than others do possesses goodwill.

Intangible Assets

While the preceding paragraph introduced goodwill, more needs to be said about intangibles generally and goodwill specifically. Capital equipment, evolving into the category of tangible assets, is associated with production of goods, while intangibles as a group are associated with their distribution. Due to law and custom, certain individuals or groups enjoyed preferential treatment through devices such as franchises, letters patent, or trade protection. After business enterprise emerged, these devices were incorporated into the system and became recognized as intangible assets to the extent they were transferable.[9]

Patents as Intangible Assets: A patent granted for an invention illustrates the characteristics of intangibles and their relationship to tangible assets. Assuming the invention is a unique production process, the equipment embodying the new idea is a tangible asset through which its owner attempts to make a profit and the community attempts to obtain a livelihood. In the absence of the patent, however, anyone with the necessary means would be allowed to make or buy similar equipment, so the only asset existing would be the tangible one. The patent subsequently gives rise to a second form of wealth based on restricting the use and sale of the equipment and its product to the patent holder. Thus the patent becomes an intangible asset since its basis is the custom and ultimately the law of society to grant them as rewards for innovation. The basis of many tangibles, by contrast, is generally technical or scientific knowledge as manifested in equipment. Therefore, the innovation itself affects the productive capability of the community, while the patent right as a legal instrument affects distribution of the benefits to be enjoyed from the increased productive capability.[10] Veblen, comparing tangible and intangible assets, stated:

> Both are assets,—that is to say, both are values determined by a capitalization of anticipated income-yielding capacity; both depend for their income-yielding capacity on the preferential use of certain immaterial factors; both depend for their efficiency on the use of certain material objects; both may increase or decrease, as assets, apart from any increase or decrease of the material objects involved. The tangible assets capitalize the preferential use of technological, industrial expedients,—expedients of production, dealing with the facts of brute nature under the laws of physical cause and effect,— this preferential use being secured by the ownership of material

articles employed in the processes in which these expedients are put into effect. The intangible assets capitalize the preferential use of certain facts of human nature—habits, propensities, beliefs, aspirations, necessities—to be dealt with under the psychological laws of human motivation; this preferential use being secured by custom, as in the case of old-fashioned goodwill, by legal assignment, as in patent or copyright, by ownership of the instruments of production, as in the case of industrial monopolies.[11]

Goodwill as an intangible asset:

Personal goodwill. In similar fashion the preceding analysis may be applied to the asset goodwill. Originally, the goodwill associated with a business appears to have resulted from a favorable attitude on the part of the customer toward the business based on the businessperson's reputation for honesty and fair dealing. The merchant quite literally enjoyed the goodwill of his customers, and, just as in ownership of a patent, possessed two forms of wealth. First the merchant possessed the tangible assets on which the trade was built, and, second, he or she possessed another asset because of the extraordinary volume of trade attracted. In the case of a patent, however, trade was restricted by law through ownership of the patent, while for goodwill trade was restricted only by the habit and choice of the customer.

The momentum idea of goodwill. A trade restriction such as the habit of a customer—however tenuous that may be—seems to be the basis, or at least may serve as one, for the momentum idea of goodwill. Anyone might go into competition with an established and reputable trader, but any new business would presumably need time for its own trade to develop. Notice that, where elementary forms of goodwill are concerned, the emphasis is not so much on building internal momentum as it is in hoping that one's customers build their momentum of trading with the firm. Such a process could occur much more slowly than it might otherwise appear because one may be depending on customers to change their habits of trading elsewhere. At any rate, the monetary value of the goodwill will be expressed in the ability either to charge higher prices, to sell more goods, or both.

Contributing to this ability, and possibly representing a more active way of pursuing momentum, may be the costs of eliminating competition. For example, Herbert C. Freeman noted that

> a theatre used for vaudeville or "legitimate" drama in a chain of motion-picture houses may be an unprofitable venture, but its ownership may prevent its use by other proprietors for motion-picture purposes in competition with one of the profitable houses in the chain. Instances of this kind can be multiplied, and similar conditions affecting manufacturing and trading concerns will frequently be met.[12]

Tangible Assets, Various Intangibles, and Goodwill—A Comparison

All assets—tangible or intangible—incorporate and/or engross some portion of a community's knowledge for profit-making purposes. In the case of many assets characterized as tangibles (such as inventory, plant, and equipment), the knowledge is of a technical nature, while intangibles universally derive value from knowledge involving law and custom. As a class, intangibles are thus technologically unproductive, representing a second way in which other assets may be made more profitable. Paton illustrated much the same point and brought in the discipline of accounting when he stated:

> In part, ... the intangible asset accounts exhibit the duplicate representation of wealth which arises out of the fact that accounting is based upon the point of view of the specific enterprise rather than that of the community.[13]

Within the category of intangibles, the value of those such as patents is sustained through law, while the value of goodwill is secured through custom. Louis O. Foster similarly added an accounting dimension to his discussion of intangibles when he wrote:

> Intangible assets are either the general claims against a whole society for a special privilege or a capitalization of probable excess earning power for which some outlay has been made. Patents, copyrights, franchises, and trade-marks are examples of the first group; goodwill, organization expense, going value, and formulas are intangibles of the second type.[14]

The fact that personal goodwill, and to some extent even location goodwill (superior returns resulting from an advantageous location of the business), is built up through habit and custom has led many writers to note how elusive and unstable goodwill is in comparison with other assets, including other intangible assets. This would also apply where superior management or good employee relations is the basis of goodwill. The difference here, however, appears to be one of degree rather than of kind. Any item, once it has been considered in its dimension as an asset, may fluctuate in value—in its ability to render an income stream to its owner—for reasons such as technical obsolescence or changing trends of fashion or population, for example.

Implications of *The New Industrial State*

Most of the preceding discussion in this chapter represents points not subject to much debate in accounting or economic literature of the past one-hundred or so years. While Veblen's evolutionary framework involving community knowledge manifested through increasingly sophisticated tools is rather unique, and while he appeared to perceive various unfavorable consequences of business enterprise, the facts, as opposed to any judgments, are generally not disputed. Notice, for instance, how easy it is to reconcile the analysis of Veblen with the remarks of Paton and Foster.

If the evolution and general nature of goodwill is not open to much question, the modern day source of the asset is. It is particularly at this point that subjectivity concerning the asset arises and the accounting issues and questions documented in Chapters III through VII begin to manifest themselves. Varying treatments are possible depending on whether the source of goodwill is deemed to be from personal factors, from the location of the business, or from advertising, for example.

So any interpretation of the source of goodwill must remain just that—a matter of opinion, no matter how logical the rationalization. Thus the choice of one economic authority and viewpoint instead of another can lead to different conclusions and is subject to legitimate question. Furthermore, others may feel that it is possible, even after a viewpoint is chosen, to extrapolate yet other conclusions from those suggested here. Beauty is in the eye of the beholder, and so, with this caveat and to provide a fuller understanding of the current nature of goodwill, the following is offered as only one possible explanation of a major modern-day source of the asset.

Galbraith's Work

In an era of small businesses, goodwill is generally thought of as somewhat incidental in its development and precarious in its continued existence. The small firm is at the mercy of its environment; consequently, its owner-manager is unable to plan its activities to any extent except in response to customer actions. The customers, at their initiative, are assumed to furnish the trade from which the momentum slowly accumulates to build goodwill. In such an instance, the incidental and precarious nature of the intangible is an indication of the type of firm possessing it.

In the opinion of John Kenneth Galbraith, a different system has emerged, and he has undertaken to describe it and its implications in his extensive economic study, *The New Industrial State.* Those portions of his arguments that throw light on the present analysis are used in the subsequent discussion.[15]

Galbraith noted that the modern economic system is dominated by a relatively few large industrial corporations. As these concerns have grown, the role, function, and importance of such groups as owners, managers, customers, and the firm itself have changed. The owners have become increasingly separated from the management of the firm, and their quest for large (or maximum) profits no longer serves as the dominant interest of the firm. Increasingly sophisticated technology, coupled with heavy commitments of resources and time, has placed a great demand on those who can bring specialized knowledge to group decision making. These individuals, whom Galbraith calls the technostructure, occupy positions deep within an organization and usually are not thought of as management. Nevertheless, the group "extends from the most senior officials of the corporation to where it meets, at the other perimeter, the white and blue collar workers" and constitutes the brains of the enterprise.[16]

The technostructure possesses control in the organization and seeks to increase its own growth, and thereby its power and prestige, through growth of the firm in terms of sales, thus financing its growth and preserving its autonomy from owner interference by maintaining at least a minimum level of earnings. The commitment to growth through implementation of advanced technology and large-scale use of resources has led to the production of goods that are increasingly related to psychological wants as opposed to physical needs. At the same time that meticulous planning is made necessary for proper utilization of the organization's time and capital, demand becomes increasingly unstable to the extent that the goods so produced relate to nonnecessary items. Demand is not and cannot be allowed to behave in this manner, however, if dire economic consequences are to be averted. An ameliorative factor sets in—the further a product is removed from satisfying a necessity, the more its demand is subject to management and manipulation. The presumption that the customer takes the initiative in purchasing goods is now open to question, for the firm will devise a sales effort that will attempt "to shift the locus of decision in the purchase of goods from the consumer where it is beyond control to the firm where it is subject to control."[17]

> Thus it comes about that, as the industrial system develops to the point where it has need for planning and the management of the consumer that this requires, it is also serving wants that are pyschological in origin and hence admirably subject to management by appeal to the psyche.[18]

Implications for Goodwill

From such an economic system, important implications result for procurement and maintenance of the asset goodwill. Goodwill could still be visualized as a differential advantage based on custom and habit and accruing to a given firm, but development and maintenance of the asset have definitely changed. The customer's desire to trade with a given firm is no longer the initial step in the sequence wherein its sales, and ultimately its goodwill, if any, are gradually built up. Advertising and other forms of sales effort shift the initiative for the procurement of goodwill from the customer to the firm. In its most advanced stage of development, the cultivation of the customer's tastes is undertaken well ahead of a product's introduction, so that when the product is ready for the market, the customer has been prepared to purchase the item at the price and quantity the firm desires. No small degree of parallelism appears to exist between this situation and the growing of crops. Given the proper environment of soil and weather and the correct stimulation through fertilization, the desired result can be reasonably predicted.

The concern's preparatory work thus becomes a monumental task and must be planned with as much exactitude as the construction of fixed assets such as factories and buildings. Creating and following a blueprint for the "construction" of consumer loyalty implies that goodwill becomes just as much a planned and created asset as anything material that could be created with the same expenditure.

Customer loyalty, like any other asset, is subject to deterioration and must be constantly reinforced if a firm is to continue to grow. In such a basic area as automotive transportation, for example, innumerable changes and differentiations of makes, models, exterior and interior design, and color are made available and recur regularly for the sake of increased sales.

> In a culture which places high value on technological change, there will be a natural presumption that any "new" product is inherently superior to an old one. This attitude will be exploited by those who devise sales strategy with the result that a great many changes in product and packaging will be merely for the sake of having something that can be called new.[19]

Any given promotional expenditure associated with a particular innovation will progressively render older products obsolete concerning the change in question, and the changes will in turn be superseded by future announcements to the same effect. These cumulative changes are not haphazard, however. Their introduction is timed to coincide with the firm's planned use of its resources, which means that the duration of a certain feature's usefulness to a firm can, within limits, be reasonably predicted. The duration of benefits to be derived from promotional expenditures associated with the new or changed feature is therefore also limited and similarly predictable. Thus customer loyalty and goodwill are not only carefully constructed but are likewise maintained by continuous expenditures that, along with the corresponding benefits, are deliberately limited in existence. This conclusion also applies to expenditures made to promote the firm in general instead of specific products or innovations. Presumably these charges would be on a recurring, planned basis coordinated to complement similar effort devoted to specific products, markets, or seasons. All of these and other similar factors would be suggestive of the expected duration of these expenditures.

Evaluating the Goal of Growth in The New Industrial State

In an earlier age, when the making of a profit was unquestionably considered to be the dominant quest of business, goodwill represented the ability of some firms to earn more profits than others. Galbraith, as the previous discussion indicates, felt the assumption of profit as the major goal was no longer applicable and that growth was the primary goal of business. Within the new industrial state, presumably some firms exist that could grow faster than others, and they thus possess a differential advantage regarding growth. Goodwill indicated a superior ability to earn profits—and still does—but the crucial assumption made in the earlier discussion was that goodwill also represented a superior ability to grow. The validity of the growth assumption and the important implications that result constitute the subject matter of this section.

To support his position, Galbraith emphasizes the technostructure and its members in relation to profit and growth.

The paradox of modern economic motivation is that profit

maximization as a goal requires that the individual member of the technostructure subordinate his personal pecuniary interest to that of the remote and unknown stockholder. By contrast, growth, as a goal, is wholly consistent with the personal and pecuniary interest of those who participate in decisions and direct the enterprise.[20]

Furthermore, Galbraith felt that not only was growth the dominant goal, it was inconsistent with maximization of even long-term profits.

Price, sales, cost and other policies to maximize growth will differ within any given time horizon from those to maximize profits. Nor will profits be maximized if, as in the case of the technostructure, there is special reason to minimize risk.[21]

Nevertheless, even using Galbraith's framework, the necessity of maximizing long-term profits appears inescapable. If the autonomy of the technostructure is so vital, it would without argument need to concentrate on growth. To preserve its autonomy, however, that growth needs to be not only absolute but relative to its competitors, otherwise its profits may well slacken as it looses its market share. It is thus hard to imagine how such expansion can be based in the long run on something other than financial growth and thus on long-run profit maximization to insure the survival, autonomy, and growth seemingly so important to the technostructure. If this one modification to Galbraith's analysis is allowed, then those firms in which the technostructure possesses and maintains the ability to grow faster than others must earn a superior profit to do so. A differential advantage in this regard is expressed as it has been for the last five-hundred or so years by possession of the asset goodwill.

Thus, a definition of goodwill based on Galbraith's analysis (as modified herein to emphasize profit maximization) is: *a differential advantage accruing to the corporation in terms of its dominant goals—the ability to generate superior profits by whatever means to finance the technostructure's growth, usually by selling goods through purposeful manipulation of the consumer's customs and habits.* If, on the other hand, one chose to stay strictly within the confines of Galbraith's analysis, then a substantially different and admittedly legitimate interpretation of goodwill is possible. Furthermore, this definition is not presented as superseding or ignoring other earlier forms of goodwill and the manner in which it may be sustained. This definition is meant to add to and build on previous ideas concerning goodwill. Insofar as smaller businesses or a less fully developed industrial situation exists, then what has been said in the past concerning goodwill is as valid as ever. Where the sort of advanced development that Galbraith describes is deemed to have occurred in the economy, then the definition just presented may have merit.

Characteristics Of Goodwill

No list of the characteristics of goodwill can be final or complete since any breakdown is necessarily arbitrary, and the nature of the asset is constantly changing as its environment changes. Over the years, however, writers on the subject have grouped their discussion of the characteristics of intangibles around certain common aspects that serve as well as any for purposes of this study. An attempt is made in the following pages (1) to extract the essence of each of these factors to further aid in understanding the asset goodwill and (2) to indicate any modifications necessitated by implications of "the new industrial state."

Intangibility

Intangibility, probably the most obvious characteristic of intangibles as a class and of goodwill specifically, is also one of the least understood. If the term "asset" is understood to mean something owned that is expected to contribute to future profits, then goodwill is no more intangible than a building. The argument might be raised that goodwill contributes certain intangible benefits to a business while a building contributes in a definite physical manner to the profitability of a firm. Anything classified as an asset, however, is only classified in that manner because it is expected to yield future benefits to a firm. Transactions related to the future have not yet occurred and at present are only contemplations of the mind; therefore, they are invisible and intangible. Goodwill has been said to be nothing but a hope grounded on a probability, but so is the future use of anything called an asset. The individual who has purchased a building has really paid for its future use that, as stated in Chapter VII, could be curtailed by fire, changed environment, or a multitude of other causes.[22]

> It would not be incorrect to say that all capital is invisible value, in that it is the present value, not of physical things, but of the hopes of the future aroused through confidence in the now invisible but expected transactions of the future.
>
> For, what is the value of lands, building, machinery, commodities, but the value of their expected "uses"? And what are their uses but the uses not yet made but yet to be made of them, either in using them directly or in selling their products for money or other products?[23]

The connotation of the term asset in the sense of the right to exclusive use of something leads to similar conclusions. The right to use a building as opposed to the right to use or enjoy the benefits of goodwill might be offered as the difference between a material and an immaterial asset, but what is the essence of a right? Discussing the difference between the ownership of land (considered tangible) and the franchise to use land (considered intangible), Hatfield noted:

> But there is no real difference between them as regards tangibility, materiality, or realness. Real estate represents a right, tracing ultimately back to the sovereign power which permits an individual to make use of a portion of the earth's surface. . . . A franchise is similarly a right granted by the sovereign power permitting an

individual to make certain restricted uses of a portion of the earth's surface.[24]

When regarded as assets, therefore, a building and goodwill do not differ.

> In a sense all property is intangible. That is, assets are at bottom the financial aspects of conditions, relationships, and tangible objects as opposed to the physical makeup or description of things; assets are economic rather than molecular in character.[25]

They are different, however, with regard to the present physical substance of the item that someone has seen fit to use as an asset, but even on this point the characteristic must be limited in application. Bank accounts, accounts receivable, investments, and prepaid insurance are all examples of assets that are just as intangible as goodwill but are not considered intangible assets. Therefore, the present intangible condition of goodwill may be considered a necessary factor but not one entirely sufficient in itself for describing the asset.

Attachment to the Business

Another important factor has been the close attachment to the business of intangibles in general and to goodwill in particular. Most intangibles could not be sold without seriously damaging the business, and goodwill—as the epitome of intangibles—cannot be sold at all without selling the firm itself or a semiautonomous segment of it. This is because goodwill relates to the superior earning power of all the other assets of a firm (or major segment of it) taken collectively; thus the sale of goodwill as a separate commodity is inconceivable. The problems associated with its transferability and realization might be compared with an attempt to sell the speed of a racehorse apart from the animal itself. In this context, Commons' remark that goodwill is the "soul" of a corporation may be more clearly understood; for goodwill is the essence of a firm, measured in terms of earning power that a firm cannot do without.[26]

Independence of Cost—A Questionable Assumption

Concerning this characteristic, Yang once wrote:

> The values of intangibles bear no definite relation to the costs of their development. This is perhaps natural in view of their differential and monopolistic character. If the advantage could be created by cost directly, it would before long cease to be an advantage.[27]

Tied in with knowledge of other traits of goodwill, this factor appears to be unquestionable as a further valid description of the nebulous nature of goodwill. In the case of a small entrepreneur, the location from which he is doing business might, quite by good luck, be responsible for an excellent trade, and perhaps he was able to acquire the land at a time when its future potential in this respect was unknown to everyone, including himself. If others could obtain a similar location, even at a price that would take into consideration the enhanced site value, they probably would do so if, in their expectations, a reasonable profit could be obtained. The problem is not their lack of ability to obtain funds but the uniqueness of the superior location that was due to a situation beyond the control of the individual able to take advantage of it.

If however, the modern situation approaches the description of the new industrial state outlined earlier, then the analysis just presented does not necessarily depict modern conditions, and the independence of cost characteristics is open to question. Within a large firm—one employing thousands of people, selling to customers on a national or international basis, and requiring heavy investment in plant, equipment, and merchandise—the extensive planning necessary to properly coordinate these factors places a strain on the assumption that the firm's superior earning power could be due to fortuitous and incidental occurrences outside the control of the firm. If the customer can be manipulated, the advantage can be created directly by cost. Yang, however, contended that cost was a universal instrument and the advantage so created could only last temporarily.[28] The answer to Yang's contention is that the ability to plan and to fit the customer to the firm's need is a function of the size of the firm, and tremendous size is not a universal characteristic of business. A large organization would therefore possess the ability to make sizeable expenditures for management of its demand and thus could better control its environment than a smaller firm with less resources. Cost, in the magnitude spoken of here, is not a universal instrument, and a differential advantage created through great expenditure might thus be maintained if the firm continues to make large outlays relative to its rivals.

Differential and Monopolistic Advantage

The idea that goodwill represents a differential advantage for a given firm illustrates that the significance of the asset derives from a comparison of one business with another or with an assumed normal firm or a normal rate of return. The benefit is a differential one because it involves the comparison of at least two firms, and it is monopolistic in the sense that the advantaged firm enjoys its advantage exclusively. In a contemporary setting, the advantage may be seen as both a cause and a result of a corporation's large size, which must be of both absolute and relative magnitude. First, the business must be of sufficient scope to exercise control over its environment, and second, it must possess the ability to do this better than its counterparts.

The idea of an ordinary or normal return is a phenomenon of business and may differ according to time and place. The concept has been defined in a number of ways, but Veblen stated:

> The precise meaning of "ordinary profits" need not detain the argument. It may mean net average profits, or it may mean something else. The phrase is sufficiently intelligible to the business community to permit the business men to use it without definition

and to rest their reasoning about business affairs on it as a secure and stable concept; and it is this commonplace resort to the term that is the point of interest here.[29]

Early economic discussions on the subject of differential advantages centered on land used for agricultural pursuits and on the ability of the landlord to obtain rent based on the productivity of his land in comparison to those parcels employed at the margin of production.[30] Preinreich felt that this rent was goodwill and noted how eventually the same analysis was applied to superior returns on other factors of production, with those returns being labeled "quasi-rents." Paton followed through with this analysis:

> Goodwill, according to this conception, is closely related to the producer's "rent" or "surplus" of economics. The producer who has monopolistic advantages, is especially efficient, or is unusually well situated for some other reason, is often said to realize a special surplus or rent. Viewing the "representative business" as essentially the counterpart of the marginal, price-determining producer, leads to the conclusion that *goodwill expresses from the standpoint of the particular enterprise the capitalized value of economic rents enjoyed.*[31] [Italics mine.]

Those early ideas and their later extensions may be placed in the more generalized framework presented earlier in this chapter. The only time any item has ever been considered productive has been when human knowledge existed to make use of it. At any given time, the level of knowledge and the circumstances conditioning its application for the needs of society place a strategic advantage on the ownership of certain kinds of property. For example, prior to the rise of the machine age, transportation conditions and the growth of population were two important factors that contributed to the strategic advantage associated with the ownership of farmland and the profits to be enjoyed as a result. The laborer, whose knowledge was employed to cultivate the land, and the owner of what industrial equipment existed at the time did not possess the same power to make profits since neither was in control of the item then dominant for utilizing human skill. With the increasing industrialization of Europe, the differential advantage passed from the owners of rural land to those who possessed industrial equipment. The value of land declined, not because it was incapable of producing crops, but because the gains to be derived from employment of the community's knowledge became greater in industry than in agriculture due to the new technological situation.[32]

Galbraith presents a similar analysis in his study, noting how power passed from land to capital, as agriculture gradually constituted a steadily diminishing proportion of the community's output. (Presumably he defines capital in terms of capital equipment—mill, machinery, factories, and so forth.)[33] He felt that the relative power of the factors of production was due to their scarcity.[34]

It will now be clear what accords power to a factor of production or to those who own or control it. Power goes to the factor which is hardest to obtain or hardest to replace.[35]

Furthermore, Gailbraith contends that control of the strategically important factor insures that the others may be obtained relatively easily for business purposes. For instance, when agriculture was the dominant industry, the ownership of land was the crucial consideration, and obtaining what little capital was needed and the required labor to work the land presented few problems. The laborer and those who possessed capital had little or no power in the system. When the machine age arose, power passed to those who owned industrial equipment, and the ownership of land no longer assured control of labor and capital. With the control of capital, labor and land were the two factors that could be acquired with few problems.

Galbraith, however, extends his analysis beyond these considerations and contends that in the contemporary economy neither capital, land, nor labor—individually or in combination—represent the strategic factor allowing for success. Galbraith believes that a new factor has arisen to control the industrial system—organized intelligence—and it is embodied in the technostructure. The success or failure of a business depends on the effectiveness of this organization, and capital appears to shrink to insignificance in comparison to this unique group within the enterprise.[36]

Galbraith's analysis brings out the importance of the human element in the modern business environment quite lucidly, but it appears to lead to certain conceptual problems. For instance, what power does the technostructure possess aside from the financial and technological resources contained within a large firm? Thus, the technostructure's strength appears to be based on the implicit assumption that sufficient resources are available to enable it to exercise its power. Shifting the analysis and looking at the problem from the viewpoint of resources, Galbraith says, "the mere possession of capital is now no guarantee that the requisite talent can be obtained and organized."[37] However, the possession and maintenance of resources of the magnitude that Galbraith discusses throughout his study would require the existence of a large, skilled group to manage their use. Therefore, how can either the technostructure or the resources long exist without the other?

The conceptual problem may be resolved if it is recognized that human knowledge cannot be exercised apart from the material or immaterial contrivances necessary to make use of it. Conceding the importance of the human factor, some of Galbraith's ideas are used in a different framework to give the following results:

In an era dominated by landed wealth, control of land was secured by its ownership, and what "organized intelligence" existed at the time to till the soil was subject to the discretion of the landlord. Two elements thus existed: (1) technology, embodied in the labor, relating to how to use the object, and (2) control of the object—land in this situation—necessary to make use of the knowledge. Later, when the machine age arose, the financiers of the late nineteenth and early twentieth centuries took the place of the landlord, while engineers and skilled labor occupied a similar role to that of their earlier agrarian counterparts.

With the rise of modern times wherein corporations reached unprecedented size and the importance of the stockholder gradually diminished, control of the industrial equipment through the corporation no longer resided with the owners. Since the era of landed wealth and throughout the machine age to the present time, knowledge of how to use resources has increased greatly along with the increased complexity and magnitude associated with their employment. As owners relinquished control of resources, those who knew how to employ them industrially took it up. For once, the two elements mentioned earlier—technological knowledge and its control—resided in the same group, which Galbraith has termed the technostructure.

While the shift of power is of prime importance, it must be seen as a shift from one group to another within the confines of the institutional framework of business enterprise. If the technostructure is to be successful, it must pursue the goals of the system within which it operates. It could not, for example, attempt to stabilize its growth, while other firms in its industry were attempting to grow, without eventually losing its standing. If it can grow faster than its competitors, it can do so only because it has a differential ability to make the profits necessary to finance this growth. This differential is called goodwill.

Where the economy or those portions of it have developed as Galbraith has foreseen, the technostructure, like Veblen's pecuniary magnate before it, controls and uses the processes of production in pursuit of its goals. It must work through the industrial equipment rather than as a separate factor. Therefore, it is concluded that a new factor has not been created, though there has been a shift in power of those who control the existing strategically important material items.

Control of the industrial processes thus allows the dominant group—at present, the technostructure—the opportunity to secure a differential advantage in comparison with some norm. If it succeeds, this advantage will result in the asset goodwill.

Instability of Value—A Questionable Assumption

Although instability of value may be particularly apparent in the case of goodwill, it is not a unique characteristic of this asset. Instability of value is a characteristic of any asset. (This discussion is based on the idea mentioned earlier that any asset is just a hope grounded on a probability.)

Goodwill is measured by the difference between (1) the fair market value of the entity and (2) the sum of the fair market values of the other assets. When the fair market value of the individual assets fluctuates, goodwill will also fluctuate—and to an even greater extent than any other one asset. Furthermore, when expectations of what constitutes a normal return in the industry change—thereby changing the fair market value of the firm—a second source of instability for measurement of goodwill is introduced. Aside from fluctuations of asset value or of industrial norms, expectations concerning the individual firm may provide a third source of instability, making goodwill's estimation appear to be little more than a haphazard guess at best.

In the modern economy, however, these remarks must be tempered somewhat. To the extent that planning by a firm can replace market uncertainty, then goodwill could fluctuate so much less that it could become a planned asset. This conclusion coincides with the idea that goodwill takes on the characteristics of the environment in which it is found. Thus, when the dominant firms in the economy must engage in extensive planning, the implication that goodwill becomes a planned asset is not especially surprising but is a logical conclusion.

Technical Serviceability

This characteristic has already been discussed, but some further clarification is presented here. While some of the other characteristics describe only differences of degree between intangibles and other assets or must be reinterpreted within a more contemporary economic system, the distinction between intangibles and tangible assets on the basis of this factor is fundamental. As Paton has stated, "The intangibles as a class make no technical contribution to production, as do services, materials, and equipment."[38] While at least some tangible assets possess the ability to make a contribution in this manner, no intangibles do.

What goodwill does indicate, however, is the ability of the firm to succeed within the economic system as it is currently organized, which represents the reason the asset manifests no productive contribution. Success is considered within terms of financial prosperity, and financial prosperity is a question of gain or loss.

Goodwill therefore (1) results from having an economic system capable of serviceability but motivated by or directed within an institutional framework designed to fulfill purposes of profitability and growth and (2) represents an ability to succeed in a superior manner in terms of these other goals.

Summary of Characteristics: A Description

Goodwill is the differential ability of one firm, in comparison with another or an assumed average firm, to make a profit. It is monopolistic in the sense that it is inseparable from the entity with which it is associated. It is measured solely in terms of profitability, has no physical existence, and, as Paton noted, makes no technical contribution to the production process. In the contemporary environment, the ability to create and maintain goodwill is often a function of a corporation's absolute and relative size—a factor that also mitigates, through extensive planning, the tendency of the asset's value to be unstable.

The Relationship of Goodwill to Its Accounting Treatment

More than one might initially suspect, the nature of goodwill has had an important bearing on the pragmatic treatment of the asset. Particularly in the twenties, attempts were made to recognize in the accounts goodwill that either was "purchased" by advertising or that merely arose independent of any cost. Practical reasons why such practices were rejected were discussed at length in previous chapters, but the fact remains that perceptions of the nature of goodwill were directly manifested in the accounts as opposed to the indirect residual approach currently used. Even so, the current treatment needs little theoretical apology for the valuation of goodwill in such a "leftover" fashion. To illustrate, those who argue against the current treatment could do so on at least two grounds. Because the valuation of goodwill is based both on the valuation placed on the enterprise as a whole and on the sum of the values attributed to the individual assets, the goodwill account could be misstated because of over or undervaluation of either. Reflecting on this fact, Canning stated:

> Goodwill, when it appears in the balance sheet at all, is but a master valuation account—a catchall into which is thrown both an unenumerated series of items that have the *economic*, though not necessarily the *legal,* properties of assets, and an undistributed list of undervaluations of those items listed as assets. It is the valuation account *par excellence.*[39]

Canning's remarks, however, should be accepted with some qualification. Goodwill is a master valuation account—not because the value of specific assets is measured imperfectly, but because the measurement of those assets is an arbitrary and subjective process at best. Proper valuation of individual assets is obscured by the fact that the purchaser has paid for the firm and the opportunity to receive its income rather than for the specific assets, which are of secondary interest when compared to the entity as a whole. The interrelationship of the assets in producing earnings may progress to such a point that imputation to individual assets might be compared to trying to compute the value of each separate key on a typewriter. The imputation problem was discussed by Paton, who even questioned the traditional methods of valuing intangibles, when he stated:

> It is true that the existence of intangible value has usually been equated with the assumption of a superior earning power, which amounts to acceptance of the view that so-called tangible resources generally stand in a preferential position with respect to the soaking up of earnings, especially when it comes to a consideration of the broader and more imponderable factors in the intangible package. But, as has been pointed out by those dealing with basic analysis in this area, this is sheer assumption. In a given case it may well be that it is the intangibles that are crucial in the generation of revenues and net earnings, not the prosaic stock of tangibles. Who knows?[40]

Summary

Goodwill may be thought of now, as it has been for the last five-hundred or so years, as the differential ability of one business, in comparison with another or an assumed average firm, to make a profit. Prerequisites to goodwill's existence include first a level of knowledge in a given community sufficiently complex to bring about ownership of the tools and equipment necessary to turn that knowledge to use. Second, ownership must exist within a framework of business enterprise. One who employs this strategically valuable property (strategic since it controls employment of a portion of the community's knowledge) more profitably than do comparably situated peers possesses goodwill.

While the remarks immediately preceding are usually not subject to much question, the source and maintenance of goodwill remain issues involving little concreteness and usually a great amount of subjectivity; they represent the origin of many of the accountant's problems of recording and subsequently treating the asset. Goodwill appears to have been originally based on the sentiments of a firm's customers, who at their initiative and by their patronage enabled the business to enjoy its superior returns.

The incidental and precarious nature of the asset appears to have changed in many important sectors of the national and world economy as the result of planning requirements inherent in business operations conducted on a large scale. Through its sales efforts, particularly its advertising, a firm now appears in many instances to take the initiative by cultivating the customer to buy its product. Creating and following a blueprint for the "construction" of the consumer's loyalty implies that goodwill is just as much a planned and created asset as anything material that could be created with the same expenditure.

In addition to such factors as customer sentiment, fortuitous location, and superior personnel, a contemporary source of goodwill may also be added involving the planned and deliberate aquisition of the asset. Thus a definition including a modern source of goodwill and building on the contemporary analysis of Galbraith could be the following: Goodwill may be defined as *a differential advantage accruing to a corporation in terms of its dominant goals—the ability to generate superior profits by whatever means to finance the technostructure's growth, usually by selling goods through purposeful manipulation of the consumer's customs and habits.*

Such a definition can in no way be the final word on goodwill since its source has always been a matter of debate, and business enterprise has always been in a state of change. At best, the foregoing and all future definitions only represent attempts to understand and interpret some portion of the business environment as it continues to evolve.

The asset has no physical existence and makes no technical contribution to the production process. It is as inseparable from a firm as is speed from a racehorse, and its creation and maintenance in the modern economy's dominant firms are a function of a corporation's absolute and relative size. In relation to accounting, the intangibles classification in which it is found indicates the type of asset that arises in successful businesses, and the limitations imposed upon its recognition in accounts are due to attempts to properly determine periodic net income.

1. E. Guthrie, "Goodwill," *The Accountant,* April 23, 1898, p. 425.

2. Thorstein Veblen, "On the Nature of Capital: [The Productivity of Capital Goods]," *The Quarterly Journal of Economics,* August 1908, pp. 517-542. (Hereinafter referred to as "Capital: Productivity."); Thorstein Veblen, "On the Nature of Capital: Investment, Intangible Assets, and the Pecuniary Magnate," *The Quarterly Journal of Economics,* November 1908, pp. 104-136. (Hereinafter referred to as "Capital: Investment, Intangible Assets, and the Pecuniary Magnate.")

3. John Kenneth Galbraith, *The New Industrial State* (Boston: Houghton Mifflin Company, 1967).

4. J. M. Yang, *Goodwill and Other Intangibles: Their Significance and Treatment in Accounts* (New York: Ronald Press Company, 1927), p. 17. (Hereinafter referred to as *Goodwill and Other Intangibles.*)

5. Veblen, "Capital: Productivity," pp. 517-535.

6. Ibid.

7. Ibid.

8. Ibid., pp. 535-539; Veblen, "Capital: Investment, Intangible Assets, and the Pecuniary Magnate," pp. 104-108.

9. Veblen, "Capital: Investment, Intangible Assets, and the Pecuniary Magnate," pp. 111-114.

10. Ibid., pp. 115-117.

11. Ibid., pp. 123-124.

12. Herbert C. Freeman, "Some Considerations Involved in the Valuation of Goodwill," *The Journal of Accountancy,* October 1921, p. 258.

13. William Andrew Paton, *Accounting Theory: With Special Reference to the Corporate Enterprise* (New York: Ronald Press Company, 1922), p. 309. (Hereinafter referred to as *Accounting Theory.*)

14. Louis O. Foster, *Introduction to Accounting* (Chicago: Richard D. Irwin, Inc., 1941), pp. 609-610.

15. Galbraith, *The New Industrial State,* pp. 6, 23-24, 71, 80-82, 110, 115-117, 166-178, 201-205, 212.

16. Ibid.

17. Ibid.

18. Ibid.

19. Ibid., p. 203.

20. Ibid., pp. 171-172.

21. Ibid.

22. See p. 144.

23. John R. Commons, *Legal Foundations of Capitalism,* (New York: MacMillan Company, 1924), p. 25.

24. Henry Rand Hatfield, *Accounting* (New York: D. Appleton and Company, 1927), p. 111.

25. William A. Paton, *Asset Accounting: An Intermediate Course* (New York: MacMillan Company, 1952), p. 485.

26. John R. Commons, *Industrial Goodwill* (New York: McGraw-Hill Book Company, Inc., 1919), p. 20.

27. Yang, *Goodwill and Other Intangibles,* p. 13.

28. Ibid.

29. Thorstein Veblen, *The Theory of Business Enterprise* (New York: Charles Scribner's Sons, 1915), p. 88. For an analysis of the origin of the concept of normal return, see Veblen's discussion, pp. 85-91, and in an abbreviated form, see Yang, *Goodwill and Other Intangibles,* pp. 91-93.

30. Gabriel A. D. Preinreich, "Economic Theories of Goodwill," *The Journal of Accountancy,* September 1939, p. 171.

31. Paton, *Accounting Theory,* p. 315.

32. Veblen, "Capital: Productivity," pp. 528-530.

33. Galbraith, *The New Industrial State,* p. 35.

34. Ibid., pp. 54-56.

35. Ibid., p. 56.

36. Ibid., pp. 46-59, 71.

37. Ibid., p. 57.

38. William A. Paton, *Accountants' Handbook,* 2nd ed. (New York: Ronald Press Company, 1934), p. 797. For the same conclusion, see Yang, *Goodwill and Other Intangibles,* p. 16.

39. John B. Canning, *The Economics of Accountancy: A Critical Analysis of Accounting Theory* (New York: Ronald Press Company, 1929), pp. 42-43.

40. William A. Paton, "Comments of William A. Paton," in George R. Catlett and Norman O. Olson, *Accounting for Goodwill,* Accounting Research Study No. 10 (New York: American Institute of Certified Public Accountants, Inc., 1968), p. 146.

Chapter **IX**

Conclusion

Restatement of the Problem

Few, if any, subjects in accounting literature have received the continuing interest accorded goodwill from the early 1880s to the early 1980s. Few, if any, subjects have been bound up with so many historically significant and currently important issues facing the practice of accounting and the accounting profession. Since previous literature involving goodwill was focused on specific problems at given points in time, a thorough history of the issues and problems surrounding goodwill was felt to be necessary and was the objective of this work. The accounting concept and treatment of goodwill was historically documented, the issues and problems surrounding goodwill were placed within a historical and institutional perspective, and the nature of goodwill was explored.

Summary and Inferences

Taking a cue from Thorstein Veblen, one can go back to a time seemingly more involved with archeology than economics to understand the way in which goodwill has arisen and evolved. In even the earliest communities of which anything is known, there existed a stock of knowledge that was applied to the materials at hand for the well-being of the group. When knowledge is quite primitive, the tools making use of this knowledge are primitive as well, and both the knowledge and the tools are held loosely by the community at large. Later, as the level of knowledge becomes greater, the tools become technologically more advanced and much harder to replace than earlier ones. Property rights then arise, and the now-strategic materials confer to their owners a differential advantage over those who do not own them. In feudal times, for example, the lord owned the property of his manor with what differential advantages in social standing and welfare it conferred. In more modern times, control of strategic materials (now industrial equipment) has been obtained through control of business enterprise.

A unique characteristic of this institution has been the manner in which any business is considered a success—its ability to make a profit. Those firms that make and/or are expected to make superior returns possess a differential advantage over those that do not. When businesses were small, this differential was due to the goodwill of a firm's customers. As time passed, when businesses grew larger and many factors contributed to the development and maintenance of this advantage, the asset representing all of these factors retained the name given those earlier sentimental characteristics—goodwill.

Many accountants would dispute little of what has just been stated concerning the evolution of goodwill. Even if broad agreement could be reached about the asset's history, its modern-day nature, source, and maintenance have been translated into exasperating practical problems of presentation and treatment for almost a century. Since goodwill is associated with above-average business profits, accountants have had to contend with the fact that "above-average" is a constantly shifting and subjective estimate at best. Furthermore, business enterprise is continuously evolving and thus continuously influencing the development of goodwill and the way in which it is interpreted.

One example of a contemporary view of business with important implications for goodwill is that of J. K. Galbraith. In the twentieth century, control of the dominant firms in the economy has gradually shifted from the owners to the technostructure—a change brought about by the unprecedented size of these firms. Proper utilization of the vast amounts of necessary resources has required such planning that a firm must take the initiative and carefully cultivate the customer to buy its products. Cultivating the consumer's loyalty requires careful planning—with the implication that goodwill becomes just as much a planned and created asset as anything material that could be created with the same expenditure. Therefore, *goodwill may be defined as a differential advantage accruing to a corporation in terms of its dominant goals—the ability to generate superior profits by whatever means to finance the technostructure's growth, usually by selling goods through purposeful manipulation of the consumer's customs and habits.* Although not meant to supersede or ignore other earlier forms of goodwill, this definition is offered as one possible explanation of a major modern-day source of the asset.

Developments in accounting generally and in accounting for goodwill specifically appear to be the direct result of changes in the business environment occurring from the late nineteenth through the middle of the twentieth century. The separation of owners from the management of a corporation has placed an important emphasis on the communication of financial information to the investing public so that statement data will not be misinterpreted. As a result, the auditor has had to be careful that the item and amount of goodwill appearing in the financial statements on which he is issuing an opinion are not subject to misleading inferences. Furthermore, the inferences to be drawn from the statements are concerned with a vital point that affects the vendibility of the shareholders' stock—the profitability of the firm. The fair presentation and proper determination of net income have become of prime importance in financial statements, and the gradual elimination by the accounting profession of alternatives for handling first goodwill's initial valuation and later its subsequent treatment has been made in an attempt to match expenses and revenues more accurately. These developments in business and accounting should be kept in mind in examining goodwill's initial valuation, subsequent treatment, financial presentation, auditing aspects, tax aspects, and its relationship to pooling of interests accounting.

Initial Valuation

The chief occurrence for accounting purposes concerning goodwill's initial valuation was the eventual adoption of and rigid adherence to the cost principle for stating the asset in accounts.

In the first twenty years of literature on the subject of accounting for goodwill, the usual emphasis was on proper determination of a figure for the asset with the discussion of all of the factors that affected it. While many approaches were mentioned, the method that eventually proved to be conceptually preferable was the capitalization of excess profits. Some accountants who were of a more pragmatic bent, however, cautioned that technique was no substitute for reality and that in the final analysis the value of goodwill was what it would fetch.

In the twenties, the optimism of the age seemed to affect accounting for the asset because a number of items were recorded under the heading of goodwill—including amounts paid for it on purchase of a going concern, advertising expenditures, capitalized early losses, and arbitrary write-ups. The proliferation of practices came from a number of conflicting objectives and other factors—deceiving stockholders, example set in other industries, proper balance sheet valuation of the asset, and proper determination of income.

In the thirties, conservative attitudes developed in the depression were coupled with a discernible shift in accounting from emphasis on determination of net worth to measurement of periodic net income. As a result, only amounts paid for the asset on the purchase of a going concern were acceptable for treatment in the accounts as goodwill, and the cost basis for goodwill became firmly established. By the thirties, the accounting profession had developed sufficiently to begin issuing pronouncements increasingly accepted as authoritative in the formulation of accounting principles. The American Institute of Accountants' Accounting Research Bulletin No. 24, written in 1944, was the first bulletin devoted specifically to accounting for intangibles and which recommended adherence to a cost basis for initial valuation.

Beginning in the fifties, increasing concern with the applicability of the cost principle in the unprecedented inflation of the post-war era led to some suggestions for periodic upward revaluation of assets, generally in supplemental financial statements. In the case of goodwill, however, such proposals were limited to general price level changes because of the relatively subjective considerations associated with the asset's appraisal.

Subsequent Treatment

Once goodwill was placed on the books, the main problem associated with its subsequent treatment was the asset's indeterminate life. As a result, a number of alternatives arose for handling the asset in the accounts. The chief change in goodwill's subsequent treatment was the gradual elimination of these alternatives until, in 1970, only one treatment was acceptable.

The two alternatives discussed most in accounting literature were permanent retention and gradual reduction of amounts recorded for the asset on the purchase of a going concern. Permanent retention was advocated by those who felt goodwill had an indefinite life and did not depreciate but only fluctuated aimlessly. Those who advocated gradual reduction did so on the grounds that no asset lasted forever. Debate between adherents of the two viewpoints continued unabated from 1884 to 1970.

Augmenting this chronic debate were developments and attitudes occurring in business generally and accounting specifically. During the twenties, for instance, emphasis had been placed on how to get goodwill on the books. In the thirties, emphasis switched to how to get it off. Whatever the justification given, lump-sum write-offs of goodwill became popular in the thirties—a reflection of the strong conservative attitudes then present. The write-offs were usually made against earned surplus or capital surplus, thus circumventing the income statement and presenting a more favorable financial picture in terms of net income, earnings per share, and return on total assets and net worth. After World War II, the authoritativeness of the pronouncements of, first, the Committee on Accounting Procedure and, then, the Accounting Principles Board gradually increased, and lump-sum write-offs to earned surplus and capital surplus were ultimately eliminated. By 1967, goodwill could be eliminated from the books only by charges to current income, and of the two main alternatives—permanent retention and amortization to current income—amortization appeared to be the preferred treatment.

Complicating the culmination of the issue of goodwill's subsequent treatment was the introduction in 1950 of the pooling of interests concept. This treatment grew in importance roughly in proportion to the elimination of lump-sum write-offs as an acceptable treatment for goodwill. The pooling treatment could be manipulated in such a manner that the accounts presented approximately the same results as if goodwill had been written off. As a result, goodwill's subsequent treatment became entangled in the general problem of accounting for business combinations. When the issue was resolved in 1970, the fight had been waged on two fronts: (1) mandatory amortization of goodwill and (2) elimination of the pooling alternative.

When the Accounting Principles Board decided the issue, mandatory amortization was still required, but the pooling treatment, though allowed, was significantly restricted. For the first time since accounting literature on the subject of goodwill appeared, the intangible's subsequent treatment was limited to one procedure, though the APB was criticized for being arbitrary in providing a maximum limit of forty years for amortizing the asset.

Financial Presentation and Disclosure

The significance of goodwill's financial presentation and disclosure was due to the fact that virtually all of the problems connected with its initial valuation or subsequent treatment, or any other aspect, accumulated and finally came to rest in the balance sheet and income statement. Of major significance was the increasingly discernible importance attached to the net income figure, coupled with attempts by firms to present that figure as favorably as possible. One way was to avoid the recognition and amortization of goodwill. These attempts were at odds with simultaneous attempts by the accounting profession to correctly determine net income, which eventually stipulated mandatory amortization of goodwill.

Through the twenties, very little significance could be attached to a figure representing goodwill in the balance sheet since numerous ways existed both to bring the asset on the books for various and conflicting reasons and to remove it. The problem was further complicated by lumping goodwill and other intangibles in such categories as land and buildings—a situation symptomatic of the general lack of reporting standards at that time.

During the depression and its aftermath, conservatism on the one hand and the recognized importance attached to measurements of net income on the other contributed to the desire to write off the asset to accounts such as earned or capital surplus in order to circumvent the income statement. When discretionary write-offs were discouraged and then became unacceptable procedures, pressure arose to avoid goodwill's presentation in financial statements by refusing to recognize it in the first place through employment of the pooling of interests technique in accounting. The accounting profession's subsequent attempts in the sixties and early seventies to limit the number of alternatives for handling the asset and to curtail abuses associated with pooling were aimed at presenting goodwill more frequently in the balance sheet than had previously been the case and restricting its mandatory elimination solely through the income statement—either as an amortization charge or as an extraordinary item.

Statistical studies made from the thirties through the early seventies indicated that in actual practice goodwill was lumped with other intangibles in approximately 80 percent of the balance sheets examined—a figure that remained relatively constant during the forty-year period. Nominal valuation was overwhelmingly favored for valuing the asset through the fifties. This practice reached the peak of its employment on a percentage basis in 1953 when the profession moved to restrict write-offs to earned and capital surplus. From then on, nominal valuation gradually and steadily declined in use until by 1973 it was practiced by less than 1 percent of the companies presenting intangibles in their statements. Although a policy of nonamortization appears to have been increasingly preferred as late as 1972, the effects of Opinion No. 17, issued in late 1970, are apparent. Amortization has increased proportionately every year since 1969.

Auditing Considerations

The importance of the auditing area stems from the auditor's functions in determining the fairness of financial reports and of the presentation in those statements of goodwill. Two main events occurred with regard to auditing aspects of goodwill: (1) the change in auditing objectives (observed by Montgomery in 1912) from the detection of fraud and error to ascertainment of the actual financial condition and earnings of an enterprise and (2) the threat to the exercise of the auditor's professional judgment through the specification of the rigid guidelines in accounting for business combinations and goodwill contained in Opinions Nos. 16 and 17.

When fraud and error detection were of prime importance, the figure at which goodwill was presented in the balance sheet became meaningless and outside of the auditor's work. Ascertaining the financial condition of the enterprise added a new dimension to goodwill's proper treatment by increasing the auditor's responsibility to avoid the possibility of misinterpretation by the public of what the figure for the asset represented. This increased responsibility came at a time when a number of ways existed to bring the asset on the books, thereby requiring the auditor to take the responsibility for the valuation of the asset by fully disclosing the method of its valuation or by disclaiming responsibility in the certificate if it could not be assumed. In the thirties and forties, as all methods for recording goodwill, other than on the purchase of a going concern, became uncommon, the auditor's earlier position was relaxed—since goodwill could by then be assumed to be valued at cost or less.

The issuance of Opinions Nos. 16 and 17 may be viewed as a continuation of the trend toward clarification of the auditor's responsibility concerning the treatment of goodwill, though at the possible cost of removing the element of professional judgment from the auditor's work. These opinions continued a trend in the direction of more specific pronouncements by the Accounting Principles Board, with rigid guidelines promulgated in an attempt to eliminate the abuse encouraged by the more subjective criteria of prior pronouncements. The auditor's guidelines could thus become his straitjacket, and he might find himself in the position of following rules that eliminated his professional judgment while only rechanneling the possibility and method of abusing those guidelines.

Tax Considerations

The importance of goodwill's treatment for taxation is due to the traditional influence of tax laws on accounting practice. The most significant occurrence in this area was the development of the tax treatment of goodwill in the late twenties and its influence on accounting practice thereafter.

Goodwill's initial valuation never presented much of a problem—it was considered a capital asset to the extent of its cost. The matter of its subsequent treatment for tax purposes, however, had to be hammered out in the courts. Since goodwill's existence was not definitely limited, no deduction was ever allowed for its depreciation, but the question of a deduction for its obsolescence was not immediately resolved. Obsolescence deductions were allowed until 1927 when a Circuit Court decision stated that it was only acceptable in the same situations where a depreciation deduction was permitted. Since 1927, goodwill has had to be retained indefinitely on the books of a business for tax purposes, and this position by the federal tax authorities has had the effect of significantly bolstering the position of those who espoused the similar position for accounting purposes, with many accounting writers mentioning the tax treatment in support of their view.

The tax law has constituted in the past, and will no doubt constitute in the future, a significant influence on financial accounting. But indications exist that this relationship of taxation to accounting is subject to change. An important reason for the traditional relationship has been the relatively strong power of the taxing authorities to determine accounting procedures for their purposes in comparison with the accounting profession's ability to determine accounting procedures for its purposes. In recent years, however, pronouncements by the Accounting Principles Board and its successor the Financial Accounting Standards Board, have been viewed and accepted as increasingly authoritative. As a result, a few attempts have been made to reverse the relationship, with some writers noting that the tax treatment of goodwill does not conform to the present accounting treatment and advocating that the tax law be changed. At present these indications are only inklings, but they do portend of possible changes to come.

Goodwill and Pooling of Interests Accounting

Pooling of interests accounting, a topic that could constitute a study in itself, was considered in this study only in relation to accounting for goodwill. Pooling of interests accounting was important in this respect because of (1) the abuses committed through its employment in attempts to avoid recognition of goodwill in business combinations, (2) the resulting criticism leveled at the accounting profession for permitting such manipulation, and (3) attempts to curtail the practice through more stringent rules promulgated by the Accounting Principles Board.

First adopted in 1950 by the Committee on Accounting Procedure, the pooling treatment was not important initially since the same effect could be achieved under rules governing accounting for goodwill, which at that time permitted discretionary write-offs of the intangible to earned or capital surplus. Conceptually, the pooling treatment was a method of accounting for a business combination where neither party to the transaction had purchased the other, thereby not giving rise to a new basis of accounting and avoiding recognition of goodwill.

In 1953, the provisions governing application of pooling were incorporated verbatim in a major restatement of all previous bulletins, but the older bulletin prescribing the treatment of goodwill was significantly modified to exclude discretionary write-offs to earned or capital surplus. The pooling treatment then became important, and attempts were made to employ it wherever possible. The subjective criteria governing its use provided ample opportunity for misconstruing and eventually ignoring the criteria altogether. Another bulletin was issued in 1957 on the applicability of the pooling concept. It further aided the demise of what effectiveness was left in the criteria, and virtually any business combination could thereafter be treated as a pooling of interests. Practices such as part-purchase, part-pooling, and retroactive poolings arose and were severely criticized both from within and without the profession.

In 1970, after several studies sponsored by various accounting organizations called for abolishment of the practice, and after more than a decade of abuse committed within one of the greatest combination movements in the history of business, the Accounting Principles Board moved to eliminate the treatment and to require mandatory amortization of goodwill in all future business combination transactions. This coordinated approach provoked a bitter fight in the business community at large, as well as within the accounting profession, due to the unfavorable effects that such recommendations could have on financial statements. After much controversy, including the threat of a class action suit against the Accounting Principles Board by merger-minded firms, the Board eventually retained the pooling treatment—though with stringent and arbitrary provisions.

In the course of events involving the business combination problem, the issues and problems surrounding goodwill in accounting came to involve much more than just the accounting treatment of the asset. The experience of the Accounting Principles Board in dealing with this and other important issues led to the eventual formation of the Financial Accounting Standards Board. The FASB has continued and even accelerated the earlier APB trend toward more technical and detailed procedures—a trend with potentially important implications for any future accounting issue as well as for goodwill, should that subject once again be the subject of a professional pronouncement.

In closing, it does appear rather intriguing that the subject of goodwill has undergone in the 1970s one of its few protracted lulls in accounting literature. The battles seem to have shifted elsewhere in accounting practice and in the profession. Where there is any significant discussion at all, it seems to be in subjects touching on goodwill such as pooling-of-interests accounting—but through the early eighties little new ground has been broken on goodwill itself.

Perhaps this trend is indicative of some new direction for accounting issues and problems, but anyone aware of the history of goodwill might recommend a wait-and-see approach. After all, the subject has died down before only to flare up again. Since it is so very illusive—an accounting greased pig, when and where the profession has attempted to define and measure it—can one really offer anything but speculation concerning current and future interpretations of the asset's nature, proper treatment, handling by the profession, and effects on the profession? As another author has done, it thus appears appropriate to close this study not with a definitive statement but with a question concerning these and many other issues associated with goodwill: Who knows?

Bibliography

"Accounting Group Moves to Tighten Rules on Mergers." *The Wall Street Journal,* June 29, 1970.

"Accounting Principles Board Proposes 'Merger' Opinion." *The Journal of Accountancy,* April 1970, pp. 9-10.

Allan, Charles E. *The Law Relating to Goodwill.* London: Stevens and Sons, Limited, 1889.

American Accounting Association, Committee to Prepare a Statement of Basic Accounting Theory. *A Statement of Basic Accounting Theory.* Evanston, Ill.: American Accounting Association, 1966.

American Accounting Association Executive Committee. "Accounting and Reporting Standards for Corporate Financial Statements: 1957 Revision." *The Accounting Review,* XXXII (1957), pp. 536-546.

American Accounting Association, Executive Committee. "Accounting Concepts and Standards Underlying Corporate Financial Statements: 1948 Revision." *The Accounting Review,* XXIII (1948), pp. 339-344.

American Accounting Association, Executive Committee. "Accounting

Principles Underlying Corporate Financial Statements." *The Accounting Review,* XVI (1941), pp.133-139.

American Accounting Association, Executive Committee. "A Tentative Statement of Accounting Principles Affecting Corporate Reports." *The Accounting Review,* XI (1936), pp. 187-191.

American Institute of Accountants, Committee on Accounting Procedure. *Accounting for Intangible Assets.* Accounting Research Bulletins, No. 24. New York: American Institute of Accountants, 1944.

American Institute of Accountants, Committee on Accounting Procedure. *Business Combinations.* Accounting Research Bulletins, No. 40. New York: American Institute of Accountants, 1950.

American Institute of Accountants, Committee on Accounting Procedure. *Business Combinations.* Accounting Research Bulletins, No. 48. New York: American Institute of Accountants, 1957.

American Institute of Accountants, Committee on Accounting Procedure. *General Introduction and Rules Formerly Adopted.* Accounting Research Bulletins, No. 1. New York: American Institute of Accountants, 1939.

American Institute of Accountants, Committee on Accounting Procedure. *Income and Earned Surplus.* Accounting Research Bulletins, No. 32. New York: American Institute of Accountants, 1947.

American Institute of Accountants, Committee on Accounting Procedure. *Quasi-Reorganization or Corporate Readjustment—Amplification of Institute Rule No. 2 of 1934.* Accounting Research Bulletins, No. 3. New York: American Institute of Accountants, 1939.

American Institute of Accountants, Committee on Accounting Procedure. *Restatement and Revision of Accounting Research Bulletins.* Accounting Research Bulletins, No. 43. New York: American Institute of Accountants, 1953.

American Institute of Accountants. *Examination of Financial Statements by Independent Public Accountants.* New York: American Institute of Accountants, 1936.

American Institute of Accountants, Research Department. *Accounting Trends and Techniques.* Vols. II-XII. New York: American Institute of Accountants, 1948-1958.

American Institute of Accountants, Research Department. "Should

Goodwill be Written Off?". *The Journal of Accountancy,* April 1952, pp. 464-465.

American Institute of Accountants, Special Committee on Co-operation with Stock Exchanges. *Audits of Corporate Accounts.* New York: American Institute of Accountants, 1934.

American Institute of Accountants. "Uniform Accounting." *The Journal of Accountancy,* June 1917, pp. 401-433.

American Institute of Accountants. "Verification of Financial Statements." *The Journal of Accountancy,* May 1929, pp. 321-354.

American Institute of Certified Public Accountants, Accounting Principles Board. *Business Combinations.* Opinions of the Accounting Principles Board, No. 16. New York: American Institute of Certified Public Accountants, Inc., 1970.

American Institute of Certified Public Accountants, Accounting Principles Board. *Exposure Draft: Proposed APB Opinion: Business Combinations and Intangible Asseets.* New York: American Institute of Certified Public Accountants, Inc., 1970.

American Institute of Certified Public Accountants, Accounting Principles Board. *Financial Statements Restated for General Price-Level Changes.* Statements of the Accounting Principles Board, No. 3. New York: American Institute of Certified Public Accountants, Inc., 1969.

American Institute of Certified Public Accountants. Accounting Principles Board. *Intangible Assets.* Opinions of the Accounting Principles Board, No. 17. New York: American Institute of Certified Public Accountants, Inc., 1970.

American Institute of Certified Public Accountants, Accounting Principles Board. *Reporting the Results of Operations.* Opinions of the Accounting Principles Board, No. 9. New York: American Institute of Certified Public Accountants, Inc., 1967.

American Institute of Certified Public Accountants, Accounting Principles Board. *Reporting the Results of Operations—Reporting the Effects of Disposal of a Business, and Extraordinary, Unusual and Infrequently Occurring Events and Transactions.* Opinion of the Accounting Principles Board, No. 30. New York: American Institute of Certified Public Accountants, Inc., 1973.

American Institute of Certified Public Accountants, Accounting Principles Board. *Status of Accounting Research Bulletins.* Opinions of the

Accounting Principles Board, No. 6. New York: American Institute of Certified Public Accountants, Inc., 1965.

American Institute of Certified Public Accountants. *Accounting Trends and Techniques.* Vols. XIII-XXIV. New York: American Institute of Certified Public Accountants, 1959-1980.

American Institute of Certified Public Accountants, Committee on Accounting Procedure. *Consolidated Financial Statements.* Accounting Research Bulletins, No. 51. New York: American Institute of Certified Public Accountants, 1959.

Andrews, Frederic. "Proposed Measurement of Corporate Goodwill May Curb Acquisitions." *The Wall Street Journal,* February 27, 1970.

"APB: Accounting for Business Combinations." *The Journal of Accountancy,* January 1970, p. 8.

"APB May Abolish Pooling of Interest." *The Journal of Accountancy,* November 1969, pp. 19-20.

Arthur Andersen & Co. "Before the Accounting Principles Board: Proposed Opinion: Business Combinations and Intangible Assets: Brief and Argument of Arthur Andersen & Co." May 15, 1970.

Avery, Harold G. "Accounting for Intangible Assets." *The Accounting Review,* XVII (1942), pp. 354-363.

Backman, Jules. "An Economist Looks at Accounting for Business Combinations." *Financial Analysts Journal,* July-August, 1970, pp. 39-48.

Basset, W. R. "What Is 'Good Will' Worth?". *System The Magazine of Business.* XXXIII (1918), pp. 556-558.

Bell, W. H., and Powelson, J. A. *Auditing.* New York: Prentice-Hall, Inc., 1929.

Beyer, Robert. "Goodwill and Pooling of Interests: A Re-Assessment." *Management Accounting.* February, 1969, pp. 9-15.

Bliss, James H. *Management Through Accounts.* New York: Ronald Press Company, 1924.

Blough, Carman G. "Writing off Goodwill." *The Journal of Accountancy,* June, 1960, p. 60.

Briloff, Abraham J. "The Accounting Profession at the Hump of the Decades." *Financial Analysts Journal,* May-June 1970, pp. 60-67.

_____. "Dirty Pooling." *The Accounting Review,* XLII (1967), pp. 489-496.

Broad v. Jollyfe. Cr. Jac. 596 (1620).

Browne, E. A. "Goodwill: Its Ascertainment and Treatment in Accounts." *The Accountant,* XXVIII (1902), pp. 1339-1344.

Canning, John B. *The Economics of Accountancy: A Critical Analysis of Accounting Theory.* New York: Ronald Press Company, 1929.

Carsberg, Bryan V. "The Contribution of P. D. Leak to the Theory of Goodwill Valuation." *Journal of Accounting Research,* Spring 1966, pp. 1-15.

Catlett, George R., and Olson, Norman O. *Accounting for Goodwill,* Accounting Research Study No. 10. New York: American Institute of Certified Public Accountants, 1968.

Churton v. Douglas. Johns. 174 (1859).

Clarke v. Haberle Crystal Spring Brewing Company, 280 U. S. 384 (1930).

Cloake, T. Reginald. "A Discussion of Goodwill." *The New York Certified Public Accountant.* IX (1939), pp. 308-312.

Commons, John R. *Industrial Goodwill.* New York: McGraw-Hill Book Company, Inc., 1919.

_____. *Legal Foundations of Capitalism.* New York: MacMillan Company, 1924.

Couchman, Charles B. *The Balance-Sheet.* New York: Journal of Accountancy, Incorporated, 1924.

Council of the American Institute of Certified Public Accountants. *Special Bulletin: Disclosure of Departures from Opinions of Accounting Principles Board.* Reprinted in American Institute of Certified Public Accountants, Accounting Principles Board, *Status of Accounting Research Bulletins,* Opinions of the Accounting Principles Board, No. 6. New York: American Institute of Certified Public Accountants, Inc., 1965.

Cox, Henry C. *Advanced and Analytical Accounting.* Vol. IV of Business Accounting, ed. Harold Dudley Greeley, 5 vols. New York: Ronald Press Company, 1921.

Cruttwell v. Lye. 17 Ves. 335 (1810).

Davis, Freeman H. "Goodwill and the Balance Sheet." *The New York Certified Public Accountant.* X (1940), pp. 33-37.

Dawson, Sidney S. "Goodwill." *Encyclopaedia of Accounting,* 1903, Vol. III.

Dawson, W. J. "Goodwill." *The Accountant,* XXVII (1901), pp. 49-50.

Defliese, Philip L. "The APB and Its Recent and Pending Opinions." *The Journal of Accountancy,* February 1971, pp. 66-69.

Dicksee, Lawrence R. *Auditing: A Practical Manual for Auditors,* [2d] authorized American edition, rev. and enl. Ed. Robert H. Montgomery. New York: Ronald Press Co., 1909.

_____. *Auditing: A Practical Manual for Auditors,* 3d ed. rev. and enl. London: Gee & Co., 1898.

_____. "Goodwill and Its Treatment in Accounts." *The Accountant,* XXIII (1897), pp. 40-48.

_____ , and Stevens, T. M. *Goodwill and Its Treatment in Accounts,* [1st ed.] . London: Gee & Co., 1897.

_____, and Tillyard, Frank. *Goodwill and Its Treatment in Accounts,* 3d ed. London: Gee & Co., 1906.

Eggleston, DeWitt Carl. *Auditing Procedure.* New York: John Wiley & Sons, Inc., 1926.

Kiteman, Dean S. *Pooling and Purchase Accounting.* Ann Arbor, Mich.: University of Michigan, 1967.

Emery, Kenneth C. "Should Goodwill be Written Off?". *The Accounting Review,* XXVI (1951), pp. 560-567.

Esquerre, Paul-Joseph. *Accounting.* New York: Ronald Press Company, 1927.

_____. "Goodwill, Patents, Trade-Marks, Copyrights and Franchises." *The Journal of Accountancy,* January 1913, pp. 21-34.

Eulenberg, Alexander. "More Comments and Replies on Goodwill." *The Journal of Accountancy,* July 1964, pp. 53-55.

Financial Accounting Standards Board. *Accounging for Intangible Assets of Motor Carriers.* Statement of Financial Accounting Standards No. 44. Stamford, Conn.: Financial Accounting Standards Board, 1980.

Financial Accounting Standards Board. *Financial Reporting and Changing Prices.* Statement of Financial Accounting Standards No. 33. Stamford, Conn.: Financial Accounting Standards Board, 1979.

Financial Accounting Standards Board. *Prior Period Adjustments.* Statement of Financial Accounting Standards No. 16. Stamford, Conn.: Financial Accounting Standards Board, 1977.

Financial Accounting Standards Board. "Status Report No. 96, January 11, 1980." Stamford, Conn.: Financial Accounting Standards Board, 1980.

Financial Accounting Standards Board. "Status Report No. 114, April 10, 1981." Stamford Conn.: Financial Accounting Standards Board, 1981.

Finney, H. A. *Consolidated Statements for Holding Company and Subsidiaries.* New York: Prentice-Hall, Inc., 1922.

_____. *Principles of Accounting,* II. New York: Prentice-Hall, Inc., 1927.

Fitzgerald, A. A. "Valuation of Goodwill." *The Chartered Accountant in Australia,* II (1932), pp. 375-379.

Fjeld, E. I. "Classification and Terminology of Individual Balance-Sheet Items." *The Accounting Review,* IX (1936), pp. 330-345.

Foster, Louis O. *Introduction to Accounting.* Chicago: Richard D. Irwin, Inc., 1941.

Frank, Walter C. "Goodwill is Not Immortal: A Proposal to Deduct the Exhaustion of Purchased Goodwill." *The Journal of Taxation,* XXXIII (1965), pp. 380-381.

Freeman, Herbert C. "Some Considerations Involved in the Valuation of Goodwill." *The Journal of Accountancy,* October 1921, pp. 247-264.

Galbraith, John Kenneth. *The New Industrial State.* Boston: Houghton Mifflin Company, 1967.

Gilman, Stephen. *Principles of Accounting.* Chicago: La Salle Extension University, 1916.

"Goodwill." *The Accountant,* LX (1919), pp. 199-200.

"Goodwill and Advertising." *The Accountant,* L (1914), pp. 287-290. 319-320.

"Goodwill: Its Nature, Value and Treatment in the Accounts." *The Accountant,* XLIX (1913), pp. 816-823.

Gundry, William H. "Goodwill." *The Accountant,* XXVIII (1902), pp. 662-663.

Gunther, Samuel P. "Financial Reporting For Mergers and Acquisitions: Current Problems with Pooling and Purchasing." *Mergers and Acquisitions: The Journal of Corporate Venture,* Winter 1974, pp. 8-20.

_____. "Financial Reporting For Mergers and Acquisitions Revisited: Current Problems with Pooling and Purchasing." *Mergers & Acquisitions: The Journal of Corporate Venture,* Spring 1977, pp. 4-8.

_____. "Part Purchase-Part Pooling: The Infusion of Confusion Into Fusion." *The New York Certified Public Accountant,* XXXIX (1969), pp. 241-249.

_____. "Poolings—Purchases—Goodwill." *The New York Certified Public Accountant,* XLI (1971), pp. 25-37.

Guthrie, Edwin. "Goodwill." *The Accountant,* XXIV (1898), pp. 425-431.

Haberle Crystal Spring Brewing Co. v. Clarke, 20 F. 2d 540 (D. 1927).

Haberle Crystal Spring Brewing Co. v. Clarke, 30 F. 2d 219 (2d Cir. 1929).

Hamilton, W. R. "Goodwill." *The Accountant,* L (1914), pp. 216-218.

Harrington, Emmett S. "Important Issues Being Discussed by the Accounting Principles Board." *Management Accounting,* December 1970, pp. 9-14.

Harris, William. "Goodwill." *The Accountant,* X (1884), pp. 9-14.

Hatfield, Henry Rand. *Accounting.* New York: D. Appleton and Company, 1927.

_____. *Modern Accounting.* New York: D. Appleton and Company, 1913.

Hill, Gordon M. "Wanted: Solutions to Three Major Technical Problems." *The Journal of Accountancy,* August 1955, pp. 44-48.

Hill, Henry P. "Accounting for Goodwill—Half Way Home." *Financial Executive,* March, 1971, pp. 42-44, 46.

"How Much Is Goodwill Worth?" *Printers' Ink,* November 21, 1918, pp. 53-54.

Hylton, Delmar P. "Implications of the Direct Write-off of Goodwill," *The New York Certified Public Accountant,* XXXVI (1966), pp. 917-919.

_____. "The Treatment of Goodwill." (Letters to the Editor), *The Journal of Accountancy,* April 1964, p. 30.

Kerr, David S. "Watered Stock and Goodwill." *The Canadian Chartered Accountant,* October 1916, pp. 89-110.

Kester, Roy B. *Accounting Theory and Practice.* II. New York: Ronald Press Company, 1919.

_____. *Accounting Theory and Practice.* II, 2d ed., rev. New York: Ronald Press Company, 1925.

Knortz, Herbert C. "Economic Realism and Business Combinations." *Financial Executive,* April 1970, pp. 48-50, 52, 54, 58, 60.

_____. "The Realities of Business Combinations." *Financial Analysts Journal,* July-August 1970, pp. 28-32.

Kripke, Homer. "A Good Look at Goodwill in Corporate Acquisitions." *The Banking Law Journal,* December 1961, pp. 1028-1040.

Leake, P. D. *Commercial Goodwill: Its History, Value and Treatment in Accounts,* 3d ed. London: Sir Isaac Pitman & Sons, Ltd., 1938.

_____. "Goodwill: Its Nature and How to Value It." *The Accountant,* L (1914), pp. 81-90.

Marple, Raymond P. *Capital Surplus and Corporate Net Worth.* New York: Ronald Press Company, 1936.

May, George O. *Financial Accounting: A Distillation of Experience.* New York: MacMillan Company, 1961.

_____. "Income Taxes and Intangibles: Two Significant Research Bulletins." *The Journal of Accountancy,* February 1945, pp. 124-129.

[———.] "Obsolescence of Goodwill." *The Journal Of Accountancy,* March 1930, pp. 241-243.

May, Robert L. "Criticizes 'Illogical' Assumption in Professor Piaker's Article" (Letters to the Editor). *The New York Certified Public Accountant,* XL (1970), p. 181.

———. "More on 'Non-Accounting for Goodwill—A Critical Analysis of Accounting Research Study No. 10'." *The New York Certified Public Accountant,* XL (1970), p. 614.

Miles, J. Royce. *The Treatment of Goodwill in Federal Income Taxation.* Nebraska Studies in Business No. 37. Lincoln: Extension Division, The University of Nebraska, 1935.

Montgomery, Robert H. "The Appraisal of Good Will." *Bulletin, National Retail Dry Goods Association,* March 1926, pp.16-17, 34.

———. *Auditing: Theory and Practice,* [1st ed.]. New York: Ronald Press Company, 1913.

———. *Auditing: Theory and Practice,* 2d ed. rev. and enl. New York: Ronald Press Company, 1917.

———. *Auditing: Theory and Practice,* 2 vols, 3d ed. rev. and enl. New York: Ronald Press Company, 1922.

———. *Auditing: Theory and Practice,* 4th ed. rev. and enl. New York: Ronald Press Company, 1927.

———. *Auditing: Theory and Practice,* 5th ed. New York: Ronald Press Company, 1934.

———. *Auditing: Theory and Practice,* 6th ed. New York: Ronald Press Company, 1940.

———. *Income Tax Procedure 1922.* New York: Ronald Press Company, 1922.

———. *Income Tax Procedure 1926.* New York: Ronald Press Company, 1926.

———. *Montgomery's Federal Taxes on Corporations: 1943-1944.* Vol. I: *Gross Income and Deductions.* New York: Ronald Press Company, 1943.

_____. Lenhart, Norman J. and Jennings, Alvin R. *Montgomery's Auditing,* 7th ed. New York: Ronald Press Company, 1949.

Moonitz, Maurice, and Staehling, C. C. *Accounting—An Analysis of Its Problems.* Brooklyn: Foundation Press, Inc., 1952.

More, Francis. "Goodwill." *The Accountant,* XVII (1891), pp. 282-287.

Mosich, A. N. "Retroactive Poolings in Corporate Mergers." *The Journal of Business,* XLI (1968), pp. 352-362.

Nelson, Robert H. "The Momentum Theory of Goodwill." *The Accounting Review,* XXVIII (1953), pp. 491-499.

Newlove, George Hillis. *Consolidated Statements Including Mergers and Consolidations.* Boston: D. C. Heath and Company, 1948.

Noble, H. S.; Karrenbrock, W. E.; and Simons, H. *Advanced Accounting.* Cincinnati: South-Western Publishing Company, 1941.

Oehler, Christian. *Audits and Examinations.* New York: Fordham University Press, 1940.

Pacter, Paul A. "Accounting for Business Combinations: the Evolution of an APB Opinion." *The Journal of Accountancy,* August 1969, pp. 66-67.

Paton, William A. *Accountants' Handbook,* 2d ed. New York: Ronald Press Company, 1934.

_____, ed. *Accountants' Handbook,* 3d ed. New York: Ronald Press Company, 1943.

_____. *Accounting Theory: With Special Reference to the Corporate Enterprise.* New York: Ronald Press Company, 1922. Also available in a current reprint as: Paton, William Andrew. *Accounting Theory: With Special Reference to the Corporate Enterprise.* Chicago: Accounting Studies Press, Ltd., 1962.

_____. *Advanced Accounting.* New York: MacMillan Company, 1941.

_____. *Asset Accounting: An Intermediate Course.* New York: MacMillan Company, 1952.

_____. "Comments of William A. Paton," in Catlett, George R., and Olson, Norman O. *Accounting for Goodwill.* Accounting Research

_____ . " 'Non-Accounting' for Goodwill—A Critical Analysis of Accountint Research Study No. 10." *The New York Certified Public Accountant,* XXXIX (1969), pp. 837-844.

Preinreich, Gabriel A. D. "Economic Theories of Goodwill." *The Journal of Accountancy,* September 1939, pp. 169-180.

_____ . "Goodwill in Accountancy." *The Journal of Accountancy,* July 1937, pp. 28-50.

Racine, Samuel F. *Accounting Principles.* Seattle: Western Institute of Accountancy, Commerce and Finance, 1917..

Red Wing Malting Co. v. Willcuts. 8 F. 2d 180 (D. 1925).

Red Wing Malting Co. v. Willcuts. 15 F. 2d 626 (8th Cir. 1926).

Revenue Act of 1921. Statutes at Large. Vol. XL (1919).

Revenue Act of 1921. Statutes at Large. Vol. XLII (1921).

Revenue Act of 1934. Statutes at Large. Vol. XLVIII (1934).

Roby, A. G. "Goodwill." *The Accountant,* XVIII (1892), pp. 288-293.

Rogers, Edward S. *Good Will, Trade-Marks and Unfair Trading.* Chicago: A. W. Shaw Company, 1914.

Study No. 10. New York: American Institute of Certified Public Accountants, Inc., 1968, pp. 143-151.

_____ . "Earmarks of a Profession—and the APB." *The Journal of Accountancy,* January 1971, pp. 37-45.

_____ , and Littleton, A. C. *An Introduction to Corporate Accounting Standards.* American Accounting Association Monograph No. 3. Ann Arbor, Mich.: American Accounting Association, 1940.

_____ , and Stevenson, R. A. *Principles of Accounting.* New York: MacMillan Company, 1922.

Peoples, John. "Accounting for Intangibles in the United States." *The Canadian Chartered Accountant,* July 1957, pp. 15-18.

Piaker, Philip M. "More on 'Non-Accounting for Goodwill—A Critical Analysis of Accounting Research Study No. 10'." *The New York Certified Public Accountant,* XL (1970), pp. 613-614.

Rosewater, Victor. "Over-Capitalization Injures the Public." *The Journal of Accountancy,* September 1907, pp. 330-332.

Saliers, Earl A., and Holmes, Arthur W. *Basic Accounting Principles.* Chicago: Business Publications, Inc., 1937.

Sanders, Thomas Henry; Hatfield, Henry Rand; and Moore, Underhill. *A Statement of Accounting Principles.* New York: American Institute of Accountants, 1938.

Sanderson, B. J. "Goodwill and Its Valuation." *The Chartered Accountant in Australia,* July 1950, pp. 20-37.

"SEC Chairman Budge Testifies on 'Poolings' and Goodwill." *The Journal of Accountancy,* April 1969, pp. 16, 19.

"SEC Chief Accountant Speaks Before NYSSCPA." *The Journal of Accountancy,* January 1970, p. 16.

Simpson, Kemper. "Goodwill." *Encyclopaedia of the Social Sciences,* ed. Edwin R. A. Seligman, Vol. VI.

Smith, Stanley G. "Depreciation of Assets and Goodwill of Limited Companies." *The Accountant,* XXXI (1904), pp. 44-49.

Spacek, Leonard. "The Merger Accounting Dilemma—Proposed Solutions." *Financial Executive,* February 1970, pp. 38-42, 44, 46, 48, 50, 54, 56, 58.

_____. "More Comments and Replies on Goodwill." *The Journal of Accountancy,* July 1964, pp. 52-55.

_____. "The Treatment of Goodwill." (Letters to the Editor), *The Journal of Accountancy,* April 1964, pp. 30-31.

_____."The Treatment of Goodwill in the Corporate Balance Sheet." *The Journal of Accountancy,* February 1964, pp. 35-40.

Stacey, Walter E. "Goodwill." *The Accountant,* XIV (1888), pp. 605-606.

Staub, Walter A. "Intangible Assets," *Contemporary Accounting,* ed. Thomas W. Leland. New York: American Institute of Accountants, 1945.

Stockwell, H. G. *How to Read a Financial Statement.* New York: Ronald Press Company, 1925.

Study on Establishment of Accounting Principles. *Establishing Financial Accounting Standards: Report of the Study on Establishment of Accounting Principles.* New York: American Institute of Certified Public Accountants, Inc., 1972.

Suttle, William C., and Mecklenburg, William G. "Pooling of Interests." *The Texas CPA,* XLI (1969), pp. 31-52.

"The Treatment of Goodwill in Accounts." *The Accountant,* XXXVI (1907), pp. 801-802.

U. S. Securities and Exchange Commission. *The Propriety of Writing Down Goodwill by Means of Charges to Capital Surplus.* Accounting Series Releases, No. 50. Washington D. C.: U. S. Government Printing Office, 1956.

U. S. Treasury Department, Bureau of Internal Revenue. *Cumulative Bulletin No. 2, January-June, 1920.* Income Tax Rulings. Washington, D. C.: U. S. Government Printing Office, 1920.

U. S. Treasury Department, Bureau of Internal Revenue. *Cumulative Bulletin 1942-2: July-December, 1942.* Washington, D. C.: U. S. Government Printing Office, 1943:

U. S. Treasury Department, Bureau of Internal Revenue. *Regulations 62.* Washington, D. C.: U. S. Government Printing Office, 1922.

U. S. Treasury Department, Bureau of Internal Revenue. *Regulations 86.* Washington, D. C.: U. S. Government Printing Office, 1935.

Veblen, Thorstein. "On the Nature of Capital: [The Productivity of Capital Goods]." *The Quarterly Journal of Economics,* XXII (1908), pp. 517-542. Also available in a collection of the author's articles as Veblen, Thorstein. "On the Nature of Capital. I." *The Place of Science in Modern Civilisation and Other Essays.* New York: Russell & Russell, 1961.

———. "On the Nature of Capital: Investment, Intangible Assets, and the Pecuniary Magnate." *The Quarterly Journal of Economics,* XXIII (1908), pp. 104-136. Also available in a collection of the author's articles as Veblen, Thorstein. "On the Nature of Capital. II." *The Place of Science in Modern Civilisation and Other Essays.* New York: Russell & Russell, 1961.

———. *The Theory of Business Enterprise.* New York: Charles Scribner's Sons, 1915.

Walker, George T. "Goodwill on Financial Statements." *The Accounting Review*, XIII (1938), pp. 174-182.

_____. "Nonpurchased Goodwill." *The Accounting Review*, XIII (1938), pp. 253-259.

_____. "Why Purchased Goodwill Should be Amortized on a Systematic Basis." *The Journal of Accountancy*, February 1953, pp. 210-216.

Walton, Seymour. "Writing Off Goodwill." *The Journal of Accountancy*, July 1917, p. 62.

Werntz, William W. "Intangibles in Business Combinations." *The Journal of Accountancy*, May 1957, pp. 46-50.

_____ , and Rickard, Edmund B. "Requirements of the Securities and Exchange Commission." *Contemporary Accounting*, ed. by Thomas W. Leland. New York: American Institute of Accountants, 1945.

Wolff, Wolfgang. "Accounting for Intangibles." *The Canadian Chartered Accountant*, October 1967, pp. 255-259.

Wyatt, Arthur R. *A Critical Study of Accounting for Business Combinations*. Accounting Research Study No. 5. New York: American Institute of Certified Public Accountants, 1963.

Yang, J. M. *Goodwill and Other Intangibles: Their Significance and Treatment in Accounts*. New York: Ronald Press Company, 1927.

Young, Norman S. "Valuation of Goodwill and Its Treatment in Accounts." *The Australian Accountant*, XVI (1946), pp. 473-486.